RAISING THE BAR ON CONSTRUCTION PROJECT TEAMWORK

Catapult Your Results from Good to World Class

RAISING THE BAR ON CONSTRUCTION PROJECT TEAMWORK

CATAPULT YOUR RESULTS FROM GOOD TO WORLD CLASS

JIM EISENHART

Force 10 Publishing, Ventura, California

Published by:
Force 10 Publishing
996 Peninsula Street
Ventura, CA 93001
(805) 650-8040

ISBN: 978-0-9837077-4-5

Jacket design by Dunn+Associates, www.dunn-design.com
Interior design by Dorie McClelland, www.springbookdesign.com

Printed in the United States of America

Cataloging-in-Publication available upon request.

Contents

Preface

My purpose in writing this book was to provide a set of values or a mindset, as well as a practical process for achieving an extraordinary level of construction project teamwork with consistency and velocity.

In working with over five hundred construction project teams worldwide, it has become clear to me that the very best of these share a common set of values which are universal to extraordinary teams in any endeavor. Yet these values or mindset are not universally acknowledged, let alone executed. Thus, I distinguish between what I will term just "Good" and "World Class" project teams. My intent in this book is to enable project stakeholders not only to appreciate and value this distinction but also to be able to bring World Class teamwork to life on their future projects.

The process I have described is based upon my interpretation of best practices or protocols for team behaviors that are empirically based and thus replicable. This is not a how-to cookbook, however. Teamwork on an individual construction project is far too nuanced and complex for that.

As one might expect, mindset or values and process are intertwined. You cannot, for example, have a winning team with only, say, passion and trust among the team players. There must also be an agreed-upon process or game plan. Likewise, the notion that you can achieve excellence by just executing a common game plan is simplistic and naive. Excellence in any human endeavor is about people, how they work together, and shared values.

Nor is this a book about partnering. World Class teamwork as I define it has been achieved and can be achieved without a formal partnering process. An effective partnering process is a tool and can be a valuable one in achieving World Class teamwork.

To communicate both values and process, I have let my clients speak for themselves in their own words where possible. Construction, to a large extent, has its own vernacular.

This book is not to be construed as the final answer for construction project teamwork. It is merely the beginning or, for many, a continuation of the conversation to bring excellence to construction project teamwork. I believe with the current construction climate of increased best-value selection, alternate project delivery methods, collaborative tools (BIM), and a challenging construction economy demanding creativity and excellence, the value of a new, higher standard of construction project teamwork is both more achievable and imperative.

Acknowledgments

I would like to offer my sincere thanks to the many people who both indirectly and directly contributed to this book.

Indirectly this book is a synthesis of my experiences in twenty-plus years of learning about construction teamwork from my clients in partnering workshops, individual conversations, and industry seminars and events. I want to acknowledge Charles Cowan, formerly of the Army Corps of Engineers, the Arizona Department of Transportation, and for over twenty-five years a partnering consultant. He is universally acknowledged as the paradigm and father of construction project partnering and teamwork.

I met numerous other pioneers along the way: Joe Brown of the California Department of Transportation, a man with a true passion for excellence and getting the job done with the contractor; Ed Ruckle of the U.S. Navy, who patiently worked with me and educated me, and thousands of others, in the real world of getting along on construction projects; Barry Thalden of Thalden•Boyd•Emery Architects, a passionate leader of overall construction project teamwork from the design profession; and Captain Mike Williamson, CEC, of the U.S. Navy, a transformational leader with a commitment to excellence who has encouraged me and contributed significantly to making this book a pragmatic tool for construction professionals.

Also, special thanks to Patrick Peterson, Project Director, McCarthy Building Companies, and John Pangrazzio, FAIA, FACHA for providing the case study in Appendix A.

My team at the Ventura Consulting Group has made a very significant contribution. Paul Crotty, Leslie Hughes, and Neal Flesner have truly been a World Class team in enabling me to bring forth this book. Thank you.

To my publishing consultant, Hobie Hobart, thank you for your encouragement and sage advice. And without my editor, Mary Jo Tate, and her patience and professionalism, this book would never have come forth.

By no means least are the individuals whom I had the opportunity to interview for this book and who graciously allowed me to use their comments (complete list in Appendix B). This book in a sense is about you and what you have shared with me. I am very grateful. I have used many of your words to illustrate the concepts to enhance the book's readability to your colleagues.

RAISING THE BAR ON CONSTRUCTION PROJECT TEAMWORK

Catapult Your Results from Good to World Class

Your Project's Best Tool for Managing Risk, Controlling Cost,

1 ≫ **2** ≫ **3** ≫ **4** ≫ **5** ≫

	COMBAT PROJECTS	BUSINESS AS USUAL PROJECTS
A	Cutting corners where and whenever you can.	You have to keep your eye on everyone. Hidden agendas are assumed.
B	Backstabbing and open hostility.	CYA mentality by all project stakeholders. Tennis, game playing, case building, and posturing.
C	Risks are realized, and lawyers mitigate issues for their respective clients.	Push risk onto others. Defer to contract with written case building. Clean up mess at the end of the job. Profit is a bad word.
D	One excuse after another. Meetings are rare and dysfunctional.	Team members blame failures on others. Accountability is avoided. Victim mentality.
E	Every man, woman, and child for themselves!	Peaceful coexistence: you do your job, and I'll do mine. Live and let live.
F	Thinking is geared toward individual survival and collection of paperwork for potential claims and litigation.	Everyone's efforts and energy are put into risk aversion or transference.
G	Open disagreement over project delivery method (PDM) and its application on the job.	Project delivery method does not acknowledge project goals and/or individuals' experience with PDM.
H	Positioning and posturing for claims from the get-go.	Disputes linger and fester. Unwilling to acknowledge mistakes or errors. Issues develop into potential claims.
I	Try to get away with anything you can. 'Cat and mouse' game.	Enforced compliance at best. Old stereotypes are adhered to and past behaviors are repeated.
J	"See you in court" or Us vs. Them. Dread coming to work. Stress and anxiety.	Relationships are bureaucratic and institutional. It's just a job. Not willing to seek or offer advice.

World Class™

and Achieving Overall Project Excellence and Personal Fulfillment

6 ≫ **7** ≫ **8** ≫ **9** ≫ **10**

GOOD PROJECT TEAMS	WORLD CLASS PROJECT TEAMS
Good intentions that at best meet schedule, budget, and quality requirements.	Measurable team goals that acknowledge but aren't constrained by contract or specs, with specific committed actions by all.
Good "fair weather" communication. With issues, default to letter writing. Complaints kept to self.	Open, direct, verbal communication that is sometimes confrontational, never personal, always constructive. Write only to memorialize.
Reactive approach to risk. Your risk is your responsibility. Profit or loss is never acknowledged or discussed.	Proactive and collaborative discussion of potential risks with mitigation and prevention plans. Notion of shared team risk. Profitability openly discussed and supported.
Can be limited by circumstances seemingly beyond the team's control. Meetings are reactive.	Team owns overall project success regardless of circumstances. No-excuses mentality. Adversity strengthens team.
Teamwork within traditional roles. Help others when they ask for it.	Organizational lines are blurred, and everyone is 100% accountable for everything. Help others without being asked.
Innovative approach to work processes, means, and methods by contractor/design-build team only.	Outside-the-box thinking by entire team, as a team, on everything. Develop schedule as a team.
Project Delivery Method or BIM implementation is formally adhered to, but not optimized to support team goals.	PDM evolves into an informal communication network that does what is best for the project. BIM is optimized.
No claims. Conflicts can be resolved, but the process can be painful. Job can be stalled, and egos get in the way.	Conflicts are resolved, or if not, quickly elevated to the next level without ill will or rancor. Still trust partner, and job continues moving forward.
"Good" is good enough. No point in trying any harder or doing any better. Individuals do what they have done before.	Continuous improvement that is measured. Ongoing review of goals and key processes. Team members learn and grow.
Clients are satisfied, and relationships last for the life of the job. Advice may be seen as self-serving.	Clients are delighted, and lifelong relationships are created. Trusted business advisor. Client, CM, inspectors as coaches Passion and pride.

PART ONE

The Case for World Class Teamwork

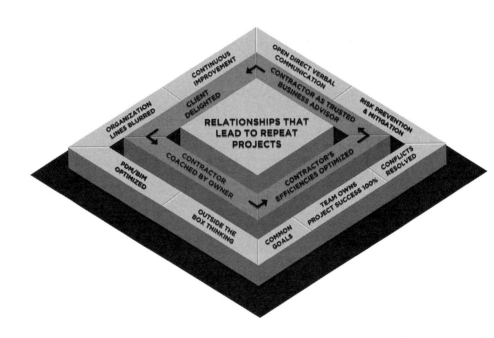

World Class Teamwork: The Model

1 World Class Project Teamwork: The Power of Shared Standards

I am not remotely interested in just being good.

—VINCE LOMBARDI—

If you have been in construction long enough—whether as an owner, designer, construction manager, or contractor—you may have had the good fortune of being part of a project that you look back upon wistfully and a bit nostalgically as being truly enjoyable, personally rewarding, and challenging and from which you developed long-lasting relationships. Chances are that job was a business and organizational success for your employer. I'll also wager with 99 percent certainty that job had great teamwork. Yet having had that experience, many of us find it frustrating not to be able to replicate it consistently on future projects.

That is what this book is about: enabling you and your fellow project stakeholders to create not just Good but World Class teams with a shared purpose, velocity, and consistency. Whether you're using conventional design, bid, build or newer project delivery methods, with or without a formal partnering or team-building process, there is much that you and your project teammates can do for yourselves. World Class teamwork is both a state of mind and a process or set of behavioral best practices or standards.

Attempting to define both behavioral practices and a mindset of World Class construction project teamwork initially sounded a bit daunting and maybe somewhat presumptuous. Clients, colleagues, and I had seen project teams that clearly stood apart, but trying to isolate key behaviors and attributes seemed elusive. Yet we realized that if you can't empirically define key behaviors, you can't change, improve, or replicate project success. In addition, many people wonder what the point is. Is there clear, measurable, and significant value in striving toward and achieving World Class teamwork? This book will demonstrate that having a truly World Class project team *is a project's best value tool for managing risk, controlling costs, and achieving overall project excellence and personal fulfillment,* bar none.

Others wonder how the distinction of World Class teamwork fits with new project delivery methods and construction methodologies. Is it just one more thing, a passing fad, or something else altogether? WCT (World Class teamwork) transcends project type and circumstances, while it acknowledges—but is not necessarily limited by—a project's legal and contractual obligations and chosen project delivery method (PDM) and construction processes.

> World Class teamwork, successfully implemented, should seamlessly integrate into your construction contract, design specifications, chosen PDM, and construction processes with the result that the project team is in committed action as a team.

At the same time, World Class teamwork capitalizes upon the varied and nuanced capabilities, experience base, intentions, and behaviors of the individuals involved as well as the unique challenges, opportunities, and circumstances facing the project team at any time.

World Class teamwork as such is a set of behavioral practices or standards that project participants execute *as a team.* The United States Marine Corps, for example, has adapted its war-fighting capabilities to new technologies and adversaries while retaining a strong, vibrant, and viable core organizational culture and organizational norms. So have enduring and innovative organizations such as General Electric and Apple.

The Genesis and Approach of the Search for World Class Teamwork

I began this search for a higher order of project teamwork several years ago after a number of my partnering clients noted that although there are no guarantees in construction, there was a fair to good probability that an upcoming job would have good teamwork without a formal partnering or team-building activity. Many of their projects were design-build or even negotiated jobs with past clients. These were organizations who had repeatedly produced genuinely good projects—many of which won awards and were completed early and within budget. But they didn't want to stop there. Instead, they challenged themselves by asking: What can we do better, faster and even more consistently? How do we provide even more value to our clients? What do we need to do to stay ahead of our competition in a dynamic construction industry?

So I looked for common phenomena of World Class projects—behaviors of the best of the best. I interviewed owners, general contractors, construction managers, subcontractors, and designers about their very best jobs. After projects were complete, I had them evaluate themselves in "lessons learned" workshops. I reviewed survey results from project teams and interviewed judges of the AGC Marvin Black Award for excellence in partnering. I also led interactive workshops at AIA, DBIA, AGC, and CMAA national conventions and regional meetings on the distinction between Good and World Class teams.

Early on I set aside the all-too-easy assumption that great or World Class teams can be defined solely on the basis of their results, such as being on time, staying on budget, following plans and specs, maybe winning awards, and, of course, being profitable. While producing results is a significant part of being a WCT, there are two variables:

1. The correlation between project results and project teamwork can be tenuous. A World Class team may complete a project very late and be over budget. Likewise, it is possible to have very good project results despite suboptimal teamwork when circumstances are favorable, such as weather, unknown site conditions being less than anticipated, funding being timely and easily available, few design errors, and few owner changes.

2. Project results do not always provide insights into empirical or observable and hence replicable team behaviors or practices. It is like saying that a football team won the Super Bowl because they had the best quarterback and the best defense, or they played hard and never gave up. These are all very subjective attributes. On the other hand, if you were able to assert that their turnover ratio was the lowest in the league, they made more QB sacks, their red zone scoring percentage was X, and so forth, you might be on to something.

The Power of Shared Standards

If World Class teams cannot be defined merely on the basis of their results, how can we recognize them? It's necessary to identify the distinctive traits that set apart World Class teams from all others. Shared standards enable us to assess, and in many cases measure, and thereby manage and control our environments.

Concrete vendors have multiple standards for concrete mix and finish. Finish carpenters can quickly and visually discern not only the type of wood but also its quality, durability, value, age, and so forth. Likewise, structural engineers can look at a physical structure and almost intuitively assess structural integrity, then do the math and drawings to back up that assessment. Shared or mutual standards enable us to deal with what would otherwise be complex circumstances and environment. They also create a language by which fellow specialists can converse using common terms, standards, and measures of performance.

Construction project managers typically are well trained in standards that enable them to manage the different facets of a project, such as scheduling, managing subcontractors and their own people, keeping a job site safe, budgeting, negotiating with vendors, etc. There are many books, programs, and seminars that can teach them how to be good project managers. Chet Widom, FAIA, current president of the American Institute of Architects, 2011 winner of their prestigious Edward Kemper Award, and Senior Advisor for the Los Angeles Community College system's $3 billion bond program, explains the challenge: "There are lots of things out there about how to manage, and we have plenty of technical and design skills in our industry. What we do not have is the consistent leadership necessary to take a project team to a high level of performance or World Class teamwork." And the ability to lead a project team to World Class teamwork, I would add, is vitally dependent on having clear, mutually agreed-upon standards or traits of World Class team behavior that you're going to lead that team toward.

Most of us have few standards of behavior for construction project teamwork. Generic terms like teamwork, good communication, and trust are pretty much universally agreed upon. They're included in just about every contractor's, construction manager's, and designer's collateral, websites, and presentations, invariably with good intentions. Yet at what point do they become clichés devoid of any true meaning, hackneyed buzz words that are bandied about because if you didn't mention them you would stand out like a black sheep? These terms have ceased to become, as one construction manager told me, "key differentiators in winning new business." And what distinguishes good communication from poor communication? What exactly is good teamwork? What does trust look like? How does it manifest itself on a construction project? How do you develop it?

Most of us can easily distinguish between what I term "Combat" projects and "Business as Usual" teams.

Combat projects are a disaster:

- Openly adversarial and hostile
- Us vs. them; winner takes all
- Complete breakdown of communication
- Unresolved claims and litigation
- Can't even agree on where to put the Porta-Pottys

Business as Usual teams aren't much better:

- Minimize or transfer your risk
- CYA mentality
- Do the minimum to get by
- Games, case building, and posturing
- Reactive/crisis management
- "Tennis" (back-and-forth paperwork)
- Cold War mentality or live and let live

But how about the distinction between Good and World Class? As we'll see, with some folks, Good is as good as it gets.

Steve Iselin, Executive Director of NAVFAC (Naval Facilities & Engineering Command) in Washington, D.C., contributes an owner's perspective: "We have over ninety installations worldwide and need to standardize our behavior on projects through best practices. This, in turn, would allow us to move from one place to another and compare, and thereby improve project and team performance."

Another problem is that if an individual or organization does have clear standards for construction project teamwork, they are rarely mutually agreed upon, let alone shared, by fellow project stakeholders. One may view explicit team goals as necessary. Another thinks the plans, specs, and contract documents are sufficient. One stakeholder believes design development on a design-build project should be done concurrently with design review. Another believes it should follow formally at 30 percent, 60 percent, and 90 percent intervals.

I assume that most projects begin with good, competent people with good intentions about working together. And yet those good intentions can easily fall by the wayside when faced with reality. The consequences? Project teamwork is all too often left up to chance and interpretation and is merely a reaction to project circumstances.

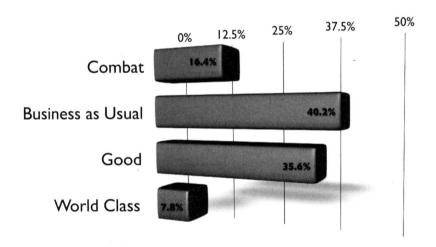

This survey data was generated from partnering workshop participants nationwide in over 125 projects and seminar attendees at over a dozen regional and national presentations from early 2007 to the end of 2010.

There's No Universal "Best Way"

There is no one, universal "best way" to manage all construction projects. Rather, the best way for any particular project evolves from having a World Class team.

Whether determining how to best execute a project delivery method, figuring out how to optimize implementation of BIM, or determining how to manage risk on a P3 project or expedite the submittal process, there is no one best way. Construction is not like flying an airplane where there are detailed, mutually agreed-upon rules, procedures, and contingency plans that cover virtually every possible scenario. On a construction project, not only are project specifications and contract documents open to interpretation, but so are the best ways to schedule the work, agree on change order pricing, and deal with conflict. On an airplane, the captain is in command, and rightly so. You do not debate the destination with him. But construction projects do not lend themselves to being directed, controlled, or managed by unilateral processes. Rather, as I will demonstrate, they significantly benefit from being enabled by collaborative processes developed by the project team.

Construction projects also have some unique characteristics that are not addressed in conventional books and articles about teamwork. For example, they often throw together individuals and organizations who have no or very limited prior experience with one another to achieve often unclear expectations in a highly uncertain, unpredictable environment for a limited time. As Jon Katzenbach points out in *Teams at the Top*, "The collective work of teams can be particularly powerful in situations where the marketplace situation is difficult to predict, where no single member of the leadership group has the answer, and where the performance upside of responding differently is very high."[1]

Bart Littell, Vice President of Parsons Brinckerhoff, program and construction managers, explains: "Before we bid a job, of course we develop contractual requirements, processes, and procedures that we believe are best practices to manage the client's project. Once a World Class team starts to take shape on a project, however, we may relax some restrictions to the overall project's advantage and let the team do what is truly best for the client."

Don't get me wrong. Experience, theory, and previous examples all have their value but do not acknowledge the complexities and shadings of the individual personalities, issues, and circumstances of a specific project.

As Jim Cowell, Associate Vice President for Facilities at Caltech and retired Navy CEC Captain, puts it, "A truly World Class team will figure it out much better than you can tell them how to do it or how they might read about it in a very prescriptive how-to book or program or by trying to copy or mimic another project." How-to books, videos, and seminars are great information sources. Yet on a construction project you can have a dozen or more very experienced professionals each with a very different idea as to how to best execute, say, a CM at Risk delivery method on that job. Without a process to align, focus, synthesize, and even benefit from this diversity, the result can be delay, added cost, and potential conflict.

Issam Khalaf, principal of Jacobs Construction Management and a 2008 Marvin Black and 2008 CMAA Project of the Year award winner, explains, "There is no 'one size fits all' process for successful construction project teamwork. A collaborative mindset is one of the key needed ingredients, coupled with a team vision and collaborative processes. These give you the opportunity to develop a best way for each job."

Paradoxically, while seemingly more collaborative project delivery methods and processes have multiplied exponentially in the past ten years, they too do not offer a panacea for teamwork. Perry Petersen of Petersen Construction Services explains: "There are so many project delivery methods and construction processes out there now that it's scary. Starting a job these days, you have no idea of people's experience with a delivery method or process nor their definition of what it means to be successful on that job with that approach."

On a construction project, you are dealing with individuals with different knowledge, experience, egos, and external demands and pressures. "Each stakeholder group, and individuals within those groups, on a project will have different levels of expectations, experience, and commitment," says Dan Gilbert, Project Director, Ontario Medical Center for Kaiser Permanente. "Making it all work together is like making a great cocktail."

And how does a team deal with unanticipated changes over the duration of the job, whether related to personnel, budget, site, or weather? How do they put all that together on a specific project and sustain it as a success? How does this happen without an individual or one stakeholder attempting to control or assert their interpretation of the best way? Insisting on or mandating a best way on a project can actually undermine teamwork. We'll also discuss the fallacy of control in chapter 3.

All of these challenges can be met by having a project team optimize its teamwork and adhere to a mutually agreed-upon set of best *team* practices or a behavioral protocol that leads to project success.

> The best way, then, becomes a consequence of or emerges
> from an ongoing execution of these processes by the project team.

Brian Cahill, Director of Operations for Barnhart Balfour Beatty, notes, "If you assemble and develop a World Class team on a project, the processes will work themselves out."

As we will see, a World Class team rarely resembles a textbook model of a project's structure or delivery method. Rather it is an informal network of personal relationships grounded in a common purpose and enabled by shared behavioral values and processes.

In this book my intent is to clearly define the significant and observable processes and behaviors that distinguish World Class project teamwork from just Good teamwork, let alone Business as Usual or Combat projects. I acknowledge that these are just one interpretation of a World Class standard. There certainly can be other interpretations or models. This is good and healthy, and I welcome engaging in and stimulating an ongoing conversation to continue to raise the bar on construction project teamwork.

2 The Imperative of Striving toward World Class Teamwork

Good is the enemy of great.
And that is one of the key reasons
why we have so little that becomes great.
—JIM COLLINS, *GOOD TO GREAT*—

Isn't being Good good enough? Maybe it is not anymore.

In March 2010, the Hensel Phelps Construction Company was awarded a $68 million Bachelor Enlisted Quarters housing project for the U.S. Navy essentially on the basis of interviews and their references. It was a design-build contract with an agreed-upon lump sum but with no schematic or even concept drawings. The Navy opted for this seemingly risky approach because it was in a hurry to expedite completion due to funding constraints.

The RFP outlined some very broad definitions of project scope, and the selection criteria were highly subjective. And guess what Hensel Phelps' references spoke about? You guessed it: teamwork, trust, integrity, an innovative approach, and truly meeting and even exceeding the client's expectations.

Best-Value Selection and Alternative Project Delivery Methods Are Becoming the Norm

It is well known that design, bid, build is on its way to becoming a minority project delivery method on larger public sector projects as best-value selection processes such as CM at Risk, design-build, lease-leaseback, public-private partnerships, and IPD become increasingly popular. Even where design, bid, build is still used, owners increasingly have the right to use prequalified bid lists. Beverly Nelson of the U.S. Bureau of Reclamation, Lower Colorado Region speaks of their selection process on hard bid projects: "Yes, we look at the bid price and technical things. But we no longer use points in rating contractors. We use adjectives. This gives us the flexibility to make a selection based upon best value. And how a contractor has previously worked with the government is now a big factor. The potential cost of conflict on our projects is enormous." The implication? As a contractor, just having a track record of good teamwork and good project results may not even get you invited to the short list.

Lee Evey, former Program Manager of the extraordinarily successful Pentagon Renovation program (PENREN) and past DBIA president, explains why Good is no longer good enough: "Ninety percent of our program's success came from selecting the right teams and writing contracts that rewarded excellent performance. Prequalification is not a solution. It is a minimal qualification. We started with a high bar right away and let only the best design-build teams compete going forward. We used past performance as the most important criteria. And we didn't just get testimonials. Where possible we went out and did face-to-face interviews with follow-up questions to truly learn about a design-build team's prior experience."

One other point: It used to be that owners, contractors, and designers collaborated out of necessity or a desire to avoid what I term "downside" risks—the costs of claims, litigation, and an adversarial relationship. In the past few years, I've been seeing contractors, owners, and CMs collaborate out of necessity to avoid what I term "opportunity lost" risks—not having a positive reputation for teamwork, not being selected for best-value projects, and not being sought after for design-build projects, repeat business, or joint ventures. We'll explore this further in chapter 8.

Mark Filanc, CEO of Filanc Construction, states it bluntly: "If you are a contractor and you are not striving toward World Class teamwork, there's a good probability you will not be in business in ten years."

And how about construction management firms? As a principal of one nationwide CM firm told me, "We all use basically the same construction management programs and software. And virtually anybody can execute them well. We need to be able to compete and differentiate ourselves on a higher plane. By offering the ability to provide an extraordinary level of project teamwork, we can provide a significant value add to our clients."

The Limitations and Constraints of
Public Project Funding Sources

Public funding for construction projects has become a more complex and convoluted process. As Bimla Rhinehart, Executive Director of the California Transportation Commission, recently said in a *California Constructor* interview, "Whether it is creative financing approaches or new procurement methods, it's very important to consider alternative procurement processes. We have such an infrastructure deficit, and funding in the state and throughout the U.S. is not available to support the amount of the deficit we are looking at."[2]

How can a World Class team help with this process? By offering owners innovative options that help them better manage risk and control costs. As we've noted, some contractors are now only bidding work that calls for a best-value selection process that capitalizes upon their proven track record to creatively and collaboratively solve challenging owner needs. Kathy Mayo, Vice President with AECOM, explains: "The funding chain is failing. It takes a lot more creativity, teamwork and flexibility to make a project go forward. This requires the whole project team to manage risks and reduce costs collaboratively. Also, people bringing money to the table are very careful about who they will do business with. If you anticipate more public-private partnerships [P3s], you need to be positioned to take advantage of these opportunities. This can be more fun and rewarding to those who can work well together."

Here's an example of such a creative, fun and ultimately rewarding approach. Don Wright, Program Manager with Bechtel, speaking of a project with a previous employer, recalls how the Air Force (end user) and Army Corps of Engineers (program manager) jointly appealed to their funding source on the A6 rocket facility project: "The COE and Air Force made a joint presentation to their funding source, who was openly skeptical about their ability to work together and deliver this complex project. So they all appeared in uniforms that were one half Army and one half Air Force crudely sewn together." The funding source got the message: They were going to work as a team.

Becoming the Owner of Choice

Another relatively recent phenomenon is the expressed intent of numerous contractors, construction managers, subcontractors, designers, and, yes, even owners to be the entity of choice. In the past, no one had much choice: the low bidder got the job. But things have changed.

As Michael Abeln, Director of Construction for the U.S. Army Corps of Engineers in the Mobile, Alabama, district put it, "We respect past performance nowadays, and good relationships can be rewarded."

As a consequence of the 2009–10 recession, public owners have also opted, often out of necessity, to be the owners of choice, which is to say, being sought out aggressively by contractors, design-build teams, and construction managers that truly meet their needs. The constituents and boards of public owners today are listening to contractor, designer, and construction management groups who advocate a relationship with their construction management that reduces project cost, better manages risk, and is more transparent through more collaborative project delivery methods and relationships. They are also willing to ask hard questions if they get just a few bids or none at all on a project.

Bob Finney, District #4 Deputy Director for Construction for Caltrans in the San Francisco Bay area, explains: "In recent times, both owners' and contractors' budgets have become extremely tight and designs have become more complex. Strong relationships that engage the contractual parties and external stakeholders are critical to manage risks and minimize costs for everyone involved." The risk to public owners of not managing those risks and costs well? Bob's colleague, Caltrans Area Construction Manager Maurice El-Hage puts it concisely: "We, Caltrans, are now competing for work with private sector funding agencies. End users have a choice between us and an often local construction management entity."

The long-term consequences of this approach for owners? Repeat, highly competitive bids by previous contractors/design-build teams who know and value the opportunity of working with that owner and, more specifically, their people again.

Enhancing Collaboration through Alternative Project Delivery Methods and New Tools

All of the newer project delivery methods are predicated on a higher and earlier order of collaboration among owner, designer, CM, and general contractor. The games of what I call "tennis" (back-and-forth paperwork), case building, posturing, and the "make it up with change orders" game that were prevalent in the design, bid, build model are not only dysfunctional but also blatantly wasteful on, say, a design-build project. The newer alternative project delivery methods set the stage for, but cannot guarantee, a truly collaborative effort grounded in common purpose and personal trust by all project stakeholders.

Barbara Jackson of the Design-Build Institute of America and author of *Design-Build Essentials*, writes, "Trust and respect are the cornerstone of successful design-build. Adversarial ways of relating do not work in a team environment; neither does trying to manage design and construction as independent functions."[3]

Likewise, the industry-wide proliferation of real-time, field-level, collaborative design and construction tools and processes (LEAN, BIM, VBM, PMIS, design-assist, and Last Planner™) has made working together at an earlier stage of project development a very real and viable opportunity.

Betsey Dougherty, FAIA, LEED, AP, principal of Dougherty + Dougherty Architects, and former AIA National Board Member, notes: "There's a paradigm shift going in our industry. We now have the ability and the tools to work together sooner and much more effectively. With this, our owners also have higher expectations. World Class teamwork should be the standard everyone on a project aspires to."

Increasingly Complex Projects

Construction is becoming more complex, whether in terms of dealing with design issues, constructability challenges, newer sophisticated ADMs, or coordinating with more numerous and vocal stakeholders and third parties. This complexity manifests itself as both a challenge and an opportunity. Let's hear from some different perspectives.

"The industry is so fragmented that no one player has the power to effectuate change. Architects are often seen as commodities, and contractors struggle with labor and process risk as they have for decades. These issues play out daily, creating inefficiencies on projects and costing billions of dollars to public and private owners," says Sue Dyer, President of Orgmetrics and CEO of the International Partnering Institute. As an example, data compiled by *The Economist* indicates that inefficiencies, mistakes, and delays account for $200 billion (that's right, billion) of the $650 billion spent on construction in the United States every year.[4]

Ron Rudolph, Regional Vice President of Turner Construction, comments: "Every day our projects are getting more and more complex. With a World Class team, you are dealing with friends, and you need this friendship to navigate through the complexity."

With this complexity comes the challenge of integrating and truly capitalizing upon the value of increasingly specialized experts. These resources include technical expertise such as membrane technology on water treatment plants, the systems integration experts on a transit project, or the baggage handling system contractors on airline terminals. Process expertise has also proliferated with scheduling specialists, commissioning agents, and BIM modeling consultants. The challenge? How do you quickly integrate this diverse and constantly changing resource base into a focused and cohesive team?

Tom Gusich, Vice President of Water Resources and Industrial Projects, University Mechanical & Engineering subcontractors in Phoenix, explains: "Being on a World Class team allows everybody to be a part of something. The talent we have now on projects is much better than it was five to ten years ago from a technical point of view. There is the potential of much more value added now from a collaborative effort. On a World Class team, we are able to tap into and take advantage of all of the team's capabilities."

David Mallik, Senior Project Manager of Whiting Turner Construction, notes: "The industry has changed dramatically in the last ten years. We know as a general contractor that we have these experts in specific fields. The challenge is taking everyone's expertise and bringing it together in harmony. This in turn provides a better value to the customer."

The Need for Greater Adaptability and Flexibility over a Project's Duration

What was important to an owner or end user at the outset of a project can often change over its duration. Nor, as we will see, do the project specifications, by themselves, always effectively communicate the end user's real intent. Additionally, changes in site conditions and permit and regulatory requirements, weather delays, new technologies, and changes in key stakeholders can significantly alter the end user's original intent. How does a project team adapt to what can be game-changing changes without defaulting to Business as Usual or the costly change order game?

Consider the Napa Creek Box Culverts and Flood Terrace project in Napa, California, which, among other purposes, was intended by Napa County Flood Control, the City of Napa, and the U.S. Army Corps of Engineers to prevent future flooding which would require evacuation of the city. The original schedule called for project substantial completion on July 1, 2013. The contractor, Proven Management, met with the other project stakeholders at the outset of the job and committed to a team or partnership goal of completing the project eight months early or no later than November 1, 2012. An extremely wet winter and differing site conditions made achieving this goal untenable. Yet when the team met in the spring of 2011, the city's Public Works Director, Jack LaRochelle, asserted the imperative of avoiding having to evacuate the city during a future flood. The team collectively agreed to establish a new team goal of "The flood control channel able to handle a hundred-year storm no later than October 15, 2012." With the creation of an additional team goal prior to the contract completion date, the team agreed to complete the remaining scope of the job on the original contract date in 2013.

My point is that World Class teams have not only the ability but also the willingness to continually ensure that they are delivering what is really, really important to the customer, regardless of changes in the project's circumstances and/or customer needs. And, as we will see, they do this as a team while minimizing any impact to the original project cost or schedule and without incurring any additional safety risks. Project circumstances will continue to be even more dynamic, particularly on large, high-technology, longer-duration jobs with multiple stakeholders.

A good example is CT scanners or MRI equipment on health-care projects. Rarely have I seen what was originally specified still be desired by the end user two to three years into the project. World Class teamwork offers a project team the means of anticipating and managing these circumstances rather than just reacting to them.

The Moral and Business (Dare I Say Profit?) Imperative

Dov Seidman, author of *How: Why How We Do Anything Means Everything . . . in Business (and in Life)*, has made a very compelling case that organizations that "out-behave" their competitors ethically will also tend to outperform them financially. His perspective challenges the conventional wisdom that winning is everything or, if not, almost everything. Seidman asserts that the business world has changed in the last decade or two primarily due to the increase in and openness of information technology. This has made everyone's and every organization's behavior much more transparent. The result? It is easy for an unhappy/happy customer, contractor, vendor, or employee to go online and bad-mouth or applaud your organization. The implications of this transparency for contractors bidding on projects with a best-value selection process should be self-evident.

Old strategies of keeping bad behavior hidden or managing it with lawyers do not work anymore. The only way to truly manage your reputation, Seidman argues, is to earn it by living and acting with integrity.

In Business as Usual let alone Combat projects, the construction process and profit are looked upon as a zero-sum game. In other words, for you to win, someone else must lose. World Class teamwork offers the very real possibility of a true win-win outcome.

Seidman uses an example of the relationship between trust and procurement costs. The least trusted companies in his study were also the least profitable and incurred procurement costs that were well over five times higher than the costs of the most trusted buyers. Also, organizations that trusted each other were more likely to share valuable information. "Trust between companies leads to more trust," Seidman says. "It sets off an upward spiral of cooperative, value creating behaviors."[5]

What is the relationship among World Class construction project teamwork, risk, profit, and future business growth? It completely shifts the game from one of prevailing or only focusing on optimizing your own organization's outcomes to one of collaborating or optimizing the performance of the overall project team's outcomes. And with the latter comes, seemingly paradoxically to many, the opportunity of even greater rewards beyond just those short-term project profits that might be gained through an effort focused on maximizing your own self-interest. Managing risk and profit now becomes a team challenge or opportunity.

Jim Link, Vice President with Skanska, explains: "When you focus on being a World Class team and developing trusting business relationships on a project, it takes your focus off profitability and you don't have to worry about it so much. It just takes care of itself. Because real profitability comes from a team clicking and hitting on all cylinders."

Scott Ashton, Industrial Division Manager of Berg Electric, subcontractors, adds: "On a World Class team, we have a much smoother project. And when our focus is on being part of the team, the profit kind of follows and comes naturally."

Not only is short-term profit a consideration, but also future profitability. Ken Schacherbauer, Vice President of Field Operations, Perini Building Company, says, "World Class teamwork allows us to maximize our efficiencies on our current jobs, but the real payoff comes on future jobs. This happens when subcontractors and designers give us a 'better look,' which is to say, their best price, and they really want to work with us again."

How do owners view contractor profit on a World Class team? In the Business as Usual world of a decade or two ago, many a public owner believed that a contractor's profitability or loss was strictly up to the contractor. Today, sophisticated owners know that they too have a stake in the success of their contractors, designers, and construction managers, especially if there was some prequalification or selection. Just walking away from a Combat or Business as Usual project and blaming it on the contractor's or designer's performance doesn't cut it anymore with their management or oversight agencies. They are held accountable for overall project success, and their ability to secure future work and funding hinges on results, not excuses. In short, they are aware of the risk of having a reputation as a difficult owner.

Captain Mike Williamson, CEC, U.S. Navy, says, "You've lost your effectiveness as an owner [coach?] if the other project stakeholders do not come to you with their problems. If other members of the team are not sharing bad news with you, and this includes their own profitability, this can lead to suboptimal teamwork and project results. This, in turn, creates a downward spiral."

In other words, if you as a contractor, CM, or designer are having issues that take your eyes off the team's common goals, let the owner know. Explain your circumstances. Give them an opportunity to support you.

As a senior manager of the largest water agency in one of this country's top five cities notes: "First of all, profit is not a four-letter word to us. If a contractor's issues with profitability are causing him to take his eye off our common goals, I want him to let me know soon. Tell us how you are doing and what would work best for you. If I understand your situation, maybe I can help you out. If not, I can at least give you a good reason why not. If a contractor is losing money and they're not open about it, things can easily become adversarial to no one's advantage."

The Correlation between Teamwork, Mitigating Personal Stress, and Having More Fun—That's Right, Fun

The Engineering News Record's March 15, 2010, cover highlighted what they termed "The Post Traumatic Construction Disorder"—personal burnout or stress:

> The factors that, in various combinations produce burnout are all there: long hours, greater workloads, job uncertainty, poor prospects for pay and promotion, ambiguous roles on projects and time and budget pressure that accelerate the risk of mistakes or compromise standards of quality and ethics. Just bringing up the subject among staff and managers violates an industry

taboo, long dictated by the industry's prevailing culture of service and sacrifice. Many professionals feel they are supposed to take whatever comes their way to keep their jobs, even if they are badly exploited. This atmosphere burns out people.[6]

The combination of the words "fun" and "construction projects" is usually considered an oxymoron. World Class teamwork cannot do much about an organization's internal culture with respect to an individual's burnout, but it can make their relationships with their fellow project team members a very fulfilling, rewarding, and even enjoyable experience. Individuals on World Class teams I've worked with invariably identify the most valued personal benefit as reduced stress or "I enjoyed coming to work on this job." And what is the primary source of stress on construction projects? The uncertainty of your colleagues' intentions and the outcomes associated with those intentions. For example, you might wonder, "Is the contractor building a case for a claim with this RFI? What am I potentially at risk for? If so, what should I be doing to protect myself?"

David Allen, Project Architect and PM for the U.S. District Court, says, "Morale on a project team is very important. You can fight tooth and nail on little things day in and day out with one another, and this leads to burnout. Individuals can lose their focus and energy at the end of the job when they really need it."

John Jansen, Senior Vice President, Kiewit Companies, explains: "On World Class teams, people enjoy going to work, and this feeds on itself and affects all team members at all levels. Once you feel comfortable in your relations on a job, you start doing social things together, and this makes the experience fun."

Attracting, Retaining, and Developing World Class Talent

World Class teamwork can significantly enhance the ability of organizations to attract, develop, and retain high-caliber personnel—particularly the younger Generation Y. Why? It helps them see the big picture, offers more opportunities for creative expression, enables personal growth, and, perhaps above all, gives them an opportunity to take more responsibility for overall project success. Also, by virtue of pushing decision making down to lower levels on collaborative processes around, say, a BIM model, individuals on World Class teams feel connected to one another in a much more purposeful and interactive way

Pat Shafter, Senior Project Manager of Swinerton Builders' 2010 Marvin Black Award-winning Flight Projects Center project at NASA's Jet Propulsion Laboratory, notes: "Being on a World Class team helps us promote from within and shows the younger members of our firm that if you want to succeed, you need to be part of a team. It also builds character and an understanding of the other stakeholders' points of view. They also get to see the big picture in a way they might not otherwise appreciate."

Vineet Nayar, CEO of HCL Technologies, writes in *Harvard Business Review*, "Generation Y is also a collaborative group. Be it on the internet or the real world, they work well in teams unlike their predecessors who grew up in a far more individualistic manner. They share knowledge, opinion, suggestions far more easily and are more open to receiving the same." He notes, "Transparency is the only way to deal with this young talent pool."[7]

Jim Cowell from Caltech agrees: "Let the young people figure it out as a team. It doesn't have to be the way the old guys say it is. They, the younger generation, have less baggage than we do."

The geographical factor also plays into attracting talented team members. George Furnanz, Senior Vice President of Stacy and Witbeck, general engineering contractors, explains: "The younger generation is not the construction nomads that we were twenty years ago. If you ask them to move every year or two, they may well tend to look elsewhere. When hiring young people in today's world, you need to be honest with them and let them know that they must be willing to relocate if the right opportunity comes their way for greater experience and to support the company. To them the company they choose must be like family."

A key element in developing younger talent is allowing them not only to take responsibility but also to make mistakes and even fail. A World Class team, as we'll see, creates the opportunity for individuals to fail, learn, and move on.

The Value of World Class Teamwork from Different Stakeholders' Perspectives

The perceived value of World Class teamwork and excellence can vary by stakeholder type and even within each discipline. So let's hear some different, yet remarkably consistent, perspectives from the different stakeholder camps.

Designers' Point of View

• Barry Thalden, Partner, Thalden•Boyd•Emery Architects in St. Louis and Las Vegas: "It costs us significantly less money in terms of our time when we're working as a World Class team. An adversarial project can negatively impact our profits by 30 percent or more. And I am personally exhausted by building projects the old way. It is no fun, and it is more difficult to deliver the best designed buildings to our clients."

• Ash Wason, Chief Operating Officer, Carollo Engineers: "The value is twofold. First is the pride that comes from being involved in a successful project and the satisfaction one gets from collaborative teamwork. Second is not having to get involved with unpleasant legal issues that nobody wants to deal with."

• Arturo Castro, President and COO, Tucker Sadler Architects: "The value in striving toward World Class teamwork is not just architectural but in that it allows the public to see the project as a major asset. It is their building, and by achieving true World Class teamwork, you realize World Class architecture that shows up in the quality and finish of the final product."

• Sylvia Botero, Senior Vice President of RBB Architects, architects on the 2010 Marvin Black Award-winning St. Joseph Mission Hospital Acute Care Tower: "On a World Class team, we are not nickel and dimed but rather are intimately involved in the project and its success. That enables a smoother running project which, in turn, allows us to optimize our fees. What it comes down to for us is very satisfied clients and repeat business."

• Craig Shulman, Senior Project Manager with LPA Architects, winner of 2010 Marvin Black Award for the Jet Propulsion Laboratory's Flight

Project's Center project: "The truly open lines of communication were invaluable, and there was no one who felt inhibited to discuss any issue. This, in turn, meant that we were able to resolve issues timely and in manner that enhanced our [LPA's] ability to make a profit and meet the owner's expectations."

• Joanne McAllister, Senior Project Manager, Anshen + Allen architects: "We work faster and more efficiently when the expectations have been clearly communicated to the entire team. In order to work faster, we need to give and take—be willing to work outside of your traditional scope of work and trust that others will do the same for you when you need it. It also fosters trust; more people will go the extra mile."

General Contractors' Point of View

• Len Vetrone, Senior Vice President, Webcor Builders: "From a business point of view, it enables us to make or better our expected profit. Personally, it allows me and my team to enjoy the construction process. It is fun going to work and enjoying people as people. Also, it builds lasting relationships which go beyond the project. For example, the construction market now is extremely dynamic. Everyone is putting together teams, which is exciting."

• Kim Grant, Vice President and Operations Manager, Swinerton Builders, winner of a 2010 Marvin Black Award for a JPL project: "Public works jobs are getting closer to negotiated work. Your next [public] job may be based on [your] relationships. World Class teamwork calls for give and take from all sides. And I enjoyed going to work on them, whereas on other jobs they can grind and wear you down way too much. You can spend a lot of emotional energy on doing things that are essentially worthless."

• Dave Niese, Area Manager, Flatiron Construction: "I wanted to be a civil engineer since I was three years old. I've worked for owners and contractors in my career. Everything I do is for the customer. Therefore it really doesn't matter who I work for. The satisfaction of being on a winning team is the same to me: quality and personal pride."

• Virgil Curtis, Project Sponsor, Balfour Beatty, and winner of a 2008 Marvin Black Award: "High-performing teams make things run so much smoother, make the job enjoyable, and decrease stress. Construction is an inherently stressful industry with ever-increasing restrictions and regulations. On a World Class team, we find a way to pull together. This makes a huge difference."

• Ken Schacherbauer, Perini Building Company: "When you're going to be spending two to three years with people, you want to be coming to work feeling good and knowing that you are accomplishing something. On a World Class team, you communicate openly, your word is honored, and you are remembered. The latter opens the door to future jobs. There's always another job that comes out of a World Class team."

• Ron Rudolph, Turner Construction: "The value of being on a World Class team is immeasurable. There's enough conflict in construction as it is and we need all the tools we can get in this economy to make our clients happy and gain repeat business. There is no alternative if we want to be successful."

• Jack Shewmaker, Construction Manager, Granite Construction: "Being on a high-performance team makes work fun. It's enjoyable to work with our partners rather than competing against them. Solving problems comes naturally. And a good, effective team will naturally be profitable—although the reality in our business is that sometimes a measure of profitability is losing as little as possible."

Owners' Point of View

• Captain Mike Williamson, CEC, U.S. Navy, in charge of over $2.5 billion of new Marine Corps construction in southern California and Arizona: "Without a framework or model, project team members can struggle in figuring out how to make teamwork work. World Class teamwork gives them a set of attributes and a process to know what it means to be on a truly World Class team. It also shows them how to work together to get beyond just the contractual obligations to understanding and executing the end user's true intent."

• Lee Evey, Pentagon Renovation (PENREN): "I appreciated the opportunity to work with some of the best people in this country. I learned early in my career that my success as an owner was always dependent upon the success of the teams I hired; when I helped them to be successful, their success equated to my success. People gravitate to this industry because they have a dream. Somewhere, in the back of their minds, they see themselves working as part of a team that strives to achieve a shared dream."

• Rick Thorpe, Chief Executive Officer, EXPO Authority, LA METRO: "We are going to a best-value selection process wherein on future contracts we will select two teams and pay them a sum of money to do preliminary project engineering and design. Our selection criteria will be on price plus a scorecard on teamwork, which is to say, we will review how they worked with us during this effort as a team. The better a design-build contractor is at working with us as a team, the better their chances of being selected."

• Michael Abeln, U. S. Army Corps of Engineers: "On a World Class team, you will get to the end of the project with more of a consensus and not a compromise. Each stakeholder satisfies their own needs but not at the expense of the project or team. We end up with a better product, and the customer gets maximum value for their dollar. The general contractor comes out ahead as well."

• Jim Bostic, Vice President for Facilities, St. Joseph Health Care System (winner of two Marvin Black Awards): "If a project is going well and there is harmony within the team, it is just so much easier and less stressful. The financial benefit is significant. It costs us so much less in management time. There is also the quality of life issue. On World Class teams everyone is happy and proud. Business as Usual, let alone Combat jobs, can burn out our employees."

• Dennis Turchon, Principal Construction Manager, Caltrans: "World Class teamwork has made my jobs more fun with the added benefit of finding a better way of doing the job. You'll always have different personalities and external pressures. When you have World Class teamwork, a project team deals with these and keeps project success as the top priority."

Construction and Program Managers' Point of View

• Issam Khalaf, Jacobs Construction Management: "We strive to be a World Class organization that delights its clients. If I and my colleagues are not behaving this way, we will lose clients and will lose out in terms of competing in the marketplace. I view my role on a project as providing the best value for my client. And even though I work for the owner, I need to build and earn the trust of the other stakeholders. When I do this and do not take sides, they will work with me as a team player and I can best serve my client."

• Mehdi Hehdari, Vice President and Regional Director, Vanir Construction Management and CM on JPL's 2010 Marvin Black Award-winning project: "Even with very good individuals from very good firms, you can never be assured of Good, let alone World Class, teamwork or chemistry. As a firm, World Class project teamwork enables Vanir CM to have a great résumé with great references which, in turn, allows us to realize new business opportunities. You cannot buy that kind of value. And on these projects I am having fun, which is earned through mutual trust and respect— that too is priceless to me."

• Kathy Mayo, AECOM: "The satisfaction and personal relationships are extremely rewarding. When I run across folks who I've worked with before and we give one another a hug and recollect our success—even though at times it may have been tough—it is a reminder to me of what's really important. Also, at AECOM we want to position ourselves to be competitive in this world construction economy by being creative and collaborative and definitely not Business as Usual."

• Larry Timmer, former Vice President, Harris & Associates, construction managers: "On a World Class team, the project comes first. My role is more as an advisor, but when I tell them (the project team) something, I do so with the overall project success in mind. We try to stay ahead of things and don't let things slow us down. For example, on a water project there was a question of an outfall injection that would be a substantive change. We got the designer, owner, GC, sub, and ourselves on a conference call and quickly, verbally, and mutually agreed on a scope of work which the contractor then priced. It expedited the process significantly."

• Don Wright, Program Manager, Bechtel: "There's nothing perfect in construction even with your utilization of best procedures and processes. With a high performance, World Class team, you can resolve things to the benefit of the project by acknowledging one another's positions and the contractual limitations and procedures."

Subcontractors' Point of View

- Ron Calkins, Project Manager, Briggs Electric (on two Marvin Black Award-winning jobs in the past five years): "Normally we really feel at the bottom of the food chain and, if necessary, have very little recourse except to take legal action where nobody wins. On World Class teams, you feel like you have a say and that your concerns are heard. Your relationships with the designers are on a personal basis. Also, they bring us in sooner and value our expertise. This creates a better flow of work for us, and our efficiencies are measurably increased."

- Frank Miller, Vice President, DynaElectric (Marvin Black Award on JPL project): "On a World Class team, I get to really know all the players and feel that we are all on the same team with the same goals. On a Business as Usual team, I am viewed as an adversary with a hidden agenda, and this barrier keeps me from fully engaging with key members of the team—especially the architect. Also, on World Class teams, I feel like I was a key part of the project, and this leaves me with a feeling of pride."

- Peter Mondery, Southern Contracting: "It is priceless and invaluable. It opens up a line of communication and expectations that otherwise would not exist for a subcontractor. We're all on the same page trying to achieve the same goals. But it also allows us to go beyond the contract specs. And when you give your word, it is your bond."

Overall Project Success = Summation of Individual Success

World Class teamwork is a significant benefit to all project stakeholders. It offers the possibility of a true win-win outcome. It also creates the possibility of a future limited only by the creativity and the freely made commitments of the individual and collective members of a project team—not the contract or specifications.

Also note the interplay between personal and institutional values or rewards. On a World Class team, these are naturally interwoven and reinforce or feed on one another. You cannot have one without the other. The personal satisfaction derived from being on a World Class team contributes to the business or institutional success and vice versa. Indeed the overall success of an organization or project is invariably a consequence of the combined success of all of its individuals. World Class teamwork is a very personal, project-specific process with both significant personal as well as institutional rewards and benefits.

3 World Class Teamwork Is NOT Conditional upon Project Circumstances

> Your present circumstances don't determine where you can go;
> they merely determine where you start.
> —NIDO QUBEIN, AUTHOR, CONSULTANT—

The vast majority of general contractors, owners, designers, and construction managers that I have surveyed attribute extraordinary project success and great teamwork to one or more of the following circumstances:

- We had good people and all got along.
- The plans and specs were clear and complete.
- Site conditions/weather were favorable.
- We had enough money. (Funding and timely payment were not a problem.)
- Third parties, regulatory agencies, etc., were supportive and responsive.
- We didn't have any major disputes.
- Everyone did what they were supposed to do.
- It was not a low/hard-bid job. (This assumes that you cannot have a World Class team on a low-bid job.)
- We utilized IPD, BIM, LEAN, Design-Build, CM at Risk, etc. (This assumes that you *should* have a high-performance team using these alternate project delivery methods or construction processes.)
- We did not have a major crisis or emergency.

Consider that maybe, just maybe, World Class teamwork
doesn't require any of the above.

Benicia Martinez Bridge

Don't get me wrong. I would not want to suggest that these processes or attributes are not desirable. But consider the possibility that you can have a World Class project team without one or more of the above circumstances. Preposterous? Not at all! In fact, it's a fallacy to assume that you need favorable, let alone ideal, circumstances to achieve World Class teamwork.

Let's look at some World Class projects that succeeded despite, rather than because of, their circumstances.

The Fallacy of Needing Good Site Conditions

Consider the $700 million-plus Benicia Martinez Bridge project completed in 2008 in the San Francisco Bay area. As the project began, it quickly became apparent to both Caltrans and the contractor, Kiewit Pacific, that the pile-driving process was killing fish. Not a good thing in the environmentally sensitive Bay area. To make things worse, the geotechnical conditions were not anything like what the plans said they would be. The result? They negotiated a $300 million-plus change order that also pushed the completion date out a full year and a half. Conventional wisdom would suggest that this doomed the project to failure.

But should unknown site conditions be held against the project team? No. Rather, they should be accountable for *how* they dealt with them *as a team*. And they dealt with them very openly and collaboratively and made the very best out of poor circumstances. The project won a Marvin Black Award for partnering excellence and was named *Roads and Bridges* magazine's "Bridge of the Year." As Kevin Mitchell, senior project manager for Kiewit Pacific, put it: "Without extraordinary collaborative efforts, the numerous challenges faced by Kiewit and Caltrans would have undoubtedly brought the project to a halt, and to this day the project would not be complete."

> I believe I did the best I could with what I had.
> —U.S. SUPREME COURT JUSTICE THURGOOD MARSHALL—

The lesson? A World Class team distinguishes between their circumstances or challenges on a job and how they deal with those circumstances *as a team.* Do not beat up yourselves or your teammates for circumstances you could not have prevented, but do work to attempt to anticipate or prevent them and, if not, mitigate them as a team. Deal with where you as a team are today—not where you should be, have to be, or could have been. As we shall see, a World Class team never underestimates its ability to deal with adversity or uncertainty.

The Fallacy of Needing Complete, Accurate Design

How does a World Class team deal with incomplete and/or inaccurate plans and specifications? They begin with the assumption that there is no such thing as a fully complete, coordinated, and accurate design—with all due respect to the designers. In fact, as many a designer has told me that owners would never want to pay what truly and 100% accurate complete plans would cost.

When a World Class team encounters a design deficiency, they acknowledge it openly, verbally, quickly, and without placing blame or taking advantage of the situation. Rather, they express their concerns in the context of the team's common purpose for project success. An example might be, "The state of the plans relative to the foundation may hinder our ability to achieve our team goal of completing this project by X date. How can we as a team deal with that on a go-forward basis?" Now of course they wouldn't state it so formally, but you get the message.

Scott Ashton of Berg Electric explains: "In these situations you've got to sit down around the table with the owner, GC, and the engineer and acknowledge the issue openly. On a World Class team, everyone is receptive and not defensive, which allows us to put forward better ways of doing things to the owner's benefit."

David Allen, Architect and PM for the U.S. District Court, speaks about such a resourceful way on his $380 million U.S. Courthouse San Diego Annex project: "We couldn't find the three-dimensional artwork for the official seal in one of our new courtrooms. So we, and a sitting judge, trusted our GC, Hensel Phelps, to go into the judge's existing courtroom, take the seal off the wall, fly it to Utah to be laser scanned, and bring it back."

A World Class team might develop an approach to complete and/or clean the design as a team to stay ahead of and support their construction schedule goal and maybe even enhance quality. This often involves bringing designers onsite for the time it takes to complete the design—maybe even the whole job. Any cost issues due to design deficiencies are dealt with later, if necessary, between owner and designer. The team stays focused on their common purpose or goals. They should not fault themselves for the state of the design unless, of course, they are operating with a design-build delivery method. But even World Class design-build teams, as the comment below indicates, do not dwell on fault or blame.

Brian Cahill of Barnhart Balfour Beatty explains: "We had an architect on a design-build job who was real uptight, gun-shy, and thought he would lose a lot of money due to his firm's potential design errors. We immediately removed that fear by affirming to him that neither we nor the owner were out to hurt him but rather were there to work with him toward the future success of the project and the team."

World Class teams and their leaders seek collaborative, go-forward solutions to design issues and recognize that working with a defensive designer incurs significantly greater costs—especially in time and mutual stress— through playing what I term the "design games." Among those are: "You should have assumed"; "The intent should have been clear"; "This is clearly an equal"; "That is a clearly a design (constructability) issue"; "It's industry standard"; and so forth by all stakeholders.

Sylvia Botero of RBB Architects notes: "On a World Class team, the entire project team works with us to ensure that our design supports the needs of all stakeholders throughout the construction phase. There's no arguing over whether the design is complete or accurate. It is all about taking the existing design and ensuring that it supports those individuals at the field level who are charged with putting our design into reality. And this is done in a supportive and collaborative manner, which we welcome."

On World Class teams, as we will see, individual and collective actions are grounded in common goals which lead to mutual support. By contrast, in Business as Usual projects, everyone's first priority is to avoid or deflect risk.

The Fallacy of Needing Sufficient Resources and Funding

One experienced project manager told me, "I would once like to work on a high-profile job that has no problem with funding." How many of you have worked on a job where funding was unlimited or not an issue? OK, now that we are back in the real world, let's talk about how World Class teams deal with insufficient funding and resources.

Consider the major remodel of the First Presbyterian Church of Bel Air, which just happened to be Ronald Reagan's old church in California. The project team members first openly acknowledged to one another that there would be changes, then very candidly guesstimated their expectations in each category: unknown site conditions, owner's additions, and design deficiencies. The result? At least 19 percent of contract value. The executive director of the church threw up his hands and said, "There's absolutely no way we can afford that!" So the team immediately initiated an aggressive scope reduction and value engineering process to bring expected costs in line with available owner resources.

Greg Simons, Executive Vice President of Bernards Construction on that job, explains how they found solutions as a team: "The project involved a remodel on a challenging site with a lot of unforeseen conditions. Once our anticipated cost projection was determined as a team, we initiated a brainstorming session with all stakeholders to mitigate the total cost of change orders. For example, when we determined that the site was sitting on solid rock instead of standard soil, the team came up with the idea of bringing in earth fill. This raised the elevation of the building but allowed us to trench and put in utilities in the fill instead of blasting and drilling the rock."

The point is that if an owner, or any other stakeholder, on a World Class team has funding or resource issues, they surface them early and verbally to their fellow team members. Yes, this is making yourself vulnerable, but making yourself vulnerable is also a key to establishing trust, as we'll see in chapter 8. The team then mutually agrees on the specific impacts, prioritizes those shortfalls, and then talks about resolving them as a team.

A key, and invariably best resolution World Class teams agree, comes through making more timely verbal decisions as a team. Most projects struggle with insufficient human resources at one time or another over their duration. On the Victorville United States Penitentiary project, the general contractor, Hensel Phelps, found themselves critically short of field engineers. They acknowledged this with their team and, as Steve Kimball, Project Manager for Hensel Phelps, put it, "We drafted two of our estimators from our regional office and sent them out there for a couple months to work as field engineers. You do what it takes with what you've got, and in this case we were able to give our estimators some valuable field experience."

As we will see in chapter 9, which speaks of the project team "owning project success 100%," most World Class teams also look first at optimizing the resources they have at hand with the assumption that through true World Class teamwork, they can do much more with less.

The Fallacy of Not Being Able to Influence Third Parties and Regulatory Agencies

On large transit projects with a duration of four to five years, there are dozens of agencies, municipalities, utility districts, and residential and commercial entities to deal with. How do you manage that cast of thousands? Mike Aparicio, Vice President for Transit Operations with Skanska, explains: "On a $900 million-plus transit project, there are daily obstacles, conflicts, crises, surprises, and even major landmines involving third parties that will, if only left up to the GC or design-build team to resolve, guarantee to stop your job. You've got to find a way to engage with them early and collaboratively. Having a World Class team with these entities as active team players makes this job much easier." We'll learn more about specific strategies for dealing with the larger, complex project in chapter 16.

A World Class team acknowledges the role of third parties and regulatory agencies on team goals early on and prioritizes them relative to their impact. The team then looks at their collective ability to genuinely engage with and enroll those third parties.

Sometimes this may require the project team going up their management ladder and using their "silver bullets" to deal with the other entity. Bringing in senior management is a last resort, but with the full project team behind the request and if expediting the issue is one of the key show-stoppers to meeting their team schedule goal, the request can be much more compelling to senior management and the third party. For example, you might say, "We're on schedule for a March 1 completion, but without permanent power after October 1, that will cost us $150,000 a week in delay costs."

The Fallacy of Not Having or Avoiding Issues or Disputes

A World Class team accepts the fact that disputes, misunderstandings, mistakes, and different interpretations are unavoidable on a construction project. Even with the best plans and contracts, it is ultimately a very human, personal experience. If you start with that assumption, the challenge becomes "How can we as a team prevent those issues that we can, mitigate the impact of those we cannot prevent, and, above all, continue to keep the job moving toward our common goals without ill will or personal animosity?" Acknowledging this protocol, in effect, makes it OK for individuals to agree to disagree at each level within the project hierarchy and then elevate issues and disputes quickly.

On Caltrans' West Bay Approach project with Tutor-Saliba Corporation anchoring the west end of the new San Francisco Bay Bridge, the project team utilized their Disputes Review Board (DRB) on one occasion, and numerous issues went all the way up and down their dispute resolution ladder. In other words, they agreed to disagree up their respective resolution ladders. How then can Mike Forner, head of the Caltrans Toll Bridge Program, call this job "the best project and team on the entire Toll Bridge Program"?

The $470 million, five-and-a-half-year project faced major technological challenges and significant impact on existing traffic, including a Labor Day weekend shutdown of the San Francisco Bay Bridge. They followed their dispute resolution protocol, kept the job moving, still trusted one another, bore one another no ill will or animosity, and worked together collaboratively while multiple, complex issues were continually being dealt with up and down their resolution ladder. That is a very mature and dynamic World Class team. We'll look at specific strategies for resolving disputes in chapter 13.

The Fallacy That Everyone Just Needs To Do Their Job and Follow the Contract

While contracts, plans, project delivery methods, and specifications can provide a foundation, they can never anticipate all the uncertainties inherent in construction. Here is how one contractor expressed it: "How can each of us on a project start by doing what we each think is the right thing and still have it go wrong?"

Gettin' good players is easy. Gettin' 'em to play together is the hard part.
—CASEY STENGEL, NEW YORK YANKEES MANAGER—

It's easy to think that if everyone just did what they're supposed to do or did the right thing, you'd have a good team and an excellent project, but there are problems with this assumption. Each team member will have different assumptions about what "supposed to do" or "the right thing" means. As any project stakeholder with more than a couple of years of project experience knows, two well qualified individuals, such as an inspector and a foreman, can take a well-written contract and a relatively complete set of plans and specs and draw two very different conclusions about how the work should be done, what the end product should look like, and who should be doing what.

Robert Develle, Manager of the Facilities Division of NASA's Jet Propulsion Laboratory, notes, "Today's jobs are incredibly more complex. You cannot do them in silos or by handing things off. Most issues require a lot of hands touching them as a team. Without that, the jobs are just too difficult."

The Fallacy That a Collaborative Project Delivery Method Will Assure Teamwork

I'll acknowledge that design-build, CM at Risk, preselection, design-assist, and employment of BIM/VBM, LEAN can all enhance the probability of high-performance teamwork as compared to a pure hard-bid project. But they by no means guarantee or ensure it. A good, collaborative project delivery method does not always translate into behavior at the project level.

Dan Gilbert with Kaiser Permanente cautions: "A new, promising alternate project delivery method or new construction process, if left alone, might actually hamper World Class teamwork. Individuals can tend to place unwarranted or untested faith in the PDM or process and may not be willing to invest time in the real hard work of agreeing upon goals, talking about risk, sharing expectations, and hammering those out together. This can doom a team. On World Class teams, you start with your model and then allow it to take on its own form based upon those conversations."

Nor should World Class teamwork be viewed as something more that needs to be bolted on to a project.

> World Class teamwork, successfully implemented, should seamlessly integrate into, facilitate, and enhance your selected PDM; construction methodologies; the capabilities, knowledge, and intentions of all the individuals involved; and the unique challenges/opportunities and circumstances facing the team at the time.

"At the time" is vitally important. All too often teams talk about what should have happened or what they believe the contract and alternative project delivery method (APDM) should call for or how it worked on a previous job. A good World Class team deals with the reality of where the job is at this moment in the minds of the individuals present and considers their expressed wants, needs, past experience, personalities, and, yes, egos. In other words it calls for genuine, verbal engagement between people in terms of what is best for that project. It also acknowledges that there is no one best way to implement a PDM or BIM and that on a specific project, regardless of its project delivery method, there will always be risk or different perceptions of risk. Only through openly acknowledging this reality can people genuinely understand, collaborate with, and trust one another. We'll learn more about this in chapter 10.

> No battle plan survives contact with the enemy.
> —HELMUTH VON MOLKE, GERMAN FIELD MARSHAL—

Barry Thalden of Thalden•Boyd•Emery Architects is a huge proponent of Integrated Project Delivery. He says, "World Class teamwork deals with the people and personality aspects of your project delivery method."

Greg Howell and Glenn Ballard of the LEAN Construction Institute note, "It is relatively easy to contract for the purchase of a thing and relatively difficult to contract for behavior. Cultural change and project leadership are required."

In his 2009 book *How the Mighty Fall and Why Some Companies Never Give In*, Jim Collins points out that one of the primary causes of organization failure is the constant searching for a silver bullet or the latest management gimmick that will make things better fast. This applies to construction project teams as well. Individuals who expect new project delivery methods, construction methodologies, or contractual models—in and of themselves—to eliminate risk, establish trust, and bring forth high-performance or World Class project teamwork and results are misguided.

World Class teamwork is not a gimmick, technique, or methodology. Rather it is a very fundamental way of relating to one another that transcends the type of project, PDM, or construction methodology.

> Your intent, commitment, and behaviors—and that of your colleagues—
> on a project count for a lot more than the technique, PDM,
> or construction processes you employ.

Neither, as we will see, is World Class teamwork just an easy pill to swallow. It requires hard work, ongoing commitment, and dealing with questions, issues, and opportunities that normally are not asked or considered.

Len Vetrone with Webcor Builders explains: "To some extent on high performance or World Class teams, you actually forget about the formal structure and processes, and it is more about the relationships and the intentions of the individuals. The structure kind of fades." As we'll see, World Class teams end up resembling informal networks or "blended teams," as Lou Palandrani, Senior Vice President for the Clark Construction Group, calls them. They relate more on the basis of common purpose and real-time, informal communication processes than they do on formal structure and written communication. More about this in chapter 12.

If your primary intent on a construction project is to minimize or transfer your risk or just win or prevail as a individual or organization, you will never achieve World Class teamwork, even with the most effective and sophisticated project management tools and methodologies. If, on the other hand, your commitment is to truly achieve extraordinary overall project success and WCT with your fellow stakeholders, then newer ADMs and technologies can enhance and benefit from a commitment to WCT.

> If a contractor's sole intent is to maximize his profit, he should invest in a CD,
> and then he'll know exactly how much money he will make.
> —ED RUCKLE, U.S. NAVY CIVIL SERVICE, RETIRED;
> INDEPENDENT CONSULTANT WITH RUCKLE ASSOCIATES—

Yet even if you are obligated to work with a hard-bid project, all is not lost. One big advantage of these projects is that the project team is much less inclined to take collaboration, let alone World Class teamwork, for granted. Consequently, design-bid-build teams are often more willing to engage in a formal process to enable and facilitate teamwork.

The Fallacy of Having to Have Good People

The most common assumption is that you really have to have competent, qualified, and trustworthy people to have a World Class team. But is that necessarily true?

On a $200 million-plus water treatment plant that was completed in the winter of 2010, the project team started by defining common goals and making very specific personal commitments to action to support those goals. A couple of weeks after the partnering workshop, the general contractor's project manager went in person to the third-party construction manager's on-site manager and asked him if there was a reason he was not following through on the commitments he made in the workshop. The CM replied in effect, "We're going to do things my way." The PM did what you're supposed to do on World Class teams: he elevated the issue to his boss, the regional vice president for the general contractor. He followed the team's protocol for dealing with disputes and brought this up verbally to his counterpart with the CM firm. The CM regional manager replaced his on-site manager.

I'm not advocating replacing people wholesale, but if individuals do not play as team players per their mutually agreed-upon teamwork standards although every effort is made to help them do so, then maybe that is what is necessary. John Sealey, former head of the Federal Bureau of Prisons Construction branch in Washington D.C., would say, "If any of my people aren't team players, they are no longer part of the team." He backed this up on more than one occasion, and the general contractors and design-build team principals on his jobs invariably articulated the same commitment and adopted the same policy with their people. This strong commitment to teamwork, I believe, contributed significantly to the Victorville USP winning a Marvin Black Award for partnering excellence in 2005.

> **TIP:** Ask this question at the initial partnering/team meeting after the team has committed to World Class teamwork or a shared set of team values: "How should we deal with individuals who cannot or will not behave in accordance with the standards of behavior we have just mutually agreed upon and committed to?"

Here's another approach to the challenge of dealing with individuals who cannot or will not act as team players. At the kickoff of a project with Los Angeles Unified School District, the whole team acknowledged that a key team member who was not present did not appear open to acting on the basis of common goals, teamwork, and trust. The team discussed this openly and agreed to try to talk the individual into a more collaborative effort. The senior project manager for the district, Anthony Sanchez, challenged the team by saying, "It would be a failure for all of us if we didn't help this guy succeed." Two months later at the next partnering meeting, the individual not only showed up but genuinely contributed to the team's efforts. The lesson? Don't necessarily assume an individual's intentions or resign yourself to the idea that they cannot change.

In a third example, the team from the San Diego Central Public Library project with Turner Construction and Tucker, Sadler Architects was confronted with a subconsultant who had what one team member generously described as a "reactive, CYA mentality." The approach the team came up with involved standing, weekly, face-to-face meetings with this individual to preempt his letter writing and e-mailing and engage with him proactively relative to future decisions.

How about not having a key player active on a project? Let's hear from Rick Thorpe with LA METRO: "If someone is not on board, we acknowledge the issue openly to the team and then ask the question 'How do we, as a team, manage this job in the interim while waiting for a new project manager?'"

The Fallacy That a Really Low Bid Can Only Lead to Unwarranted Change Orders and Claims

When the lowest bid is significantly lower than the other bids and from an unknown firm, an owner might assume that their job would be a claim and change order nightmare and that they should prepare to act accordingly. Unfortunately, as we will see, this can become a self-fulfilling prophecy.

It's a new world out there. Even the best and most reputable firms are bidding jobs well outside their traditional expertise and geographical locations with razor-thin margins. Does this negate the possibility of World Class teamwork? Not necessarily.

Here's an example of how one contractor is experiencing an owner's willingness to engage and coach the project team. George Delano, Senior Project Manager of Granite Construction, explains: "In the old days the notion was that the owner left us to our own devices and we succeeded or failed on our own. Now we see more owners and CMs who appreciate the big picture and the value of a collaborative relationship reaching out to us as general contractors and saying, in effect, 'We know you guys are up against it on this bid. How can we make this job go well for all of us?' Likewise, we're more willing going into a job to be candid about the assumptions in our bid and where we need the owner's and CM's help for our mutual success."

How about from the owner's or program manager's point of view? Brian Jordan, Senior Vice President and Regional Manager with AECOM, comments: "On a major wastewater treatment plant, the low bidder was well beneath the second low bidder and had little local prior experience in this type of construction. You need to approach these types of situations with an open mind. So we and the owner met and talked with the contractor and learned that the schedule really drove their bid. Fortunately, it was in the owner's interest to expedite the work as well. This enabled us to find common ground. You've got to be open and share one another's critical assumptions and motivations ahead of construction actually beginning."

Of course, there will still be organizations who believe the claims/change-order game is the best way to make up for a low bid, but those are fewer and fewer. We will talk more about this in chapter 8.

The Fallacy That Significant, Pervasive Adversity Negates Teamwork

The worse the project circumstances, the easier it may be to build a World Class team. It sounds counterintuitive at first. I couldn't understand this for a while until Josh Randall, Vice President for Tutor Perini Corporation, explained it during the LA METRO Red Line projects of the late nineties when the city, press, and residents were openly against the projects. Site conditions and access were miserable. Even the Los Angeles MTA senior management, which was a revolving door at the time, had a very dysfunctional organization culture. It has since become a model of excellence for transit projects nationwide.

"It was a consequence of a 'Circle the Wagons' effect," Josh said. "We all at the project level quickly realized that the only way these individual station jobs would be successful would be if we came together at the project level as a true high-performance team. We succeeded in spite of the circumstances or maybe because of them."

Bob Finney, District #4 Deputy Director for Construction for Caltrans in the San Francisco Bay area, adds, "A World Class team will find a way to make a project work and make it better. They can take a project fraught with risk and peril and keep it going."

In fact, it may even be true that you cannot have a World Class team *without* limits, constraints, and challenges. If these do not exist, a World

Class team creates its own challenges. True trust, some pundits postulate, can only arise out of challenge, adversity, and risk. World Class teams, as we will see, can actually thrive on adversity. And the reality today is that most large, urban construction projects are nothing more than a continual string of challenges, adversity, and sometimes nasty surprises. So how do you deal with it without naively assuming adversity will go away or should not exist? You come together as a World Class team before you encounter those challenges. More about this in chapter 8.

The Fallacy That Achieving World Class Teamwork Is a Short-Term, Feel-Good Experience

Most of us have been through team-building experiences that merely left a temporary, residual feeling of good will and intentions, and consequently we are rightly skeptical of anything that promises a quick, easy fix. World Class teamwork is not a quick, easy fix. Often it is hard, sustained effort. Yet, as we will see, it is purposeful, collaborative effort that is grounded in very specific personal commitments to action to which the individuals and project team hold themselves accountable. It is, in other words, about committed action, not vague intentions. If individuals and organizations are not willing to engage on such a basis, this process is neither meaningful nor worth the effort.

In my experience, professionals and craftspeople in design and construction are the ultimate pragmatists. They are decidedly leery about "rah-rah" experiences, games, or psychological processes, let alone exhortations from senior management to "win the big one." Such techniques have, at best, a short-term effect. Being from California, I have fun with workshop participants at the outset of a partnering workshop by reaffirming to them that we will do the traditional team-building exercises, starting, of course, with the hot tub (clothing optional), the group hug, the chant, and of course a good "Circle of Trust" and a soulful rendition of "Kumbaya," followed by the capstone event—the human sacrifice, for which invariably, a subcontractor is chosen.

Talking and learning about listening or communication skills is useful, as can be psychological profiles. But these at best produce a better understanding and do not, by themselves, generate what I term committed action. As we will see, on a World Class team, individuals will actively seek to listen, understand, and communicate with one another because of their shared commitment to a compelling purpose and an agreed-upon protocol (our ten WCT behaviors) that support achieving that purpose.

What construction professionals do value is the opportunity and freedom to excel and express their skills on a project they can be proud of.

What World Class Teamwork Really Requires

If you take away all the conditions (excuses?), as we have above, what does World Class teamwork really require? In my experience, it comes down to a commitment by senior management to working on the basis of shared values of trust, common purpose, and teamwork with a mutually agreed-upon protocol or process that leaves their team in committed action toward common goals.

Ken Schacherbauer with Perini notes, "I take our commitments very seriously and try to project a positive attitude toward the owner and design team that we are committed to World Class teamwork." Psychologists call the power of expectations the Pygmalion Effect; it is more commonly known as the self-fulfilling prophecy.

That is why it is imperative to differentiate between achieving or striving for project team excellence and conventional measures of project success. By declaring yourselves successful as a World Class team, you can assert your effectiveness without being dependent upon the ultimate success of the project. As in the Benicia Martinez bridge example, you can be late and over budget and still be a World Class team. It is a bit of a word game, but a team that believes itself to be World Class in the face of disadvantageous circumstances or at least is continuing to strive toward WCT has a big leg up on project teams who resign themselves to being victims of their circumstances.

John Wooden, the ex-UCLA basketball coach who was recently selected as "Best Coach of All Time," never tried to motivate his players or exhort them to win a game or tell them that "It's important that we be #1 or that we had to be the NCAA Champions." Rather, he was challenging them consistently, individually and as a team, to be the best they could be as individuals and as a team.

Here is how Dan Gilbert of Kaiser Permanente put it:

> The value of the World Class team process and approach springs from three sources: First, the alignment of the personal and professional goals of the individual participants and the business interests of their respective firms with that of the other stakeholders. This, in turn facilitates the establishment of the team based on those common goals and purpose for the project. Second, establishment of partnering language that enhances communication and negotiation of individual commitments among the stakeholders. Third, development of and commitment to specific and measurable project goals, along with detailed processes necessary to accomplish and review the team's performance of them.

World Class teamwork is like any other collaborative human behavior. If you and your teammates have mutually agreed upon clear standards of excellence—goals and behaviors—which you all commit to striving to achieve and you continually measure your performance by that standard, you stand a very good chance of eventually getting there . . . or at least getting close. World Class teamwork is a mindset as well as a set of behavioral practices backed up by committed action.

4 Taking Away Our Mental Constraints to World Class Teamwork

One of the most difficult aspects associated with transitioning people from design-bid-build to design-build project delivery is mental.

—BARBARA JACKSON,

"TAKING AWAY THE MENTAL RESTRAINTS OF DESIGN-BUILD"—

If you look at World Class teams in any endeavor—whether sports, business, or construction projects—a common thread is that they are rarely led or managed in a conventional way. Construction project team members often resent being contractually limited, rebel against being motivated, and dislike being directed. So where does that leave us?

Let's hear from Peter Drucker, perhaps the foremost management thinker of the twentieth century:

> The leaders who work most effectively, it seems to me, never say "I," and that's not because they have trained themselves not to say "I." They don't think "I." They think "we"; they think "team." They understand their job to be to make the team function. They accept responsibility and don't sidestep it, but "we" gets the credit. . . . This is what creates trust, what enables you to get the task done.[8]

The Most Significant Constraint: Assumptions

The biggest barrier to a construction project team being a World Class team is the assumptions that senior management of each the major stakeholders may have about the ability of a project team to work together collaboratively on the basis of trust, teamwork, and common goals.

How did this situation come about? We may need a little history lesson.

Since the early 1960s, construction in the United States began to become a very risk-averse industry. In his seminal book, *The Death of Common Sense: How Law Is Suffocating America*, attorney Philip Howard made a strong case:

> Law began infiltrating the nooks and crannies of our lives in the 1960s and crowding out our common sense. Rules replaced thinking. Process replaced responsibility. One false idea lay at the bottom of these developments: that human judgment should be banned from anything to do with law. We fell for the idea that all could be laid out in a tidy legal system where decisions were pre-determined, social choices pre-made.[9]

Nowhere did this manifest itself more than in public sector construction. Private construction was also significantly tainted. The notion was that if construction contracts were comprehensive and detailed enough, the owner could avoid (or transfer) all risk. The game was not to win but rather to minimize your risk and loss. How uninspiring!

Betsey Dougherty of Dougherty + Dougherty Architects explains: "The liability insurance crisis of the 1970s and 1980s coached designers to diminish their liability during construction, which in turn led to the erosion of the role of the design professional relative to construction support services."

Can you imagine the length of the contracts that would address all the possible risks and scenarios that might occur on a construction project? The idea of World Class teamwork didn't even occur to those individuals writing or managing construction contracts. Has anyone ever been truly inspired by a written contract? OK, maybe the U.S. Constitution, but that document essentially reasserts individual rights and freedoms rather than seeking to limit or constrain them. I'm not advocating ignoring construction contracts altogether. We'll explore their role more in chapter 8.

One example of this dependence on contracts was in the way major public agencies trained their construction/project managers back in those days. For over twenty years, Ed Ruckle was Resident Officer in Charge of

Construction for the Construction Battalion Center, Port Hueneme, California, the training base for naval construction management. Ed recalls: "In the 1980s through early 1990s, Navy contract managers and ROICCs (Resident Officer In Charge of Construction) attending the Naval Civil Engineer Corps Officer School were basically instructed in how to implement and enforce contract requirements. The fundamental assumption behind this training was that our contractors needed to be watched, controlled, and closely managed."

Contractors and designers were not about to roll over with this trend. They hired attorneys and claims consultants who were able to effectively counter even the most bulletproof contracts. This resulted in project teams that, at best, were characterized by Business as Usual.

Constraint #2: The Assumption that Construction Is a Zero-Sum Game

With this assumption comes the notion that you must out-game or avoid being out-gamed by your fellow project stakeholders in order to win.

I used to have a lot of fun in workshops by having project teams identify the "games we play" in Business as Usual and Combat projects, where the intent is not to win or play as a team but rather to prevail as a single stakeholder, minimize or transfer risk, and control behavior. Here are just a few of the games they came up with:

- The high/low change order pricing game.
- "You may beat me down this time, but I'll get even later." (unspoken)
- Using the schedule as a weapon
- "It's not my job."
- Case building by accumulating paperwork. In the U.S. Navy they used to call it the "rule of gross tonnage."
- Posturing
- "I didn't bid it that way."
- "Do you have a different set of plans/specs?"
- "They let me do it this way on the last job."
- "My intent was . . ." or "It's industry standard" vs. "It's not industry standard."

- Tennis (back-and-forth paperwork or e-mails)
- Stonewalling
- Flood them with RFIs
- "Just read the contract."
- "Rejected"—with no explanation
- Minimum to get by or "Just build it per plans and specs."
- "The other inspector said it was OK."
- Taking the maximum amount of time to approve an RFI/submittal
- The blame game
- Cat-and-mouse game played between inspectors and foremen

One project team actually came up with 65 games! So who wins once game playing, case building, and posturing start on a construction project? No one. It's hard to consistently prevail at game playing, particularly on larger jobs where you're dealing with experienced professionals (fellow game players?). If you have a reputation as a good game player or by-the-book, litigious stakeholder, word gets out. There are large public works owners who cannot understand why they get few bids or the bids they do get are always 20 percent over the designer's estimate.

What is the invariable consequence of game playing? Everybody gets sucked into it, hunkers down in their foxhole, and builds their Maginot Line, and the whole job stalls. Who started it? Who knows? You could waste a lot of time and money trying to figure it out for no real purpose. Captain Mike Williamson, CEC, with the U.S. Navy explains, "Game playing occurs when you have imperfect information and people perceive other stakeholders as withholding information. It has a trickle effect, and everyone goes into a defensive mode."

So we're back to senior management's role. All it takes is one stakeholder's senior manager or principal to be convinced that Business as Usual is the best/only way to play the game, and your project team is dead in the water as far as achieving World Class teamwork. You can be sure that this attitude will be adopted by their subordinates on the job. More about dealing with Business as Usual in chapter 13.

Constraint #3: The Assumption that World Class Teamwork Will Require You to Work Harder, Longer, and at Greater Cost

Those of you who have been a part of a World Class team know this to be a fallacy. Yes, World Class teamwork is characterized by more verbal communication and meetings in the beginning. The trend toward design-assist, BIM, and VBM is an open acknowledgement of the value of having the contractor, designer, and owner communicating collaboratively before the design is finalized to minimize future design conflicts, changes, and errors.

The assumption behind this initial investment in time and resources is that it will pay off in spades in terms of avoiding misunderstandings, different interpretations, and constructability issues/RFIs, thereby expediting delivery, reducing cost, and enabling the team to avoid claims and disputes at the end of the job.

World Class teamwork is work, but it is a stimulating, positive, and above all a meaningful and *purposeful* type of work. It's not unusual on World Class teams to see individuals working ten- and twelve-hour days, six days a week. But they're doing it not because they have to but rather because they are truly personally committed to supporting their team to achieve a compelling goal and the intrinsic satisfactions they realize from that effort.

John Jansen of Kiewit explains: "Purposeful work adds a lot more pride to what you're doing as an individual. You're more energized and you see where you effort and long hours are being rewarded. People on these jobs are much more engaged and want to keep contributing to the project's success."

Constraint #4: The Assumption that There Is No Evident Payoff to You or Your Organization for Being Part of a World Class Team

A very valid concern. But this is one that *only* comes up from folks who have never been part of a World Class project team.

Let's look first at the role of work in personal happiness. Yes, I said *happiness*—a word that many people do not equate with working on a construction project. According to Dennis Prager, author *of Happiness Is a Serious Problem*, work can be a "major source of happiness—if the work is joyful and meaningful." He goes on to state:

When a person engages in work primarily to make money and achieve success, the work is rarely joyful or ultimately meaningful to that person. This is why unpaid volunteers can easily derive more happiness from their work than millionaires do from theirs. A simple test to ascertain how much you enjoy and derive meaning from your work is to ask yourself whether you would continue doing it if you won the lottery.[10]

So what do members of World Class teams have to say about the personal value of the experience?

• Don Eng, Director, Construction Management Division, City and County of San Francisco: "Less personal stress and the confidence that the job will get done."

Less stress and greater peace of mind surface as key benefits for over 70 percent of World Class team members. Some say that the ability to go home at night, not worry about the actions or intentions of your fellow teammates, and look forward to going to work tomorrow is priceless.

• Boone Hellmann, Campus Architect, University of California, San Diego: "I can sleep at night because I know that my project manager has my interests protected, and so do my contractor and designer."

• Barry Thalden, Thalden•Boyd•Emery Architects: "Pride in the team and being part of it. Seeing where your success is tied to the success of the team is very rewarding to me."

• Kirk Hazen, Vice President, Hensel Phelps, Orlando: "On a World Class team, everyone gives 100 percent. That makes my life a lot easier and gets me excited about the project. It gets my inner juices flowing by seeing the joy of the team in fulfilling their goals."

• Mike Aparicio, Skanska: "It's an emotional, personal thing which leaves me with a true love of the game (construction). There's a passion and pride that comes from these jobs."

Several years ago I attended a UCLA business school alumni weekend where our keynote speaker was legendary coach John Wooden, then 97 years of age! We had the privilege of asking him questions, so I asked: "Coach, you've spoken of passion and love. What's the difference?" He said,

"It's easy for a coach to get a team passionate about a game. But to enable them to truly love the game is something altogether different."

• Commander Whit Robinson, CEC, U.S. Navy: "I've been in the Navy 18½ years. I am really excited to see how far we are able go with World Class teamwork on our Naval Hospital Camp Pendleton."

• Craig Shulman, Senior Project Manager with LPA Architects on the Jet Propulsion Laboratory's 2010 Marvin Black Award-winning project: "Personally, I could honestly say that I was sad that this job was over. I had never had that happen before. I truly enjoyed going to work."

• Wayne Lindholm, Executive Vice President, Hensel Phelps Construction: "The value of the personal relationships that come out of jobs like these is huge. And not just from a business perspective. It is kind of neat to stay in touch with clients and vice versa when you're not involved in a job with them. It's a life, not just a job, and it is a lot more fun this way."

TIP: The best way to deal with this constraint of "What's in it for me?" is to have those individuals who have been part of a World Class team to share their experiences.

Daniel Pink, author of *Drive: The Surprising Truth about What Motivates Us,* challenges the notion that people are primarily motivated by the carrot and stick. For algorithmic tasks (those with routine, predictable outcomes), extrinsic motivators like money and tangible rewards work well. But for heuristic tasks which involve more creative, innovative thinking and collaborative problem-solving, the work itself can be inherently enjoyable. In other words, as construction projects become more complex and the opportunity for truly innovative and collaborative thinking increases, the need for extrinsic motivators decreases for contractors, owners, designers, and construction managers alike.

World Class teamwork optimizes an individual's ability to realize intrinsic motivation. On Business as Usual and even Good projects, most individuals' work is essentially algorithmic—you do your job, hand it off to me, and I'll do mine—and therefore precludes intrinsic motivation.

Constraint #5: The Assumption that Although You May Be Committed to World Class Teamwork, You Don't Know about Your Colleagues, So Why Risk It?

Let's face it: It's easy, safe, and predictable to default to stereotypes and our lowest expectations of one another. "It is easier to work on the basis of Business as Usual," says Jim Linthicum with the San Diego Association of Governments (SANDAG). I'm not about to drop my shield when there's a risk that you might take advantage of me.

What's the risk of committing to work together on the basis of WCT or common stretch goals, teamwork, and personal integrity? Team members often respond, "Well, the contractor might not follow through on their commitments." True, but how many times are you going to let this happen before you bring up your shield? The risk is really minimal. No one is going let someone continually eat their lunch.

Virgil Curtis of Balfour Beatty in Seattle explains: "Yes, trust is risky. But it's a question of risk versus reward. The reward of trust is great when your partner reciprocates. If this doesn't happen, it's only risky one time. And then at least I know what I'm dealing with."

> I have found that by trusting people until they
> prove themselves unworthy of that trust, a lot more happens.
> —JIM BURKE, FORMER CHAIRMAN AND CEO, JOHNSON & JOHNSON—

As one contractor told us, "On a World Class team, both of us trust one another never to come up with an 'I gotcha.'"

Pink's hypothesis that we are all motivated fundamentally by similar circumstances challenges the assumption that most project stakeholders have: that the others on a project (those not in their own tribe or profession) are solely motivated by self-interests that are inherently incompatible with their own. These assumptions or expectations, as we know, have a way of becoming self-fulfilling.

For example, what do owners and designers often assume about the intentions of **contractors**?

- Only in it for the money.
- Change order artists
- Just trying to meet the minimum to get by
- Sharks/used-car salesmen—take your pick
- Cutting corners where and when they can

Likewise, what assumptions do contractors and designers have about **owners?**

- Just a bureaucratic process for them
- Cannot or will not make a decision
- Change their minds, don't know what they want
- Want a Cadillac on a Chevrolet budget
- Can't even agree with one another

What do contractors, owners, and designers think about **construction or program managers?**

- No real personal stake in the success or failure of the job
- Paper pushers
- Justifying their own existence
- Not at risk

What do contractors, owners, and CMs think about **architects and engineers?**

- Never willing to acknowledge a mistake, defensive
- No experience or interest in constructability
- Building a monument to themselves
- In it for their ego

In one workshop exercise where team members were encouraged to state their stereotypes, architects were accused of being "God-like." With that, the principal of the design firm stood up and asserted in a loud voice, "I am not God-like; I *am* God!" There is nothing like a self-deprecating sense of humor to allow us to overcome our stereotypes.

Ken Schacherbauer with Perini Building says: "The biggest challenge to World Class teamwork is breaking down preconceived barriers or stereotypes. Only by getting your subcontractors in a room with your owners to set common goals can the owners really see the passion that most subcontractors have for doing first-class work."

Stereotypes by definition are a bit of an exaggeration, but for many they are or have been reality. In fact, there are more than a few in the construction industry who are hard-wired this way. As one client put it, "It is unfortunate not only for our industry but also for these individuals and their firms. They are on their way to becoming dinosaurs."

I had an experience with such a contractor involved in a local project in southern California. He was brazen enough to openly acknowledge to all that he was going to make up for his low bid through change orders. The city bent over backward to be accommodating, but nothing they did could change his conviction that he had to play hardball to win and that the city was intentionally out to get him. Frankly, I left feeling sorry for his two sons, both recent graduates of a high-caliber engineering school. They were being trained in a moribund business ethic that, in the long run, is a professional, personal, and business dead end.

What would happen, for example, if all project stakeholders on your next job assumed that all of their fellow team members were there for the same intrinsic rewards or satisfactions as you were? What if they all wanted to be part of a team that truly challenged them professionally and offered the opportunity for creative and collaborative thinking, which in turn generated a true sense of pride and accomplishment?

Likewise, what would be the consequences if, on your next project, you and your fellow team members related to one another on the basis of their mutually shared future commitments (see chapter 6 on goals) rather than on the basis of expectations and assumptions?

Bart Littell of Parsons Brinckerhoff explains: "The more World Class teams you participate in, the more you realize that the personal needs, wants, and satisfactions of all of us are essentially similar."

This realization that we're all here for similar reasons as human beings creates the opportunity for a very fundamental bonding. We are not all the mercenary or egocentric individuals that we might fear.

Daniel Pink goes on to validate this notion: "A study of 11,000 industrial engineers working at companies in the United States found that the desire for intellectual challenge—that is, the urge to master something new and engaging—was the best predictor of productivity."[11]

Pink goes on to relate one of our literature's most memorable classics and maybe one of our nation's earliest construction fables from Mark Twain's *The Adventures of Tom Sawyer*. As most of us recall, Tom was faced with whitewashing Aunt Polly's 810-square-foot fence. No open bidding here. Pink summarizes:

> But just when Tom has nearly lost hope, "nothing less than a great, magnificent inspiration" bursts upon him. When his friend Ben ambles by and mocks Tom for his sorry lot, Tom acts confused. Slapping paint on a fence isn't a grim chore, he says. It's a fantastic privilege—a source of, ahem, intrinsic motivation. The job is so captivating that when Ben asks to try a few brushstrokes himself, Tom refuses. He doesn't relent until Ben gives up his apple in exchange for the opportunity. Soon more boys arrive, all of whom tumble into Tom's trap and end up whitewashing the fence—several times over— on his behalf.[12]

Pink explains: "In other words, rewards can perform a weird sort of behavioral alchemy: They can transform an interesting task into a drudge. They can turn play into work. And by diminishing intrinsic motivation, they can send performance, creativity, and even upstanding behavior toppling like dominoes."[13]

Returning to construction—and let's be honest here—how many of you would be willing to operate a D-9 for just a day without pay? I sure would, although I would certainly wreak a lot of havoc on the job site.

Constraint #6: The Assumption that Because You Have Never Been Part of a World Class Team, It Sounds Like Fantasyland and Will Never Happen

I do not blame individuals or organizations who have this mindset. If you have been on three to four projects in your career, it's not uncommon that none of them have been World Class teams (see data graph on page 12). Or if all of your prior jobs have been Combat or Business as Usual with maybe a Good or two, World Class teamwork is something you may not be able to even conceive of. It is kind of like trying to explain democracy to someone who has only experienced dictatorship. The concept doesn't even compute.

Above all, Business as Usual is comfortable. You do not have to change or really engage with your colleagues and address the possibility that there might be a better way, let alone concede that you might be wrong. We all have a tremendous proclivity to act solely on our assumptions and previous project experiences. While experience can be good, it can also be limiting.

Some individuals will spend the better part of a hour arguing with you why contractors can't be trusted, why public owners won't be flexible, or how BIM should work. They are more committed to prevailing with their own opinions about their assessments than they are to even entertaining the possibility that there might be a better way through a collaborative process.

I distinguish here between skeptics and cynics. Skepticism is OK and can be prudent on a construction project when dealing with a new concept or idea, strangers, or new technology. But how do you deal with cynicism, which according to Dictionary.com is characterized by "an attitude of scornful or jaded negativity, especially a general distrust of the integrity or professed motives of others"? Cynics are not open to even considering new possibilities. Their minds are made up. As we will see, all we can do is give them a choice.

> Cynicism is not realistic and tough. It's unrealistic and kind of cowardly
> because it means that you don't have to try.
> —PEGGY NOONAN, *WALL STREET JOURNAL* COLUMNIST—

Constraint #7: The Assumption that You Will Lose Control of the Project If You Let the Team Run It

The first question here is: Are you more committed to controlling the project or to striving to achieve World Class teamwork and extraordinary project results? Behind the notion of having to control a project is the assumption that if I do not control the project, it will not turn out well or in my best interests. Additionally, a fundamental assumption in a control-based construction process is a continuation of the past. The word *control* actually carries with it a negative connotation: without it, we are "out of control." Would it not be better to speak instead of a "process that leaves each member of the project team assured that the project is tracking toward an extraordinary success"?

Do not get me wrong. I am not equating control with abdicating accountability or responsibility. Accountability and empowerment are not mutually exclusive. On a truly World Class team, individuals are accountable to and for one another. Somewhat paradoxically, this provides for a higher order of control or better yet, assurance that the project is moving toward success. Responsibility, of course, continues to rest with senior management.

Let's examine this a bit more. Construction, like the rest of our economy, is changing. Decision making is being delegated more and more to the project level. Information availability and the need for speed have brought forth tools like BIM, PMIS, and VBM, which, in effect, enable project-level players to make real-time decisions based upon shared information in an online or face-to-face environment. This eliminates data silos. The technological means for real-time collaboration are here.

Len Vetrone of Webcor explains: "The virtual building modeling (VB) process becomes the nexus. Cost, schedule, and quality decisions are made in the field. The VB model, in effect, is part of everything." The implication? Top management day-to-day involvement in, let alone trying to control, any of these processes would paralyze most projects.

> My research suggests that the dramatically decreasing costs of information technology (IT) are changing the economics of organizational decision making, with the result that decentralized control is becoming more desirable in many situations. Moreover, our very notions of centralization and decentralization may be changing.
> —THOMAS MALONE, MASSACHUSETTS INSTITUTE OF TECHNOLOGY, SLOAN MANAGEMENT SCHOOL—

Let's also look at the idea of whether those whose primary intent is to control a project can truly control it. What really happens? At best you get compliance. Truly controlling anybody is an illusion. The vast majority of stakeholders on construction projects today resent being controlled and are smart enough to protect or assert their own self-interests if one stakeholder insists on controlling their behavior. Attempting to control someone very explicitly communicates to them that you do not trust them to do what is right—or at least what you deem as right.

Scott Ashton of Berg Electric explains: "On most jobs we as subcontractors are used to getting beat up. On a World Class team, there's a huge amount of trust instead of an emphasis on control. Everyone is willing to give up some control so that the team can succeed."

When you try to control, you will definitely not get any results that go beyond just meeting the contractual requirements. The best you will get is Business as Usual along with its attendant characteristics of boredom, "it's just a job," game playing, case building, posturing, and people trying to get away with as much as they can.

Self-described "bottom feeder" Peter Mondery of Southern Contracting subcontractors says: "When someone is preoccupied with attempting to control the project, the result is that it slows us down because we end up spending so much time and effort trying to get issues resolved."

The control versus empowerment issue often comes up relative to the role of the third-party construction or program manager. More than a few construction managers feel that if they are not controlling the project, they are not providing value or justifying their existence to their owner. Issam Khalaf with Jacobs CM provides a more contemporary view: "I view my role as managing the contract to provide a best value for my clients. Although I work for the owner, I do not view my role as taking sides or controlling the contract. Rather, it is building and earning the trust of the other team players. If I am able to do this, they will work with me and my organization and its resources to achieve mutual success."

Mehdi Hehdari with Vanir Construction Management explains: "On a World Class team, I view my role as facilitating everyone else's and the team's work. I earn this through listening, being very patient, demonstrating that

I respect everyone else, and being open-minded. This creates a forum for resolving the construction issues and finding the best solutions with win-win outcomes for all parties."

Constraint #8: The Assumption that Collaboration Is Too Risky and that It's Safer and Faster to Operate Independently and on the Basis of Unilateral Decision Making

A June 2008 study by the Economic Intelligence Unit of Pricewaterhouse-Coopers, LLP on "Managing the Risks and Rewards of Collaboration" drew some interesting conclusions.[14] Most notable was that the more formal and highly structured the nature of the collaboration, the higher the associated risk by stakeholders. The author, for example, speaks of joint ventures as having significant or very significant perceived risk, whereas trust-based collaboration or relationships based upon verbally and mutually agreed-upon principles, as in World Class teamwork, have relatively minor perceived risk.

Any collaboration, including World Class teamwork, certainly entails risk, which we will consider further in chapter 8. Among these risks are being taken advantage of, which experienced World Class team players acknowledge as only a one-time event. A second risk is the investment of time in developing, engaging in, and nurturing the collaborative process on a project. This is a question of risk versus reward. A third risk is that the effort spent in engaging in World Class teamwork may fail. This, as we will see, is invariably a consequence of lack of commitment and the absence of a viable model or process.

What are the consequences of failure? As I will suggest, the downside risk of attempting trust-based collaboration (World Class teamwork) is minimal. You can just walk away from it and default to Business as Usual. And, as one client put it, "At least you know where you stand a lot sooner than you would otherwise."

On World Class teams, participants value the more substantial risk of not collaborating and are more willing to genuinely commit and engage in a process to make it work. They also appreciate that today's construction projects are far too complex for any one entity to have all the answers and go it alone—whether formally or informally.

Constraint #9: The Assumption that Because You Have Good People from Good Organizations, You Do Not Need to Strive toward World Class Teamwork

At one workshop, one of the owner participants asserted: "We've selected one of the top five largest contractors in the country as our design-builder. This job will be good, and we don't need to talk about it [being good]."

I asked the team, rhetorically, "Why is it you can put together good people from good institutions and still have less than good, let alone World Class teamwork?" None other than the regional vice president for the contractor stood up and said, "It always comes down to the individuals and how they work together." If there is one sure thing in construction, it is that you will never know how individuals will interact when they come together on a project. As we will see, a World Class team deals with one another on the basis of their future commitments, not their history or reputation, regardless of however great or lousy that might be.

That said, Larry Kolves, Superintendent with Pinner Construction, told me: "We not infrequently have subcontractors give us discounts on a project bid depending on who our project manager was. They're asking themselves, 'Is this someone I can work with?'"

At the outset of partnering workshops, I ask participants to identify the characteristics of "good" projects. Once they've come up with a very predictable list of five or six (good communication, teamwork, no claims, on budget/schedule, good quality, etc.), I ask if anyone disagrees with any of these. The response, of course, is "Not at all." I then ask: "Can we not assume on jobs of this scope nationwide that likewise 95 to 98 percent of owners, general contractors, design-build teams, designers, construction managers, and subs would agree on these?" They think about this a little and invariably respond Yes.

Next I ask the million-dollar question: "Why is it, then, that you and I both know that nowhere near 95 percent of those projects end up having those characteristics you just agreed upon? Why is it you can start projects like this one with good people who have good intentions and still a project team can go south?" This question invariably generates some thoughtful introspection and comments like different goals and agendas, personalities, misunderstandings, unresolved issues, conflicts, egos, and so forth.

Richard Welsh, Regional Construction Engineer, U.S. Bureau of Reclamation, notes, "Every person on a project team may have good intentions in his or her own mind at the outset, but those are rarely congruent with everyone else's."

"Good intentions," says George Furnanz of Stacy and Witbeck, "are a one-time thing at the start of a project. They too often end up getting compromised by subsequent project circumstances. And, if good intentions are just left on the table, they will certainly not take you to the next level of teamwork."

Very few people need to be reminded that individual "good" intentions rarely lead to team excellence.

As Jerry West, former NBA All-Star, former manager and GM of the Los Angeles Lakers and former owner/GM of the Memphis Grizzlies, put it in a conference we jointly spoke at in the mid-80s, "I'll take the NBA champions any day over the NBA All-Stars. Good individuals who play great as a team will beat great individuals who play good as a team any day."

Constraint #10: The Alpha Male Construction Syndrome (AMCS)

There's another phenomenon that I call the Alpha Male (it's mostly a guy thing) Construction Syndrome or AMCS. Two guys—let's say the project managers for the owner and contractor—meet for the first time. Both, very sincerely, are out to subtly or not so subtly persuade one another that they are "good guys" and that they can get along. "Do I need any help?" is code for "Is either of us not capable of working with one another?"

Should they spend time on an activity designed to help improve their ability to work together to make this a good project? Should they even invest a little time really understanding what each of them is committed to and exactly how they and their organizations are going to work together to make the job an extraordinary success? Or should they even acknowledge that down the road there will be disputes or different interpretations between them and that it might be useful to develop an agreed-upon means for dealing with them? "Nah, I don't need any help, do you?" "Of course not. Hey, man, let's just get going and build this thing."

In *How the Mighty Fall: And Why Some Never Give In*, Jim Collins uses the term *hubris* to describe a common source of the failing of successful organizations run by very smart individuals in the recession of 2008–2010. Hubris is arrogance, a sense of infallibility, an overconfidence that comes from previous success. We're all vulnerable to it, and the more successful we are, the more vulnerable we become. In construction we're particularly prone to it after having a positive experience with a construction methodology or how a PDM successfully worked on a previous job. We tend to assume that this identical process and how we executed it will work equally well on our next job with a different project team.

Remember the Coronado Navy BEQ project with no concept drawings, a lump sum, and a design-build PDM? Hensel Phelps' Project Manager, Bill Welch, said, "There's really no precedent for going forward on a project like this." So he and his Navy counterparts invented one. Sometimes having a blank sheet of paper and no expectations can be a source for extraordinary teamwork and innovation.

When Lee Evey took over the job as program manager for the Pentagon Renovation in 1997, he had managed large defense contracts but had virtually no construction background. Therefore, Lee says, he had no expectations. There's no baggage, past precedents, or assumptions to take for granted inhibiting the team in those circumstances.

Projects that are especially vulnerable to hubris are often the most complex and involve the most experienced, talented, and highly educated individuals and organizations. It's easy to think, "Hey, we've handled lots of projects more complex and bigger than this one" or "There's nothing to worry about; we've seen this before." In other words, "Leave us alone and let us build it."

How then did John Wooden, winner of ten consecutive NCAA titles at UCLA, maintain a coaching process that enabled both him and his teams to avoid falling victim to hubris for such a long period of time? His humbling adage "It's what you learn after you know it all that really counts" may have had something to do with it.

Constraint #11: The Assumption that Because You Already Know How the Project Is Supposed to Work, There's No Point in Spending Time Talking about It

An individual in one of my recent workshops asserted this about an hour into the partnering session. I acknowledged, "Yes, you may know how this project is supposed to work, but there are thirty-nine other people in this room here today. What do you want to bet that each of them exactly shares your opinion? Secondly, none of them nor you know how you are going to work together as a team on this project. Are you willing to leave that up to chance and circumstances?"

Vitas Rugienius, Operations Manager, Hensel Phelps Constuction, says: "When we start a project and get an 8,000-page stack of drawings, it's important that we try to understand the owner's meaning behind them. Talking about why they want what they want and how the system is really supposed to function for them makes it easier for us to truly satisfy them."

Constraint #12: The Assumption that World Class Teamwork Can Only Happen on High-Visibility, Negotiated Jobs with Top-of-the-Class Stakeholders

Some folks tell us, "Hey, we are only building a pipeline or a waste water treatment plant" or "It is not really possible to get people excited or passionate about a hard-bid public works project."

Hogwash. No project type is inherently uninspiring. Likewise, all project types can be made challenging by open, creative goal-setting. Conversely, some high-profile, private sector, showcase projects with blue-chip firms are characterized by lousy teamwork. It happens—most directly attributable to hubris.

Jack Shewmaker with Granite Construction notes, "We've had World Class teams on $5,000 driveway pavement projects with private homeowners."

It is not what you're constructing that counts. Rather, it is what you and your team make out of what you are constructing that really matters. And this is where World Class teamwork can transform any project into a true World Class project.

So What Can You Do?

If you take away all of the constraints, assumptions, and excuses as we have done, how do you initiate World Class teamwork? Bart Littell of Parsons Brinckerhoff explains: "You cannot force World Class teamwork. It starts at the top. If senior management is committed, they create the atmosphere and the confidence of striving toward it." As we saw at the conclusion of chapter 3, senior management commitment is the key.

Nor can you sell anyone on it. You cannot even motivate them to do it. You definitely cannot contract for it. It is kind of like riding a bike. People have to experience it for themselves. All we can ask is that they go forward with an open mind. Senior management can help them, as we will see, by giving them choices and helping them create the distinction of World Class teamwork vs. Good teamwork and Business as Usual. You can also have them hear from others on their project that WCT is really possible and share their personal experience with it and passion about striving toward it. Then have them talk about the specific value that it might have were they to successfully implement World Class teamwork on this job.

Another approach? Get them talking about challenges and opportunities and have them turn these into measurable goals. Then have them talk about how they will work together to make them happen—not just by sharing good intentions but rather by creating a future through specific individual requests and commitments.

> Whatever you can do or dream you can, begin it.
> Boldness has genius, power and magic to it. Begin it now.
> —GOETHE—

Stephen Sharr, Director of New Construction for the Central Region of the Los Angeles Unified School District and four-time Marvin Black

Award winner, explains: "If you change their actions, this will change their minds and ultimately result in trust." Don't mess with their minds or what's going on inside their heads. Most folks in construction find games, psychological stuff, and lectures on teamwork boring, meaningless, and not having much specific relevance to their project. They mentally check out.

So if you take away people's assumptions, baggage, and stereotypes about one another, what might you be left with? How about this?

> The vast majority of project stakeholders truly want to be part of a project
> that is characterized by a self-generated common purpose
> that truly challenges them, genuine teamwork, and trust.

Call it what you want. I call it a World Class team. Why settle for anything less? Sure, a lot of us are covered with a couple of levels of scar tissue. We have all been burned and are rightly skeptical. Yet even working in some of the most bureaucratic of bureaucracies and with some of the most hardball of contractors, I have rarely seen individuals so embedded in past, adversarial, or Business as Usual beliefs that they are invulnerable to the possibility of World Class teamwork.

PART TWO

The 10 World Class Team Behaviors

5

Delight the Client, Coach the Contractor, and Build Relationships That Lead to Future Projects

Business as Usual: Relationships bureaucratic and institutional. Minimal compliance at best. Advice = "Just build it per contract."

Good Teams: Client satisfied = plans and specs met. Advice given, but intent questioned. Contractor/DBT on their own for profit.

WORLD CLASS TEAMS: Client/end user truly delighted. Contractor/DBT seen as trusted business advisor—no spin. Long–term relationship. Owner and CM work with contractor/DBT as coaches to enhance their efficiencies.

NOTE: This behavior is really the consequence of the following
nine World Class team behaviors, but I decided to share it first to establish
the end game and give you a view of our destination.

Delighting the Drill Instructors

The project was a $60 million design-build led by Whiting-Turner Construction for two dining facilities for Marines at Camp Pendleton, California—one facility for recruits and the other for real Marines. The concept specs were virtually the same for both facilities. So what was the difference? Major Cava, the officer in charge of the area, explained in a partnering session: "The recruits are there to learn how to be Marines. The other facility for Marines can actually be a little nicer because they have a choice where to eat." We were brainstorming team goals at that point, and Russ Nicholson with Clark Nexsen, the Whiting-Turner design-build team's design manager, asked, "Well, what if the recruit facility actually contributed to their ability to learn to be Marines?" With that, the floodgates opened. Murals of past Marine battles on the walls, the ten rules of conduct, displays promoting the various Marine specialties (aviation, recon, etc.), and models of weaponry were all suggested. Finally someone asked, "Who do we need to talk to in order to find out what they really need to learn?" Major Cava said, "The DI's" (drill instructors).

But they didn't stop with that facility. Someone asked how we would know that we had delighted the customer/end user of the Marine dining facility. One person replied, "Well, they currently eat a lot at McDonald's, Burger King, and another Marine facility on base." So, Chief Warrant Officer Sullivan asked, "What if this facility was the 'go to' place?" Great, everyone agreed, but how would they measure that? "Easy," said a Marine. "We can monitor their use of their personal dining cards." So the project goal #2 was that "The Marine facility was a 'go-to' facility by choice on a measured basis over all of the other three choices combined."

When this book went to press in the summer of 2011, this project team was well on track for their above goals and had achieved the highest level of World Class teamwork—as measured by survey—sooner than any previous project team I have worked with. As one team member told me, "We have a compelling purpose that goes well beyond just building two structures."

Delighting the Customer Comes from a Personal Conversation— Not a Set of Specifications

Do not be afraid of asking the end user or owner what would delight them or really make them happy from a *personal* point of view.

Let me relate a personal experience. I recently went to several orthopedic surgeons about a back problem I had. Most said something to the effect of "Well, here's your problem, and this is the procedure I would recommend." One, however, started by asking me, "What do you do?" I told him I'm a passionate trail runner and skier. He replied, "OK, so what would make you happy?" I quickly responded, "If I could ski and run again consistently." The doctor then said, "All right, that's what I'll do for you. This minimally invasive procedure will give you an 85 to 90 percent probability of doing that without major surgery." I was sold.

Most owners are not asked what would delight them or what is their real intent for the structure or facility. At the same time, most contractors and construction managers *assume* owners would be satisfied if they merely conformed to the plans and specs. Most owners, in turn, assume that expressing or requesting project results beyond the contract documents, concept design, or specifications would be presumptuous and futile and would leave them open to exorbitant extra costs and change orders.

Why is this? As one owner put it, "Opening up this way requires a huge amount of trust. You risk being taken advantage of if you talk about what's really important to you."

In truly World Class teams, owners are asked what would delight them. Not only that, but they also feel comfortable expressing it. The contractor can always say that it is not in their scope and provide a cost impact if useful. In other words, air it out, make an extraordinary request, and tell them what you would really like to see. What have you got to lose?

Delighting the customer does not necessarily equate to what *you* think or believe would delight them. It may not, for example, be of particular value for a client to have a finish that is better than specified. You must make a genuine, sincere, personal inquiry into what the individual client believes would delight them.

Paul Ligocki, Operations Manager of Hensel Phelps, relates what happened when the senior management of his company invited their owners to come in and talk with them about quality—real quality. "To our surprise, it really had not much to do with meeting plans and specs and so forth. As an example, the woman in charge of the Smithsonian Air and Space Museum told us, 'You know, we have a lot of priceless objects in here, and if they get wet, they will be irreparably damaged.'"

Yes, you should always acknowledge the contract and the specs, but what separates World Class teams is that they make the construction process a truly personal experience that allows for personal wants, needs, and desires. Isn't that how we all want to relate to one another?

Your reputation is in large part based upon the personal experiences individuals have had with you and your people. As Johnny Pinner, President of Pinner Construction, observes, "'Was the project pleasant or not?' That's what they remember."

Delighting Third Parties on a Design, Bid, Build Project

On the Lombard Reservoir seismic retrofit project for the San Francisco Public Utilities Commission, the project team had a big problem. The local residents—a very vocal, affluent, and well organized group—were up in arms about the impact that the project would have on the adjacent park and tennis courts. They were threatening to stall or force the city to effect a major design change. So Boon Lim, Construction Manager for the PUC at the time, did a gutsy thing: he invited them to a partnering workshop. Many of the other project team members rolled their eyes at the risks involved.

Three residents came in with arms crossed and facial expressions that said, "We're here to do battle with the indifferent, bureaucratic city and the greedy, profit-at-any-cost, slash-and-burn contractors." So we started brainstorming goals. At one point I asked them what would they really like to see on this job. A lady said indignantly, "Do you realize that you'll be blocking access to our tennis courts for over a year?" The contractor replied, "Well, I don't think it would be a big deal if we were to temporarily fence in a walkway directly to the tennis courts from the street during construction." "You really would do that?" the lady asked in amazement. "Sure," said the contractor, looking at Boon, who readily agreed.

One gentleman then pointed out that because of the construction fencing, they would have no grassy area to walk their dogs on. The contractor offered to set aside at all times at least a third of the park's grassy area for the public. Over lunch the residents, contractors, and city attendees were talking away like old friends. Boon Lim, currently Construction Manager for Wastewater for the San Francisco Public Utilities Commission, says, "By incorporating the residents in the decision-making process, they felt that they had some genuine control and say over the job. They became very reasonable and willing to work with all project stakeholders on future decisions—many of which were compromises—to our mutual success."

Trusted Business Advisor—No Spin

Hopefully you've had a relationship with a financial advisor or accountant to whom you looked for honest, candid, personal advice about managing your unique financial future and with whom you could be completely open. You received advice and counsel that did not seem self-serving on the part of the advisor. Mark Norris, Assistant Public Works Director with the city of Oxnard, California, describes this as "a contractor coming up with advice to us that does not necessarily benefit him."

This kind of relationship can be invaluable. The biggest payoff? An outcome that truly meets your needs and not having to second-guess an individual's intentions. One client expressed it as peace of mind.

Tony Ferruccio, Executive Vice President of Mactec general contractors in Atlanta, explains: "Achieving this kind of relationship is the pinnacle of success on both a personal and business level. On World Class teams, they [owners] will seek you out for future work and ask you to bid. I had one owner who was so persistent that he was virtually begging us to bid. I'm honored to work with a client on this basis."

As owners are increasingly awarding construction projects on the basis of best value, they are looking for the same kind of trusted relationship with their designers, contractors, and construction managers. These entities are likewise placing value upon developing long-term relationships with owners and with one another. Fundamentally, all of us value a relationship that is open, trusting, and completely aboveboard. Being a trusted business advisor does not mean that you must forego profit. It does mean that your primary commitment is to provide ongoing genuine value to your client on a business and personal level.

Ongoing value also means that you provide and discuss with your client choices and options, not non-negotiable, unilateral notices of potential changes via letter (see chapter 8 on Risk and Changes). These choices are often trade-offs among schedule, cost, public impact, and quality, and they seek to enable the client to make a good business decision that speaks to their real intent for the project given where it is at that point in time.

George Furnanz of Stacy and Witbeck says, "Being seen by your client as a trusted business advisor is priceless. Once you get to that point, you will win, or rather be selected for, future work with that client. We are now bidding negotiated work that focuses on our past track record and references. The bar keeps going up for us, but we always challenge ourselves to find a way to reach it."

Here's an example of a mutually beneficial, long-term relationship between an owner and a general contractor. Jim Bostic of St. Joseph Health System describes their relationship with McCarthy Building Companies: "We have had what I'll term a strategic partnership with McCarthy over some six projects with different project teams. Nevertheless, our shared core values have been constant and remain so on current jobs—those being trust, mutual respect, openness, and a confidence that we can manage and resolve any and all disputes. This allows me to have an informal conversation at any time with anyone from McCarthy without circumventing protocol. I also feel assured that I can go to McCarthy's senior management and they will immediately address my concerns. With other contractors, my experience has been that when you do this, they often put their head in the sand."

Patrick Peterson, Project Director of McCarthy Building Companies, adds, "As a result of this effective partnership, St. Joseph Health System, the designers, McCarthy, and many of the subcontractors and other project team members are continuing to work together on new projects, with prospects for several more in the future. The St. Joseph Health System has contracted McCarthy and the applicable subcontractors for four additional large-scale construction projects."

Mark Filanc with Filanc Construction shares his experience on a design-build treatment plant project: "The owner took us in, and we basically looked at his cost model with him and came up with solutions that optimized his overall plant costs. This was well beyond the initial scope of our engagement. All of our clients have needs, but in most cases they have needs that they are not even aware of. We view our role as providing, or offering, solutions to those needs. In a trusted business advisor relationship, doing this and doing what you say you are going to do are critical."

Construction managers of the old "control" type may see this as a threat.

Someone who attempts to control project performance is not a trusted business advisor—even to the owner. The vast majority of us resent being controlled even by those who ostensibly work for us, and we deeply question the intentions of those who seek to control us. Would you want your financial advisor to control your financial future? Or would you want him or her to genuinely listen and work with you to provide the best value solution to fit your unique needs and circumstances?

On the other hand, construction managers who look at themselves as trusted business advisors see unlimited opportunity to add value to their clients, secure repeat business, and potentially develop new services altogether. Issam Khalaf of Jacobs CM says, "We strive to delight our clients by providing superior and innovative services and results." Likewise, Kathy Mayo of AECOM states, "We endeavor to understand our clients and bring them along to the idea of working with the contractor. We need to respect and understand how the client really wants things done."

Leading general contractors, designers, and even subcontractors are seeking to position themselves as trusted business advisors both on projects and in securing new work. Being viewed as a trusted business advisor can create not only new business but also completely different kinds of new business opportunities. Len Vetrone of Webcor explains: "I'm excited that the market is going this way. We're learning from one another. Recently, we even had a structural engineer recommend us to another team."

> Synergy is the highest activity of life; it creates new untapped alternatives; it values and exploits the mental, emotional, and psychological differences between people.
> —STEPHEN COVEY,
> AUTHOR OF *THE 7 HABITS OF HIGHLY SUCCESSFUL PEOPLE*—

David Mallik of Whiting Turner Construction adds, "We've seen greater success and truly delighted customers, which is part of our mission at Whiting Turner. World Class teamwork allow us to establish goals as a team and be honest and open about what's going on. This is the basis for delighting our customers."

So how do you start developing a relationship with a customer/client that earns you the distinction "trusted business advisor"? Wayne Lindholm of Hensel Phelps explains: "There are no shortcuts; you have to earn it every day." And, I'll add, it becomes a consequence of engaging with your client and customer as a World Class team. Chapters 5 through 14 will explain how you do this.

The Owner, Construction Manager, and Inspectors as Coaches

So far we've considered the benefits of World Class teamwork to the owner in terms of being delighted and having a trusted business advisor relationship with their contractor, design team, and CM. But what value do these project stakeholders gain from this relationship apart from potential future business? Is the owner or CM just a passive player on a World Class team?

Not at all. On a World Class team, the client or owner is actively helping you, as a contractor or design-build team, succeed—not only in terms of overall project success but also in terms of managing your efficiencies and profitability. I call this kind of relationship one where the owner or CM is a coach.

Why is this important? Because the specs, contract documents, and pre-construction meeting rarely give a contractor, CM, or designer an accurate understanding of what's truly important or desired, let alone how the decision process really works within the owner's organization.

Summit Builders Division Manager Mike Tylwalk explains: "When we have a relationship with our clients as trusted business advisors, they reciprocate by helping us steer around potential project potholes and roadblocks that we are unaware of. When an owner is actively coaching you on a project, you develop a level of trust like no other. They alert you to major pitfalls and how to deal with certain individuals and personalities, and they actually share their expertise with you in working within their organization. For example, if we're having trouble with payment, an owner on a World Class team first of all will listen to me and then tell me very specifically how we need to package and put forth our pay application to expedite payment. This is invaluable in helping us maximize our efficiencies."

A true coach, according to Jim Selman of Serene Ambition, who pioneered management coaching in the late 1980s, is more committed to your commitments than you are and is willing and able to support you in achieving your success. As we will see, this requires common goals or shared commitments, which can only be achieved through collaborative action. With common goals, each stakeholder has, in effect, an incentive to enable their fellow project stakeholders to achieve their goals. In other words, you help me succeed, I help you succeed, and we both come out ahead.

A good example is an elementary school project where there was an issue over the HVAC system relative to what was specified and bid on by the subcontractor and what was currently not available. The owner, subcontractor, and GC had a mutual problem: how do we now select an acceptable HVAC system in a manner that meets the owner's needs as well as budget, enables to subcontractor to realize a fair profit, and does not hinder the team's aggressive schedule? The owner coached the GC and subcontractor on how to communicate to the district in a way that left the district in a position to make a good, fair, and expeditious business decision.

The Lone Ranger Is Dead

As we will see, going it alone as a GC or DBT on today's more complex, larger jobs with large "multi-headed" owners is like Indiana Jones walking into the Temple of Doom without a flashlight. There is no telling what is coming at you or what is around the corner. Some inside knowledge is required to work through a maze of departments and third-party agencies whose formal organization charts and job descriptions often bear no relationship to how decisions are really made or what is really wanted relative to what was specified.

Virgil Curtis with Balfour Beatty shares this observation: "There needs to be someone on the owner's team who will step up and take responsibility and be supportive of you and your efforts. If that individual isn't apparent, you, as a contractor, need to be very vocal and open about finding someone." In other words, on World Class teams, contractors and design-build team members are not reluctant to ask for help or coaching. This can be a big step for some contractors who, quite naturally, have taken pride in their ability to go it alone.

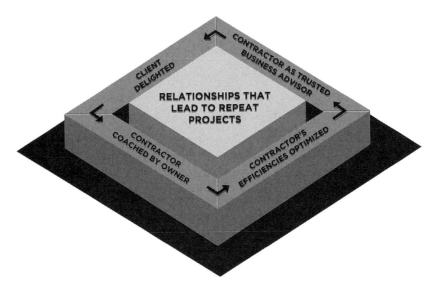

World Class Teamwork: The Relationship and Payoff

There's a distinction between being a effective coach and directing the work, which, on a construction project, can carry contractual obligations. A effective coach enables his players to see opportunities or challenges that they cannot see or may not be aware of on their own. These in turn allow the player or players to optimize their performance.

Steven Boehm, South Region Director for New Construction for the Los Angeles Unified School District, notes: "Coaching goes a lot further than just telling a contractor to perform 'per the contract and specs.' It involves giving them the 'why' and the big picture in a way that allows them to make a good business decision for themselves that also supports our overall project success. It also communicates to them that we'll be fair and open."

Consider for a moment that on a World Class team everyone is willing to coach their fellow project stakeholders. I call this a project culture of mutual support. It is, perhaps, the epitome of working relationships on a construction project.

Kathy Mayo, now with AECOM, explains: "It is a two-way street. When I was with BART [Bay Area Rapid Transit District], if I listened and attempted to understand the contractor and showed an interest in helping him solve his problems, then when I needed something, he was there for me and willing to bend over backwards."

Yes, this requires clear common goals; open, direct verbal communication; 100 percent accountability by everyone for everything; the project team owning overall project success; and the notion of shared risk—all of which we will talk about in subsequent chapters as characteristics of World Class teams. And yes, coaching can be risky—but only one time. If you as an owner extend yourself to help a contractor and they take advantage of that assistance exclusively for their own self interest, it's back to Business as Usual—World Class teamwork over.

The ultimate consequence of having a trusted business advisor and coaching relationship on a construction project? I've heard owners, designers, and contractors say it: relationships that lead to repeat projects.

6

WORLD CLASS TEAM BEHAVIOR #2

Define and Commit to Team Goals:
The Foundation for Trust and Teamwork

Clear, common goals that the whole project team buys into are the centerpiece.
They ensure we are all in alignment with common expectations.
These need to be set early.
—JIM BOSTIC, ST. JOSEPH HEALTH SYSTEM—

Business as Usual: Have to keep your eye on everyone. Hidden agendas assumed. Plans and specs are there to be enforced.

Good Teams: Good intentions that at best meet schedule, budget, and quality specifications or requirements. Absence of personal committed action.

WORLD CLASS TEAMS: Measurable team goals that acknowledge but are not constrained by the contract or specifications. Collaborative processes backed up by specific personal commitments to action.

I asked each of the 127 construction managers, architects, engineers, owners, and contractors I interviewed who had been part of a World Class team about the value of having explicit, measurable, and common team project goals and their relationship to a construction project team's ability to achieve World Class status. Here is what they said:

Not really necessary:	0%	Yes, that is correct—zero percent!
Necessary:	10%	
Absolute prerequisite:	90%	

More specifically, here's what several senior executives had to say:

- Wayne Lindholm, Hensel Phelps: "What's the point of having a team if you don't have common goals?"
- John Jansen, Kiewit: "Team goals are key. They enable a basis of discussion by the team that is focused. They also bring forth conversations about collaborative solutions to overcome predictable challenges that might impede the team from achieving their goals."
- Dennis Turchon, Caltrans: "Common goals are essential. Otherwise you don't know what you're working for."
- Cynthia Meinhardt, Project Officer, City of San Diego New Central Library: "Through bringing people on board a project with common goals, you are able to resolve issues and conflicts in an effective way as well as develop relationships with other members of the city, the contractors, and consultants. This enables us to deliver the best overall project to the citizens of San Diego."
- Carlos Gonzales, Senior Project Manager, Clark Construction Group: "Having common goals gets everyone thinking about their contribution to the team and the actions they can take."
- Scott Ashton, Berg Electric: "Stretch team goals are very important. They allow us as a team to identify impediments early and then get everyone involved in attacking and resolving them."

This has led me to the following conclusion—one of the few absolutes I have discovered in writing this book:

You cannot have a World Class project team without common team project goals.

Above all, do not fall victim to the assumption that just building the job to specification and contract requirements constitutes common goals. Steve Iselin of the U.S. Navy explains: "A team can have what appear to many as common goals, but if these were not developed by the team as a team with the opportunity to hear all sides out, then they are nowhere near as valuable as any one individual's assumptions or the contract requirements."

The feedback I get from partnering workshops is that the real value comes from the *process* of establishing common goals as a team and reviewing them periodically over the course of the project. It's the inter-action and communication that take place between individuals during these processes that provide the real value. Paul Ligocki of Hensel Phelps explains: "If you don't flip possible project goals back and forth between the owners, designers, and contractors several times, the team never really explores the possibilities."

Dan Gilbert of Kaiser Permanente adds, "At the outset of a project, there are some individuals who overestimate what can be done. There are some that are more cynical. On a World Class team, the team needs to hear from both. It can be challenging but extremely valuable to get everyone to be open and honest. In this interplay is the real value."

Goal setting is also, as we shall see, the very best way to build genuine trust among construction project stakeholders. Why? While talking about trust is useful, it is often too abstract, particularly for folks in construction, who tend to be goal- or task-oriented. Lectures, simulations, psychological tools, or games that attempt to establish trust are of marginal value. As my colleague Neal Flesner from Missouri says, "Show me."

When project stakeholders start talking about project goals not con-strained by contractual requirements, they begin to find out what is really important to one another and discover they really do have a lot in common. They also begin to realize that they cannot achieve these stretch goals with-out one another's support, contribution, and genuine commitment. They also begin to generate a personal "at stakeness" in the project's success—a commitment not just grounded in meeting contractual requirements or specifications. They also begin to see the intangible and intrinsic benefits and satisfactions that come from working as part of a World Class team and owning the game.

As we learned from Daniel Pink in chapter 4, human beings crave meaning and purpose from their work, and this meaning has no relation-ship to their financial compensation. To the extent that this meaning and purpose are shared via common goals, the real foundations of a team begin to develop.

Thirteen Tips for Setting World Class Team Project Goals

While just sitting down and attempting to define common goals is useful, establishing guidelines and having a semi-structured process for this conversation can significantly enhance its value.

1. Start by asserting that we are not in any way going set goals that change, relax, or compromise any stakeholder's legal or contractual obligations or the specifications. At the same time, we will not necessarily be limited by them.

Team members tell me this is very liberating. Nobody likes to be constrained by contracts or specs. This step allows team members the freedom to begin to define and then own their own definition of project success instead of one that is imposed upon them by contractual requirements. This makes a huge difference and leads to committed action, not merely compliance. Compliance, as most of us know, tends to foster a "minimum to get by" attitude. Compliant team members also simply mimic acceptable behavior (try) and condition themselves to say and do the right thing—which is another form of game playing as discussed in chapter 3.

On a World Class team we can, in other words, mutually commit to work toward goals that better or exceed our legal and contractual requirements and the project specifications. Steve Van Dyke, Project Director for McCarthy Building Companies, explains: "Everybody on a project team wants to build something that is not just limited by the project's specifications."

In other words, we, as a team, all commit to working toward those goals as a shared future. We may end up short, and that is OK. It is important to stress the distinction between merely trying and genuine personal commitment. How do you know if you've created genuine personal commitment? There is resultant action or what I term "committed action," which is vital to project team members of a World Class team. Without it, goals can become just good intentions which may or may not be pursued. Creating a clear delineation between committed action and intentions or just trying is critical when bringing together individuals from different organizational cultures whose definition of these terms may be at significant variance.

"A mutual commitment to working toward goals that go beyond those you are contractually obligated to elevates every individual's and the team's game," says Vitas Rugienius of Hensel Phelps, "and unless you challenge yourself through these goals, you will not know your limits as an individual or as a team."

Mike Ghilotti, CEO of Ghilotti Brothers Construction, insists, "Committing to and striving toward stretch goals is the only way to do business. Most project stakeholders find that setting stretch goals and achieving them brings out the best of everyone. And individuals are willing to commit more. This saves time and cost and delivers a much better value to the customer." Having your own goals also leads to optimism which, many psychologists assert, is a key to individual well-being and happiness.

In *Teams at the Top,* Jon R. Katzenbach notes that "Circumstances involving challenging performance requirements create the need and opportunity for teamwork."[15] For example, you might start by asking the team what is the earliest they will complete this job if they limit themselves to just meeting the contractual completion date. They inevitably reply "on the contractual completion date." On the other hand, try asking, "If we set our team/partnership goal for three months early and we miss it and come in only two months early, what's the penalty?" None, of course. And they will know as a team that they did the very best they possibly could.

2. The goals should speak to the owner's real intent, not just the plans and specs. Involve the owner/end user in the goal setting process.

As we'll see in chapter 8 and as we saw in chapter 5 with our example of the Camp Pendleton dining facilities, rarely do project specs speak to the true intent of the owner and end user. What do they really want this structure to accomplish? Is having one lane of the interchange open to traffic before the whole project is complete desirable? Put it on the table. Involving the end user in setting goals creates the opportunity to truly delight the customer by finding out what is really, really important to them.

Consider another example. When San Francisco's MUNI—the aboveground street car line—was upgrading its Fisherman's Wharf Loop (the most popular tourist attraction in California), the general contractor, Stacy and Witbeck, put forth the idea of finishing a twenty-eight-month project eight months early. Initially the response was "No way! Are they crazy?" George Furnanz of Stacy and Witbeck explains: "We opened everything up to them and asked them 'What do you think?' The key was establishing credibility, and we did this through three actions: We were early on our schedule commitments; we were open and honest; and we did what we said we were going to do."

Through the good fortune of having the CEO of Scoma's Restaurant in the partnering workshop, the team quickly determined that he and his fellow constituents (the other restaurateurs and retailers) were very open to modifying the contract document's street closure requirements *if* this would support shortening the overall project. So instead of the contractor having to close each end of a street to vehicular traffic for three weeks, the Scoma's CEO declared if the entire street was closed for a week—with the understanding that this would help complete the whole project eight months early—they would support it.

After a subsequent brainstorming session, San Francisco MUNI, Stacy and Witbeck, and the third parties hit their goal together—a true win-win outcome. Don Chee, former Senior Project Manager with the City and County of San Francisco, commented, "If someone had told me that this job could be done eight months early, I would have thought they were hallucinating."

The lesson? Including the owner and end user not only enhances the outcome but also personalizes the project: "We're not building this hospital for the county, but we're now building it for Dr. Fred and his patients." Additionally, the end user sees the critical and potentially costly trade-off relationships between their initiated changes and overall project cost and schedule. The result? They are part of our team. They need us and we need them for project success.

3. It is important that the goals be stretch goals at the time they are being defined by the team and given what the team knows about the project then.

In *Built to Last*, Jim Collins and Jerry Porras advocate setting BHAGs—Big Hairy Audacious Goals. A good BHAG is something that you currently do

EXERCISE FOR DESIGN-BUILD TEAMS

NOTE: This is designed to bring forth possibilities similar to those considered for the
Camp Pendleton dining facilities in chapter 5.

• Have the end user state their desired intent for the facility if it were truly to
meet the needs of its occupants or the beneficiaries of its function.

• Break the group up into teams of four to five individuals, preferably from different disciplines. Tell them they are to acknowledge but not necessarily be
constrained by the concept drawings or schematics. They should think truly
"outside the box" and put themselves in the role of the end user. Each team is to
come up with one or two really good ideas.

• Go around the room and have each team share their best idea. Don't evaluate
them at this point.

• Then give each individual two points that they can use to vote for the two ideas,
or they can put both votes on one idea, Read through the ideas and ask individuals to raise their hands for the ideas they want to allocate their points to.

• Discuss the best ideas. If necessary, delegate to a task group with deliverable-
by date with champion.

---

not quite know how to do. Think of President Kennedy in 1961 declaring
his commitment to "put a man on the moon and return him safely by the
end of this decade." Conventional wisdom at the time suggested that a realistic goal would be at least two or three decades out.

A good BHAG gets people outside of their box or comfort zone, as we'll
discuss in chapter 11. It is slightly unrealistic and requires true outside-the-
box thinking by the whole team as a team. Perhaps even more importantly,
it can be achieved *only* through extraordinary or World Class teamwork.

Dave Takamoto, Principal with Takamoto Ventures, Inc., explains: "Initially when we set our BHAGs, we thought they were unachievable based
upon our prior history, but now, at the two-thirds point, we really do

believe they are a possibility. By establishing and achieving goals higher than we've ever done before, we've set a standard for us to strive toward that will last for a long time."

4. It is absolutely imperative that the team be crystal-clear about their definition of the end game and that they set end game goals before they start to figure out the how-to.

The contractual definition of substantial completion, for example, is almost always subject to interpretation. Rather than argue about the minimum to get by, as a team would do in Business as Usual, a World Class team asks the owner, "What would you really like it to mean? Is phased completion/turnover something that would really be of value to you? What is your real intent for this facility?" Is it, as in our Marine dining facility example, just to feed people, or could it be for something else?

In the military, you start with defining the mission or purpose; then you can determine how you are actually going to fight the battle. Likewise, Michael Abeln with the Army Corps of Engineers says, "You need to start with a clear definition of the end game in sight of all team members. If you do not, there's a tendency for the team to focus on means rather than ends."

In our culture we are trained to commit only when we have figured everything out. This is natural and comfortable, but I term this only a conditional or qualified commitment: "I'll commit if/after you show me how this and this will happen first." For example, someone might say, "I'll commit to an early completion date *if* someone shows me how we will expedite MEP coordination using BIM." It is much better to set the goal first and get the team commitment to it. Then the team will be in a much more powerful position to figure out how they *as a team* are going to expedite MEP coordination to support their project completion goal.

If a construction project team starts with focusing on the how-tos, they invariably resort to working harder, longer, or better at doing what each *individual currently* knows how to do. This is very limiting and precludes true, outside-the-box thinking and, at best, produces marginal or incremental improvement. It results in a Business as Usual project and team. They also get bogged down in detail.

Consider a design-build project team that creates a process to concurrently execute both design development and design review. All stakeholders would invariably agree this is a good idea. But it is a process, not a goal. What, I would ask, would be the consequences of having done so at project conclusion? Some of the responses:

- Job completed 2 months early
- No customer changes after 90% design approval—excluding those due to new technology
- No design changes that involve additional funding after 90% review

A good criterion for determining if you have end game goals: If you read them back to the owner and/or end user, would they resonate with them? Would they say, in effect, "Great—that would truly be extraordinary and would not just meet the specs but also my real intent for this job"?

5. The goals must be measurable.

A lot of teams start with goals like "Quality is very good." In workshops I ask, "If quality were to be very good, what would that produce? What would be the consequences at the end of the job? And then how do you measure this?" Project teams then typically come up with more measurable goals like these:

- Punch list complete within fifteen days of substantial completion
- No rework
- No written Notices of Noncompliance (They are addressed at the verbal stage.)
- All deviations have a recommended action plan agreed to within 48 hours.

Without measurable goals, a team can easily become unfocused and lose its sense of priority. Pat Peterson of McCarthy Building Companies explains: "You have to have measurable common goals for World Class teamwork. Without these, stakeholders can go off on different paths with different assumptions, and it can take a whole lot of effort to bring them back together. That effort takes you away from meeting the end goals of the end user."

Kim Grant of Swinerton Builders adds, "Measurable common goals are very important in order to establish the finish line. In the old days, things were very subjective. Construction is too complex for that anymore."

6. The more uncertain and unpredictable the construction environment, the more imperative it is to have truly measurable stretch goals.

On the Salinas Valley Memorial Hospital retrofit of an operating, sixty-year-old hospital, the team members had a strong tendency to say, "There's just too much uncertainty on this job to set a completion goal. When we open up a wall, there's no telling what we'll find." Actually, it works the other way around. The more uncertain your environment, the more important it is for the team to set goals. Why?

Here's how Doug Strout, Principal and Director of Healthcare for KMD Architects, San Francisco, counseled the team to deal with it: "If we do not truly challenge ourselves in the face of uncertainty, the greater the tendency to just react to circumstances. Setting a truly challenging goal can allow us to look for real outside-the-box solutions, to anticipate and, when necessary, mitigate uncertainty, whether it be in the form of site conditions, unclear drawings, or third-party response, as a team."

There will always be issues on a construction project that are uncertain or unpredictable at the outset of the job. That's what makes this business challenging for many of us. If President Kennedy had waited until all the systems and studies had been conducted before he set his goal of landing on the moon, we'd still be struggling to get there according to some scientists.

After setting a goal in an uncertain environment, individual team members are always amazed by what the team collectively can come up with to anticipate and/or mitigate that uncertainty.

7. Paradoxically, a good project stretch goal may even be less than the contract requires.

Why would a World Class team set a goal less than the contract requires? For example, a contract/baseline schedule might require completion in one year or no later than December 21, 2012. On the specific date the team is meeting to establish their team goals, weather, unknown site conditions, or a delayed NTP may make December 21, 2012, completely unachievable. So the team may agree that completing this project NLT February 22, 2013, is really an empowering, WCT goal. Recall the Benecia Martinez Bridge project where their revised BHAG was a year and a half beyond the original contractual date due to unknown site conditions.

8. Team goals should not be "have to's" or "shoulds."

As we have already seen, goals should acknowledge, but not be constrained by, the owner's needs and contract documents. They can be better than, equal to, or in some cases less than them. Owners often state, "This job has to be done no later than _____" or "There is absolutely no way we can exceed our contingency." Yet owners should be open and candid about their expectations. "Contractors need to clearly understand our expectations relative to the contract documents and specifications," says the district manager of construction for a metropolitan school district.

Try using language that is less controlling to bring forth genuine commitment. For example, you might say, "We have, as you know, a GMP of Y dollars on this project. Given where we are today and what we know about the site, conditions, plans, etc., what would be an extraordinary team or partnership (no contractual obligation here) result for us as a team to strive to attain relative to cost?"

Dave Cavecche, Executive Vice President and General Manager of the Suffolk Construction Company, explains: "This is not 1945. Today you cannot just produce edicts that people are supposed to follow. You have to involve them in the whys and help them understand what is critical and how important their role is in making the project successful. And then seek their genuine commitment. You do not do this by making a bunch of rules or mandates."

I was recently involved with a large, luxury condominium project in Las Vegas. The owner's representative, Deutsche Bank, had a "have-to" goal of a certain date. The contractor's vice president overseeing the job felt there was absolutely no way to achieve this. This had produced a certain acrimony between the two of them which they had danced around, wasting time and avoiding confronting the issue.

The solution? The team acknowledged the owner's desired goal and then challenged themselves as a team to come together and strive to develop a plan to achieve it. What was the value of this approach? First, it took the onus off the contractor, challenged the whole team to collaborate, and allowed for the possibility of breakthroughs that the contractor had not considered. Second, even if the team came up short, the owner would know that everyone—including his on-site staff—had done their very best as a team to meet the goal. Third, everyone committed to achieve whatever goal they came up with. It was not just the contractor's schedule. Fourth, the owner had a high level of confidence that whatever date they came up with, there was a good possibility of achievement. Certainty on a construction project, even if less than desired, carries with it a high value.

Boone Hellmann, Campus Architect, UC San Diego, notes, "A 'have-to' goal can impose constraints and limit a project team's creativity. I've found it best to verbally acknowledge our needs—which often may be contractual—to the team and then challenge the team to be the best that they can be."

As Boone states, a "have-to" goal precludes the team from coming up with creative and more realistic solutions that might come close to meeting the owner's real needs. For example, on an office building project, the team could agree that beneficial occupancy of the first six floors might take place by a certain date which corresponds to the owner's ability to lease those floors and the contractor's ability to complete them. The remainder might follow at a more realistic construction date with no harm to the owner.

Fred Powell of NBBJ Architects says, "On a World Class team, you're honest with one another and do not tell others what they want to hear. This truth can be painful. But everyone on a construction project, sooner or later, knows when they're getting gamed."

Don't get me wrong. It is certainly the owner's prerogative to express concerns about cost or the imperative of opening the facility by a certain date. But the owner should then allow the team the freedom to express what they view as possible. If participants do not believe they have that freedom, they are all quite adept at telling owners what they want to hear—and then dealing with the reality of the job later, with very predictable consequences.

World Class teams are brutally yet empathetically honest with one

EXERCISE: SETTING A COST EXPECTATION AS A WORLD CLASS TEAM

Most project stakeholders are reluctant to talk about project costs openly at the outset of the project. There's an assumption that the bid amount or GMP is all that needs to be said. Owners, naturally, want not only to minimize change orders but also to drive home the point that they expect few. In workshops, I say, "Let's get real and honest with one another if we're a WCT and 'put the moose on the table.'" I have them do a little exercise which first acknowledges the reality that on 99 percent of projects, there will be changes. They will be due to one of these causes:

Unforeseen site conditions =   _____% of Contract Value

Design deficiencies (not on design-build projects) =_____% of CV

Owner scope additions =   _____% of CV

Grand total =   _____% of CV

To a large extent, they are going to be what they are going to be, and the team will end up pricing them fairly. There is one notable exception which has arisen in the past several years, and that is where a team is using some form of design-assist and/or BIM/VBM methodology which truly enables the team to minimize changes, particularly those due to design deficiencies (see chapter 8).

So I ask team members to guesstimate their expectations in each category as a percent of contract value—not what they'd like it to be to meet their contingency, and not what it has to be to meet their budget, but what they honestly expect knowing what they know today about the job, the site, the drawings, and similar projects.

In dealing with anticipated cost, it is interesting what teams come up with. Sometimes the range can be significant. It is important to let them kick it around a bit but then quickly compromise on some number. Again, it will be what it will be. With World Class teams, it's very useful to align or at least acknowledge expectations openly, even if it is something the owner does not want to hear.

another. At the same time, they are willing to seek to truly understand one another's needs and come up with innovative solutions to meet them.

Change order expectations are really not goals unless you are working in a design-assist mode and/or with a BIM technology. World Class team goals imply you have the ability to influence them. So either include change orders as a current expectation in your list of team goals or leave them out altogether. Most elect to leave them in. (We'll learn more about change orders in chapter 8.)

Some teams do, however, set team goals for themselves to offset expected cost increases or define a value engineering goal. A team can influence this by establishing a dedicated team process to facilitate the consideration of value engineering ideas. More about this in chapter 11.

9. The team's goals should not be mutually exclusive and should benefit all project stakeholders.

World Class teams do not compromise the project's safety goal to expedite the schedule. Nor do they compromise quality (keep in mind completing the job per specifications is a contractual obligation) for schedule. *They're going to achieve them all.* Sometimes this in itself becomes a BHAG. This avoids what some organizations call the either/or fallacy, such as the notion in this country back in the sixties that you couldn't produce a quality car without it costing much more. The Japanese taught us otherwise. In *Built to Last*, Jim Collins and Jerry Porras call this "the tyranny of OR."

In construction, a safe job and an expedited job are not necessarily mutually exclusive. A lot of good contractors argue that they are, in fact, mutually supportive.

It is not unusual on a construction project for the owner to express no desire or need for expedited completion. Yet this may be a need or desire of the contractors. A World Class team puts this on the table: "Is the owner willing to accept early completion even though that has no tangible benefit to them?"

10. Ensure that goals are comprehensive—and not just limited to contractual items.

Jim Wyatt, Director of Field Engineering at the Eastern Municipal Water District, warns, "Quite often these days, the bid documents don't relay the bigger issues for the contractor to be aware of. These can include regulatory time frames, environmental restraints, and system demands."

Make sure the team goals cover all facets of the project which the team can influence. (See chapter 9 on owning the game.) Obviously they should include safety, schedule, cost, quality, impact on neighbors and third parties, conflict resolution, LEED status (Hey, why not try for Platinum rather than Gold?), and environmental impact. A good way of testing this is to ask "When—not if—we achieve all of the above, can everyone in the room say that this project was an extraordinary success? If not, what is not included our list?"

11. Err on the side of setting the team goals a little too hairy. Reinforce that it's OK if they try and come up short.

On a bridge project in Seattle, the owner brought up the idea of trying to complete the bridge in one season (thereby avoiding two wet-weather winters). They spent some time in the workshop developing a process for which they would have to get critical County Board of Supervisors approval. I then asked, "Let's suppose you come up with this concept and develop it as a team and the council rejects it. Then what?" Most agreed it would be a worthwhile endeavor and, even if they failed, they would have failed knowing that they did the best they possibly could as a team.

As one owner said, "When you get the team thinking about 'going to the moon' commitments, they need to know that failure is not fatal." Many people do not commit if there is any possibility of failure. Why? It is safe, and they are more committed to being safe than they are to producing extraordinary results. Jim Cowell of Caltech adds, "The leader provides the space for the team to fail without being executed." What can a World Class team learn from failure to achieve a goal? How about perseverance and resilience? It can also test their trust and create the opportunity for a creative solution.

Individuals coming onto a project team are always a bit conservative when it comes to their confidence in a World Class team's ability to come up with innovative solutions to seemingly impossible situations. This is particularly true if they come to the project with a mindset that sees fellow stakeholders as passive contributors, let alone adversaries.

Remind the team that these are partnership goals and intend nor imply no contractual obligation. That does not mean, however, that they should be taken lightly. These are personal and team commitments.

12. Avoid "don't walk on the grass" goals.

A "don't walk on the grass" goal is by definition limiting, constraining, and ultimately uninspiring. It's like a football coach saying to his team at the beginning of the season, "Our goal this season is not to lose more than five games."

A good example is considering impact to the public or end user during construction. Typically teams come up with goals like "no surprises" or "no complaints." Such limiting goals do not get the team thinking of positive and proactive outreach efforts they could implement to favorably impact those third parties to prevent most complaints. (We'll explore such efforts in chapter 11.) They only result in thinking of ways to avoid mistakes and to react to complaints. These represent two significantly different ways of looking at a project. For example, instead of setting a goal of "no rework," a World Class goal would be "all work done right the first time."

What if a team set a goal that this project would "actually *increase* retail sales during construction"? This was the team goal on the Valencia Streetscape project in San Francisco. Not only that, but by having a member of the San Francisco Bike Coalition in the partnering workshop, they came up with a goal of "Valencia Street is a sought-after bike route *during* construction." Don Eng of the City and County of San Francisco explains: "We did not just want to react to complaints. This would put the team in a defensive and very uninspired mode."

Some of the how-to's they came up with later included flyers and a link on the Bike Coalition's website talking about how to navigate the street during construction and the things to be seen on this route of interest to bike riders. They also planned to give bike riders water bottles with the city's logo.

13. Team goals can, and often will, change over the duration of the project.

It's important to remind the team that today's team goals may not be meaningful as the project unfolds. As demonstrated in the Napa Creek Flood Control project in chapter 2, a World Class project team is flexible and adaptable to changing project circumstances. At the same time, they should not abandon their previous goals too easily. For example, perceptions of the schedule completion date will vary significantly among stakeholders at any one point in a project. It's important to hear all sides and particularly to let the optimists have their say.

My experience is that initial project team goals are still viable perhaps at best 30 percent of the time at the end of a project. The longer the duration, obviously the more prone a project is to changing goals. More about resetting team goals in chapter 14 on "Refocusing a Challenging Job."

> An effective leader allows exceptions to the rule for exceptional results
> or when circumstance demands.
> —COACH JOHN WOODEN, UCLA—

Testing the Team Goals

The true test of good World Class team goals: Are the project superintendent's palms a little sweaty? And, I might add, the hands of the key subcontractors. Quite seriously, most good superintendents are the ultimate pragmatists—and that's what they are paid for. Suppose the superintendent says something to the effect of "Well, the only way we're going to make this happen is if everything works and we somehow figure out how to do this, and that, and expedite this." Explore what they mean by "everything" and "expedite this," and then ask, "OK, suppose we do all of that. Now is it possible?" If they grudgingly say "I think so" or "Yeah, but it will be real tough," then you know you have a good WCT goal!

As we have seen, it's best to err on the side of the goal being a little too hairy and audacious. Challenge the team, as a team, to creatively come up with how-to's that none of them individually could figure out. But as one contractor told me, "There needs to be a sanity check as well."

Grounding the Individuals in the Team's Goals

Here's a way to affirm and ensure individual commitment to team goals. Ask each of the project stakeholders, "What do you, personally, have at risk or to gain in achieving all of the team goals?" Emphasize *what they have at risk or have to gain personally*—not organizationally. Ash Wason of Carollo Engineers explains: "It is important that the goals involve the personal commitment by the team members and not just an institutional commitment by an organizational entity. People will go a lot further when they make personal commitments than when they had no say." In other words, each individual needs "some skin in the game," as another contractor told me.

> Until one is committed, there is hesitancy, the chance to draw back,
> always ineffectiveness. Concerning all acts of initiative,
> there is one element of truth, the ignorance of which kills countless ideas
> and splendid plans—that the moment one commits oneself,
> then providence moves all.
> —GOETHE—

What are the payoffs of personal commitment?

The answers are very predictable if you do indeed have compelling goals as we saw in chapter 2:

- Pride
- Challenge
- Learning
- Job security
- Less stress—remember, this is the most valued payoff
- Enjoying coming to work every day
- Reputation

How far are individuals willing to go to commit to team goals that beat their contractual obligations? Here is what one third-party construction manager whose firm had a time-based services contract with the owner's organization said about personally committing to a team stretch goal of

What do you personally have at risk or to gain in achieving all of these goals?

World Class Teamwork: The Personal Value

completing his project sixty days early: "Completing this job sixty days early will cost me and my firm money, but my reputation is my best job security. On that basis alone, I'm more than willing to support the team's early completion goal."

The art of coming up with true World Class team goals on a project that truly evokes the passion, contribution, and commitment of all stakeholders can be daunting and requires patient perseverance. A leader or facilitator does not want to manipulate or impose their own agenda, but at the same time they want to enable the team to genuinely consider its true outer limits—without any quick assumptions about where these might be. Do not rush through this process. In some full-day workshops, we've spent the better part of a half day working on WCT goals. Post-workshop critiques by participants report that this was always the most valuable part of the day.

Never Underestimate What a Team Committed to Common Goals Can Accomplish

Almost without exception, individuals on a construction project begin a job by defining project possibilities based solely on what they believe they and their organization can do by themselves *and* those they are limited to by the contractual requirements. They have rarely considered what's possible with a true collaborative effort with all their fellow stakeholders actively supporting one another. They cannot have. This can only come from a free, open, and interactive process. As Jim Linthicum of SANDAG says, "I hire my people for their brains and not just to manage a checklist." More about this in chapter 11.

Goal Setting: The Foundation for Passion and Committed Action

Why have I spent so much time talking about setting goals? In my experience and that of my clients, it is the Maypole around which all of the other WCT behaviors revolve or from which they are sourced. To put it into construction terms, it is the foundation upon which the rest of the team structure and effectiveness is fundamentally dependent.

A goal-setting process that establishes compelling goals is also the source of passion and commitment. It brings forth the kind of passion that makes a designer want to put in the additional time to expedite an RFI response to a subcontractor. The passion that brings forth the extra effort by an owner to fast-track a pay request. The passion from an inspector that makes him or her want to show up after hours on his or her own time to ensure that overtime work is done right.

What is the ultimate validation of true team commitment to common goals? Mike Aparicio, currently with Skanska but previously with the Washington Group, notes, "Our team on the LA METRO Eastside Extension taped the team's schedule goal in big, bold numbers on the wall inside the men's restroom in our trailer."

AN EXAMPLE OF PROJECT TEAM GOALS

NOTE: This 2010 Marvin Black Partnering Excellence Award winner was a $70 million-plus design, bid, build project for a facility that would enable JPL/NASA to develop space satellites and vehicles in a modular format. The owner was the Jet Propulsion Laboratory (NASA), the architect was LPA Architects, and the general contractor was Swinerton Builders, Inc. The construction manager was Vanir CM.

Jet Propulsion Laboratory Flight Projects Center
Partnering Workshop Proceedings

Our Partnership Goals/BHAGs:

1. Project complete/punched no later than June 6, 2009, with JPL able to fit in on a floor-by-floor basis beginning on that date, with project close-out documents submitted no later than July 6, 2009

Key processes we need to expedite, figure out, invent, make happen to realize goal number 1 above:

    a. Identified access/laydown areas

    b. Expedited submittals, especially metal panels

    c. Developed a BHAG schedule for 6/6/09 that we all contribute and commit to

    d. Expedited RFIs

    e. Facilitated personnel access (NOTE: This was a secure site.)

    f. Expedited inspections

    g. Expedited change orders

    h. Identified and expedited procurement of long lead items

    i. Expedited commissioning/startup/close-out

    j. Submitted close-out documents and record documents

2. Project complete at contract value + 7.5% of additive change orders minus 1% of deductive changes (value engineering) = net 6.5%

3. Zero recordables/zero incident rate

4. Zero rework. Zero punch list (complete) at June 6, 2009. Punch as we go.

5. Achieve LEED Gold (NOTE: Contractual requirement was LEED Silver.)

6. Zero unplanned business interruptions to JPL during construction

7. 90% of issues resolved at the Pat, Sam, Tony, Craig, Scott level (project level). No claims.

7

WORLD CLASS TEAM BEHAVIOR #3

Practice Open, Direct, Verbal Communication

On World Class teams, you can call "bull____" on one another and be open.
Your pride is checked at the door. On Business as Usual teams,
you're very cautious with one another and don't expect anyone to bend at all.
—MIKE GUSICH, VICE PRESIDENT,
UNIVERSITY MECHANICAL & ENGINEERING, SUBCONTRACTORS,
PHOENIX, ARIZONA—

Business as Usual: CYA mentality by project stakeholders with a lot of intentional tennis (put it in writing). Case building, posturing, and game playing.

Good Teams: Effective fair-weather communication. With issues, can suppress, avoid, delay, play tennis, and write letters.

WORLD CLASS TEAMS: Open, direct verbal communication that is sometimes confrontational and always constructive. Implicit trust, but verify. No surprises.

"Jim, why don't you just shut up and sit down," the CEO of one of the top twenty-five civil engineering contractors in the U. S. told me midway through a partnering workshop on a major bridge project back in 2001. I meekly mumbled something and took a seat. The team's conversation continued, quite well actually, without the benefit of a humbled facilitator.

This WCT behavior is the most highly valued by all WCT teams. The ability to talk straight to one another—without any game playing, posturing, storytelling, nonessential letter writing, or case building—can be a project team's best asset. Consider what our clients and seminar participants have told me are the consequences of the alternative:

On Business as Usual, let alone Combat teams, over 65 percent of an individual's time can be spent in letter writing, case building, or posturing.

Think about that: over two-thirds of the time of all the human resources on a project team wasted, and for no purpose. If you stop and figure out the actual dollar cost, it is staggering. *The Economist* recently estimated that the U.S. federal government now employs a quarter of a million people to write and enforce regulations alone.

David Allen, Project Architect and PM for the U.S. District Court. relates, "I've seen quite a few projects where the amount of time spent in nonproductive, defensive activity of team players is well in excess of 65 percent. You cannot have anything close to a World Class team by just playing defense."

On the Hard Rock Casino project in Las Vegas, the team was just starting with its teaming process, and Perini's general superintendent—a hard-bitten, crusty fellow, in other words, a real pro—sat there with his arms crossed and with his body language saying to the world, "This meeting is an absolute waste of my time."

When we got to an issue involving RFIs, I asked him, "Fred, what do think about that?" He said something to the effect of "Well, if the d____ architect would just do their job." I asked, "What specifically do you want the architect to do?" He said, "They could give me the curtain wall RFI back quickly." "How quickly?" I asked. "Three days." I asked one of the design team members, "Who within your design team is responsible for that RFI?" Jack raised his hand and said, "I guess that would be me." I then asked Fred, "Why don't you make your request of Jack and see what he says?" He begrudgingly did so ,and Jack immediately responded, "No problem—you got it." Fred, taken aback, leaned forward in his chair and asked, "Can I make another request?"

Ron Hall, Regional Manager for McCarthy Building Companies, notes, "While some people are naturally inclined to communicate and discuss issues, there are others who will need to be coaxed. There needs to be one or more leaders in the group who are committed to drawing out these very important team members."

A Communication Protocol that Leads to Committed Action

The reasons why team members do not communicate openly and directly on construction projects are endless. Lack of trust. Not knowing whom to communicate to about what. Believing that the other party will not do what you request, so why bother? Being wary of upsetting someone if you make a request they might not like. Reluctance to ask for help or assistance because you might be perceived as weak or unqualified or could even be taken advantage of. It is easier—or at least is perceived as being easier—to avoid direct communication. You don't have to put yourself out there. As Don Eng with the City and County of San Francisco says, "Open, direct, verbal communication is hard to do and not natural for many, but it is essential for World Class teamwork."

What are the consequences of failing to communicate openly, directly, and verbally? Most people default to a reactive mode at best, communicating with and to the other parties only when they deem necessary—which is to say, after it was really necessary. That communication will often be in writing or via e-mail, and the receiver will reciprocate in kind. This, in turn, predictably leads to Business as Usual.

With time, many construction project teams move beyond Business as Usual and get to Good communication. Heck, you can play checkers with a stranger for four hours and begin to communicate on a personal level. But how does a project team get to World Class communication with velocity, which includes being very direct, open, and transparent? Again, it starts with the foundation of common goals and the process of developing them, which leads to trust.

We are all more open and direct with people whom we perceive as having the same intentions as we do. To the extent that we question their intentions, we are guarded and closed, especially on a construction project. Stephen Sharr with Los Angeles Unified School District says, "Through goal setting and following up on actions, you generate earned and learned trust." It is not prudent to start a construction project by laying all your cards on the table or by making big requests of other players whom you only just have met.

A process of goal setting is one of the best tools I've seen to accelerate individuals' ability to communicate with one another. It's positive and forward looking, and it reveals our personal, common, future interests in achieving something other than just meeting our contractual obligations. To the extent that goal setting truly challenges individuals and the team to go beyond their comfort zone, it creates a basis for open, direct, personal communication. With that understanding, I find teams willing to adopt the following protocol, which I call the World Class communication rule:

> I will not question your intentions unless and until you do something blatantly obvious that causes me to raise my shield, game over, back to Business as Usual.

1. Talk first and document only to memorialize. No "tennis."

"Tennis" is back-and-forth letter writing or e-mailing, which wastes time and can also breed an adversarial relationship. Eventually, of course, everyone will document what they need to document. This is best done to memorialize an agreement reached through verbal communication.

On project station B-271 of the LA METRO Red Line subway back in the mid-nineties, the team came up with a rule which they called Rule 271: No project team member will write a letter or e-mail a fellow team member without a preceding telephone call. Here's how Doug Duplisea, currently Senior Vice President and Southwest Regional Manager with the Kiewit Companies in Phoenix, recalls it: "You don't blindside your partner with a letter. So before you send it, you walk over to him and tell him what you're thinking of putting in writing. We had a situation where we did this, and the owner actually coached us, saying, 'You'd be making a stronger point if you referenced this spec section in your letter.'"

Another project team acknowledged that the use of e-mails was OK to get an issue on the table or, in some cases, on the record, but verbal communication was the only way to resolve issues. Increasingly, however, I am seeing World Class teams establish a protocol of no matter what, talk first and then document only if just to memorialize. This may require a subcontractor, for example, talking to the GC before they speak to a subconsultant.

2. Communicate on the basis of specific requests, not demands.

A request is a call for a specific action by a specific individual by a specific date that supports our common goal. You do not make requests of organizations, such as "I would like the owner to _____." Make a request of Charlie or Fred or maybe both. Nor do World Class team members demand action. A demand does not offer the recipient a choice. As we'll see, always having a choice and being able to say no are key tenets of a World Class team.

World Class teams are very personal, and relationships are not institutional. Rob Robinson, Vice President of URS Construction Management, explains: "Being on a World Class team breaks down the walls that exist between stakeholders and enables you to deal with individuals and personalities, not impersonal institutions."

Let's get personal and relate on the same basis as your local bank or insurance company wants you to relate to their organization. Very few of us feel any personal commitment to other institutions that we work with or purchase products or services from. You may like the dealer you bought your car from, but I'll bet that had more to do with the individual salesperson than it did with the organization per se.

3. Respond with personal commitments to action with a deliverable and date.

"I'll try" or "I'll see what I can do" does not cut it. It is either yes, no, or an alternative. And it is OK to say no. People tell me that stakeholders on World Class teams say no to one another more often than on Business as Usual or Good teams. Why? They're being honest with one another. Offering an alternative solution or compromise is also acceptable. For example, you might say, "I cannot get back to you by Friday as you requested on the status of that submittal, but I can get back to you no later than next Monday. Is that OK?" or "I can give you this part of what you're requesting by that date and the rest NLT than the following Tuesday. Is that OK?"

On one project, one of the designers was reluctant to make any commitments at all. "No," he would say. "I don't want to lock myself in" was his justification. Yet that is a commitment, albeit an unspoken one. That is it is a commitment not to commit oneself. It also communicates a lack of commitment to the team goals.

How do you deal with that? Ask the individual "what additional information would you need in order to make a decision or be in a position to consider the request?" Or, "OK, if you're not committed to that idea to achieve our common goal, what are you committed to?"

4. Avoid complaints and history.

Recounting the past (who should have done what) and complaining do not result in action and just waste people's time. Communicate on a go-forward basis only.

> TIP: To quickly stop complaining in its tracks, ask the complainer,
> "What is it you want me to do?"

Sara Loughead, Project Manager for Rady Children's Hospital, says, "On our team I was told what actually happened and what's being done to recover. And the answers were forthright and verbal. Everyone cared and took the time necessary."

World Class Team Members Ask for Help and Make Big Requests of One Another

Let your fellow team members know what you need. Lay it out there. Here's the understanding that makes extraordinary requests OK if not downright essential on a World Class team: the need/urgency required by *our* common goal—especially the schedule. Dave Niese of Flatiron Construction explains: "On a World Class team you should never be too embarrassed to ask and never be too offended by what's requested."

Certainty, even if later than preferred, is of much higher value to contractors than not knowing or an indefinite response.

Without a common goal, if someone makes an extraordinary request of you, you might have good reason to question their intentions: "Why do they want this? They've got to be up to something. Hmm, safer to say no, defer, or tell them to put it in writing." Common goals take the assumption of any personal agenda or ulterior motives out of the request. The request has nothing to do with you personally; rather it is essential to expedite a process which, in turn, is necessary to achieve *our* goal.

Avoid Written "No's" and Openly Acknowledge Why You Cannot Do What Is Requested

In a recent workshop, one of the owner's managers said he often felt obligated to write letters denying the contractor's requests due to his senior management's or third parties' possible reaction. So I asked the team, "How does a World Class team respond when faced with pressure by higher-ups or third parties?" The majority of the participants agreed: call/talk and be open about it, explain the situation, and try to find some compromise. Minimally the conversation might be something like this: "Jack, I'd like to help you out with your request, but my hands are tied by such and such. And that would require..." or "The Water Board will really come down hard on us if we let you do this. Here's what they'll be looking for. Do you see another way?" You might also say, "Here's how you'll have to approach this with So and So." This is what I referred to as coaching in chapter 5.

Example: Open, Direct, Verbal Communication at the Field Level

What about World Class communication at the field level between superintendents and inspectors?

On Los Angeles Unified's Central Region Elementary School #14, the district's Inspector of Record, Bill Davis, has what he describes as the best relationship he's had with a superintendent in over forty projects spanning his entire career. Here's what he has to say about Swinerton Builders' Project Superintendent Roland Muller: "He's willing to work with you, and he's a problem solver, not a problem maker, yeller, or screamer. He's the epitome of a team player, which makes all things possible. I go to his office every day, and we work things out verbally, not confrontationally. He is truly in it for everyone's benefit. Most supers want to kick butt, and there's an 'I don't care what your problems are' attitude. Not with Roland."

And what does Roland Muller think about Bill? "There's real teamwork between Bill and me. We're both looking out for the greater good of the project, and both of us recognize we cannot succeed alone. When we work together, it is always about looking ahead—as in I tell him 'This is what is going to come up,' and he tells me what he'll be looking for. We're open with one another, and neither of us has totally made up our mind. If you do not have this working relationship, it is an uphill battle with both parties looking for ways to stop or delay the other. The result? On this job things are done right the first time all of the time."

It's OK to Be Passionate, But Don't Be Personal

Open, direct, verbal communication does not preclude heated argument. Disagreements, different interpretations, misunderstandings, and mistakes will occur even on World Class teams.

It's OK to be passionate and feel strongly about your beliefs, but remove the personal attacks. In other words, lose the attitude. Again, it is the context within which these expressions are made that makes the difference. If the passion and feelings are about the issue and not your counterpart, fine—let it out.

> Politeness is the slow poison of collaboration.
> —ANONYMOUS—

Make requests; let go of the history and stories. Remember, you are all on the same team playing the same game. It is always better to surface differences now verbally rather than ten months from now in the form of a written request for change or claim.

Many individuals believe that expressing personal feelings and emotions is not productive. I disagree, and so does Dave Tatevossian, South Region Deputy Director for New Construction with the Los Angeles Unified School District: "When you love what you do, you are passionate about it being done to the best of your ability and that of the project team. With some people, construction is just a job. On World Class teams, your collective love of the work enables everyone to be passionate and to sustain that passion even in the face of day-to-day challenges and circumstances. With that passion can come disagreements, and these can be heated, but that's OK. These disagreements can bring out the best of us."

Lonnie Morelock of Kiewit Companies adds, "Passion is the driving force of successful outcomes. Where passion is lacking, there is no follow-through. But true passion unleashes a tidal wave of energy and focus which eventually leads to what had been perceived as unachievable results."

As one World Class team contractor remarked, "The good thing about these situations is that at least you come away very clear about where everyone really stands on an issue. Better that than having people put them off until the end of the job when you hear about it in a letter."

Most folks in construction do not get involved because of a desire to write. They get involved in construction because of a passion to build and design. Minimizing unnecessary documentation allows people more time to do what they love to do and do it with people who share that same passion.

8

WORLD CLASS TEAM BEHAVIOR #4

Minimize Risk, Manage Change, and Maximize Profitability

*It is a pretty shallow victory if at the end of a job the owner, designer,
and contractor all did not win. World Class teamwork creates a scenario
where all stakeholders can win and everyone is concerned
about everyone else's success.*
—BARRY THALDEN OF THALDEN·BOYD·EMERY ARCHITECTS—

Business as Usual: Push risk off onto other stakeholders. Defer to contract well after the risk has occurred. Written case building. Stakeholders in trouble pursue own self-interests surreptitiously.

Good Teams: Reactive approach to risk by each stakeholder individually. You are responsible and on your own for your risk and profitability. No explicit acknowledgement of shared risk.

WORLD CLASS TEAMS: Open, proactive, and collaborative verbal anticipation of potential risks and ways to prevent/mitigate them developed as a team. Notion of shared risk. Profitability openly discussed and supported.

Risk. The very word conjures up negative connotations when associated with construction projects. Common reactions include: "Get rid of it," "Deny it," "Avoid it," "Shift it," "Let's not talk about it openly with one another because it will foster a negative or defensive conversation," "Let's spend a lot of time debating it and attempting to determine who, according to the contract, it belongs to," or "Hey, our contract or IPD agreement should cover everything. No need to worry." World Class teams view it differently.

The context or perspective with which a project team approaches risk determines how they will respond to it. Change the context and you can change the response. Sounds easy, but let's look at it more closely. On a construction project, risk is a very personal phenomenon. It is what you and each of your individual fellow stakeholders perceive it to be at the time, acknowledging the contract and specs.

Brian DerMatoian, Vice President, SJ Amoroso Construction Company, says, "Different owners and individuals have different preferences and philosophies regarding risk. You as a contractor need to encourage them to talk openly about theirs and how you can, with this understanding, work together toward mutual success."

Consider this analogy. When is a strike in baseball—excluding batter whiffs and foul balls—a strike? Most people say when the pitch is in the strike zone. Wrong. It is when the umpire calls it a strike. As any major league batting coach will tell you, different umpires have different definitions of strikes. Some call 'em high, some low.

Furthermore, World Class teams consider risk a natural consequence of individuals interacting with incomplete information, uncertainty, and limited funds with a contract and specifications all of which can be open to interpretation. If we all agreed that the drawings were perfect, the contract was crystal clear, and we were able to anticipate all unknown conditions and changes we could, theoretically, eliminate risk. But we can't, and we would never be willing to incur the expenses to do this even if we could.

Every World Class team needs clear, compelling, common team goals and a protocol for dealing with risks, including unknown conditions, change orders, incomplete drawings, and conflicts. Without these, individuals will default to protecting their (or their organization's) perceived self-interests relative to those real or potential risks. Such reactive, defensive processes are natural and normal, but unfortunately they can lead to Business as Usual or even, as we will see in chapter 13, Combat. Collaborative PDMs and construction processes (BIM) can help a team manage risk but never entirely eliminate it. Nothing can. If we could eliminate risk, the construction process could be managed by computers, not people.

So can risk actually enable World Class teamwork? In *The Death of Common Sense: How Law Is Suffocating America*, Philip K. Howard writes: "Uncertainty, the ultimate evil that modern law seeks to eradicate, generally fosters cooperation, not the opposite. The contractors (CC Myers) and the state officials (Caltrans) rebuilding the Santa Monica Freeway after the Northridge earthquake in 1994 had a lot to lose by being unreasonable. Humans are driven to be reasonable with each other because uncertainty puts both at risk."[16]

With this understanding, a World Class team recognizes the tangible and intrinsic rewards that exist in collaborative approach to risk through:

- Mutually anticipating potential risks as a team that could hinder their ability to achieve their common goals, while acknowledging their contract, in an ongoing, open, and verbal process
- Acknowledging openly to one another that most of these risks are shared
- Recognizing that the individuals or stakeholders in the best position to control the risk should handle it

But there are other risks today that were not as present in the construction industry when Mr. Howard wrote his book. These were alluded to in chapter 2 as "opportunity lost" risks—the risk of being excluded from future best-value selection processes by owners, the risk of not being seen as a desirable partner for a design-build project or joint venture, or the risk of being an owner who does not receive aggressive and creative bids by numerous well-qualified contractors or design-build teams. I also call these the "short list risks." How does a contractor, owner, or CM assess those risks, which are very real and potentially costly?

The 85/85 Rule—Mutually Anticipating Potential Risks Relative to Achieving Project Team Goals

Once a World Class team has established common goals, the process of looking at potential risks becomes less of a one-time, defensive effort by individual stakeholders and more of a collaborative, proactive, and ongoing process. In my experience, at the outset of a project and on an ongoing basis, a truly World Class team can anticipate 85 percent of the major potential risks to their common goals and significantly prevent or, if not, significantly mitigate 85 percent of those. (See the BOMS Board exercise on page 140.)

THE 85/85 RULE

A World Class team can effectively anticipate 85 percent of potential challenges to their team goals and then significantly prevent or mitigate 85 percent of these.

Mike Ghilotti of Ghilotti Brothers says, "A key advantage of a World Class team with a proactive meeting process is that you can talk about potential risks in the future relative to your common goals. This is a much more positive, open process and is very effective in dealing with those risks."

For example, a conversation like this might occur: "Accepting what we believe our contract says, and given our goal of completing this project six months early, and our cost and quality goals and our commitment to contractor/DB team profitability, what could get in our way? How can we then prevent, or if not, mitigate these risks?"

On Good—let alone Business as Usual or Combat—jobs, individuals are reluctant to speak openly with one another about potential risks, and there's a tendency to attempt to shift the risk. In the absence of common goals, speaking about potential risks might make an individual appear weak, incompetent, potentially vulnerable, whiny, and very self-serving.

Brian Cahill of Barnhart Balfour Beatty notes, "If a contractor is given a set of drawings with off-site work under a different area or jurisdiction that they believe they have no control over, without open, honest communication about that risk with the other stakeholders, they're going to put a very high number on it. And this does not bode well for teamwork or trust."

So how does a World Class team speak about risk and uncertainty?

Jeff Lage, Vice President of Skanska, explains: "We manage risk by talking, communicating, and being open. This starts by dropping your barriers and assumptions about one another and making yourself a little vulnerable. But also key is looking ahead as a team toward your goals—this is the biggest thing. This way you're doing the planning so that you've got your arms around the risk, should it occur, as a team. This puts you in the best position to deal with it to all parties' benefit."

Intellectuals solve problems. Geniuses prevent them.

—ALBERT EINSTEIN—

Shared Risk, Vulnerability, and Transparency

Talking (not writing) and listening sometimes requires "putting the moose on the table" and speaking openly and transparently about potentially sensitive issues. These can include:

- If we proceed on the basis of just a verbal authorization, am I at any risk?
- What if a subcontractor goes broke?
- How do we deal with an individual/stakeholder organization not being a team player?
- How do we as a team expedite the work with incomplete and/or uncoordinated drawings?
- How do we minimize late payment or financial difficulties by the owner?
- What if there's a faulty execution by a vendor?
- What if there's a delayed response to a critical submittal?
- What if permanent power is late?

A truly World Class team will accept that the majority of these potential risks and uncertainties are shared and can best be dealt with through a collaborative process. For example, what can we do as a team to prevent or at least mitigate late submittal responses? Designer, owner, and contractor all have something to contribute here. Michael Abeln with the Army Corps of Engineers explains: "On World Class teams, you jointly identify risks which may be different for each stakeholder. But we're cognizant of one another's risks and recognize that most are shared. And on World Class teams, everyone accepts their share."

Again, going through an exercise of developing common goals creates the foundation of trust that can allow individual team members to speak openly about potential risks to "our goals." Project team members have more at stake, individually and institutionally, in identifying, preventing, and mitigating risks as shared risks. The result? Managing project risks becomes an ongoing team responsibility and commitment.

The mutual understanding of both the concept of and specific potential
for shared risk is absolutely critical for long-term project success.
—TONY FERRUCCIO, EXECUTIVE VICE PRESIDENT, MACTEC, ATLANTA—

Once the team accepts the notion of shared risks, it is a short jump to making the determination as a team of who on the team is the best informed, is best qualified, or has the influence to deal with a potential risk. Which team members, for example, can best contribute to helping us put together a storm water pollution plan that will allow us to work through the winter that, in turn, supports our early completion goal?

Kathy Mayo of AECOM notes, "There needs to be a joint, ongoing process to openly discuss and share risks on a project. With this comes the mutual understanding that ultimately, for the benefit of the project, a specific risk best belongs to that party who is in the best position to control or influence it."

Determining this is invariably a team effort, and it capitalizes upon the blurring of organizational lines and everyone being 100 percent accountable for everything, We will consider these in chapter 10.

Perspectives on Transparency

Let's hear some other thoughts on transparency. How transparent can or should one be on a World Class team? Are there any limits?

Stephen Sharr with Los Angeles Unified School District notes, "Transparency is one behavior trait that is fundamental to a trusted business advisor relationship. By that I mean a willingness to be open and discuss normally cloistered business issues—for example, sharing potential risks with your partners that you might anticipate which could impact you and your organization. At the same time, it is OK to have things that you do not talk about with others, although not in the sense of hiding them. There's a mutual respect and sensitivity to those areas that are genuinely proprietary to one another."

My experience is that willingness to be transparent, to be open, or to acknowledge uncertainty is a function of the degree of perceived risk or reward by the individuals on the team. There is no One Best Way or degree of transparency. One design-builder might feel comfortable with an open book on change order pricing. Another may feel that just verbally talking about the scope is sufficient. The greater the potential risk or reward, generally the more willing individuals on a project are to open up. It is useful, however, for a project team to continually test their limits and err of the side of vulnerability.

When not taken advantage of by a stakeholder, this process of transparent discussion tends to foster increased trust and greater levels of transparency. This in turn creates a greater opportunity to find common ground and a mutually satisfactory solution or mitigation measure.

A effective third-party neutral or facilitator can help expedite this process and bring people out. Robert Develle of NASA Jet Propulsion Laboratory explains: "A good facilitator has no skin in the game and is totally neutral with no axe to grind other than to make the team successful. They can ask questions that project stakeholders may not want to ask or be able to ask."

Interestingly, on World Class teams, many risks are associated not with the downside (something going wrong in just building this job to plans and specs) but, perhaps more importantly, with the upside risks of pursuing extraordinary team goals. What are the risks if we attempt to expedite the job? What are the risks associated with proceeding on a verbal authorization?

For example, a contractor might state to his partners, "Given our goal of completing this job six months early, I'm willing to start construction on Buildings B & C before the design is complete. Starting this way is risky for us, but it is a lot cheaper than waiting for complete and approved documents." Risky, yes, but a World Class owner/designer might then reciprocate this openness by their teammate and explicitly agree, for example, to help their teammate facilitate his construction *with* incomplete documents. Herein lies another opportunity for an owner or CM to act as a coach. This again involves open, transparent discussion of potential risk with a teammate who's willing to share that risk.

The Role of Management in Facilitating Transparency

In his current best-selling book *The Five Dysfunctions of a Team*, Patrick Lencioni writes, "The most important action that a leader must take to encourage the building of trust on a team is to demonstrate vulnerability first. What is more, team leaders must create an environment that does not punish vulnerability."[17]

On World Class teams, senior management challenges their team to deal with seemingly unspeakable "What if?" scenarios. Mike McKinney, Operations Manager with PCL Construction, Inc., explains, "A key part of my job is to challenge a project team to consider potential risks and how they, as a team, might prevent or mitigate them."

Senior managers are also in the best position to acknowledge to the team the possibility of failure, uncertainty, misunderstanding, or even incompetence on the part of their organizations and to explain that failure by any stakeholder does not call for punishment or provide an opportunity to take advantage of one's teammate. In other words, they make failure, within acknowledged limits, OK. A willingness to verbally acknowledge and tolerate uncertainty by the team can be key to fostering transparency and trust. For example, a contractor on a World Class team is more inclined to express to their client the potential uncertainty of, for example, encountering differing soils conditions well in advance of actually breaking ground. With this information, the owner is willing to engage in a conversation relative to potential alternatives to mitigate potential scenarios as a team as opposed to a hard line that results in a "put it in writing" change order.

Captain Mike Williamson of the U.S. Navy says, "You need to understand where and when you, as a team, can take a risk and where you should not. To do this, a World Class team will endeavor to mutually understand the overall goals of the job and the environment and intentions of teammates. Likewise, everyone needs to appreciate one another's strengths and weaknesses, including their own. For example, we might decide as a team to get a little closer to a deadline because we know that the trade leading this effort is really good. And the trade needs to know that the rest of the team is there to support him. He also knows that we will not take advantage of the situation should he fail or fall short."

Profitability Is Not a Bad Word

Conventional or Business as Usual wisdom states that each project stakeholder only looks after their own self-interests, especially when it comes to money. It also teaches that no one but you is, or can expected to be, interested in enhancing your profitability, especially if you are losing money. It was not that long ago in the industry that some owners would brag that "no contractor is going to make a profit on my job." Conversely, of course, contractors would blatantly play the change order/claim game. For owners even to speak about contractor/designer profitability was seen as opening themselves up to being taken advantage of or perhaps even violating ethical or organizational policy. But is this mindset even in the project's overall best interests, let alone in the best interests of the organizations and individuals involved?

Cost, profitability, or job security issues are unquestionably a key trigger of personal stress and anxiety. The solution? Creating an project culture where it is OK to talk about them. Without this there is an inherent tension on a project, particularly if it is not going well, which can lead to further misunderstanding and conflict.

Let's challenge conventional wisdom about talking about profitability with some comments from World Class team members:

• Fred Powell, NBBJ Architects: "Respect for a contractor's profitability is essential to getting them to work with you to achieve the overall goals of the project. If they feel I'm holding up their schedule, that works against all of us. I will make a point of going to the sub trade's trailer a couple times a week. This communicates, I believe, my respect for and understanding of their work process."

• Paul Ligocki, Hensel Phelps: "It's unfortunate, but often we see subcontractors arguing their position on a cost issue because they believe they've gotten to a point where they have no choice. If they're open and honest early on with us, we're willing to work with them to help them maximize their efficiencies."

• Wylie Bearup, City Engineer, Phoenix: "On a World Class team, you shouldn't be afraid to talk about contractor profitability and margin. Without that understanding, there's always an underlying anxiety on a project, and this can lead to an dysfunctional team. If, for example, a subcontractor is having problems and I'm aware of it, this helps me understand the correspondence I'm getting from them. With that, I may be more receptive to value engineering or lower-cost options they put forward."

- Virgil Curtis with Balfour Beatty on the Marvin Black Award-winning C-510 project with Seattle's Sound Transit: "Sound Transit's willingness to support our ability to be profitable was huge. It is a trust thing. Early on in the project when we didn't know them and vice versa, we kind of negotiated back and forth. We were both able to appreciate that you can't ask without giving. We both appreciated that construction on this project is a two-way street. It is tricky to manage and to ensure that you're open and don't spring surprises on one another."

- Dave Cavecche, Suffolk Construction Company: "World Class teamwork makes a lot of sense from a business perspective. When you understand where everyone is coming from and are working together in a collaborative way, at the end of the job, everyone will speak highly of your company. And that is worth money in and of itself. I can take that and parlay it into other projects. Doing the right thing consistently will make us more profitable."

Change Orders—Opportunity for World Class Teamwork

Business as Usual Teams: The high-low pricing game played *intentionally.* Independent estimates with inflated and deflated assessments about scope, risk, and schedule impact.

Good Teams: The high-low pricing game played *unintentionally* with different assumptions about scope, schedule impact, etc. Tennis and delays.

WORLD CLASS TEAMS: Verbal, on-site, joint agreement on scope, merit, schedule impact, risks, and breakdown of cost estimate. GC/DBT involved early in owner design development to minimize/mitigate impact and offer fresh ideas. Owner willing to offer partial payment.

Change orders and the risks associated with them are usually considered the bane of construction projects—necessary evils that have a tendency to bring out the worst of a team's performance. As Tony Ferruccio of Mactec asserts, "On Business as Usual teams, there's a tendency to wait until the end of the job to deal with claims and associated change orders."

In my experience, if the change order process is not discussed in advance by a project team, there's at least a 65 percent probability that the team will end up playing the high-low change order pricing game—if not intentionally, then unintentionally due to different assumptions about merit, scope, and potential schedule impact of potential changes.

Mike Scott, Assistant Vice President with Parsons Brinckerhoff, notes, "Another game we see on Business as Usual jobs is the contractor saying something to the effect of 'Let's do this one big settlement and then everything will be OK.' This usually works for a week or so, but six months later they're back asking for the same thing."

Talk and Walk Before You Write

World Class teams look at change orders differently. As one owner told me "Change orders are not necessarily a bad thing. They can be opportunities for teamwork and enhancing project value." So how do World Class teams deal with change orders? Here are some examples.

Wylie Bearup, city of Phoenix, who recently managed completion of a $600 million convention center and $250 million hotel, says, "A high-performing, collaborative project team that gets it together early to talk about potential changes gives me the certainty that I don't need to go out and get more money. Also, my end users can plan better for their needs, and there is just a very high level of certainty all along the line."

Ray Hughes, Regional Manager with Flatiron Corporation, adds, "On our Taxilane S project with Los Angeles International, we recommended constructability reviews where we would meet and talk with the owner and our subs when an owner was about 50 percent complete with his change. This way we could help them ensure a change that met their needs, minimized costs, and avoided future misunderstandings about scope." Call it a form of informal design-assist.

On the Salinas Valley Memorial Hospital remodel and retrofit, the team agreed to meet on site as a ceiling was uncovered. Designer, sub, CM, owner, and GC were all represented. Robert Van Kirk, Construction Administrator of Mazzetti and Associates, design consultants, describes the purpose: "The intent is to rapidly agree as a team on the intent of any RFI and then confirm this verbal understanding in a confirming RFI in writing if there's a potential change order. The team would also agree on possible design solutions and potential cost impact (ROM) if any, again verbally."

> TIP: When uncovering ceilings or other potentially unknown areas,
> discussions can be initiated at the site by the field level
> to mutually agree on RFIs that may lead to changes.

The JPL Flight Projects Center team suggests that the change order process should include:

- Subs willing to proceed with work without a signed change order
- Owner willing to pay immediately for that part of a change order that they can currently agree to, with the remainder to follow further review
- Willingness to give and take if close on pricing; no changes for issues under $500 and no credits for issues under $200
- Subs able to talk to construction manager directly to clarify scope, risk, and schedule impact

How about on design-build projects? Vijay Daniel, Senior Project Manager for Whiting Turner, explains: "On a design-build project with a fixed fee, there's a lot of anxiety on our part when there's a change by the owner of one thing for another. To ensure that it's apples for apples, there needs to be an open, verbal process that involves all stakeholders to achieve a fair resolution."

The above examples rarely happen serendipitously. They need to be part of an explicit understanding reached between project stakeholders prior to encountering the first change.

And notice the commonality of all of them. They all involve talking and verbal communication prior to initiating any written correspondence.

The change order process can also develop real trust and even a trusted business advisor relationship, as we discussed in chapter 5. Kim Grant at Swinerton Builders observes, "Owners used to not view contractors as trustworthy. Now I like it when owners trust me with offering changes. I feel good about people asking my opinion. I am also not reluctant to ask them, for example, 'What is it about this change order that is bothering you?'"

Dealing with the Schedule Impact of a Change Order

A $25 million project at a major urban wastewater treatment site was well underway, and the schedule had been pushed out at least a year by unforeseen site condition and owner adds. There were numerous change orders, for which the owner acknowledged merit and constructability cost, but the contractor was reluctant to estimate schedule impact. From the owner's point of view, the contractor's intent was to wait until the end of the job to hit him with a big change order. The contractor, on the other hand, felt the owner was being unrealistic in pressing for schedule impacts that he could not foresee given the uncertainty of future work and feared he would be obligated to hold fast to any estimate he gave at the time. All of their communication was done via e-mail and written correspondence.

So how would a World Class team deal with this situation? Here are three different perspectives.

• Don Eng with the City and County of San Francisco suggests, "You first need to verbally acknowledge that there will be some schedule impact and candidly and mutually discuss the certainties and uncertainties of that. Develop some mutual estimate and then expedite the change order. Both parties need to accept a shared risk in doing this. On a World Class team with trust, if the true number turns out to be significantly larger or smaller, then we would both be willing to compromise later. The important thing is to talk about it openly with one another and try first to minimize the impact. For the GC to wait until the end of the job to estimate schedule impact puts all the risk on the owner."

• John Jansen with Kiewit advises, "You need to mutually agree on a process ahead of time to use for time impact analysis. Use that as a tool for 'what if' discussions. This allows you to look at schedule impacts as risk avoidance measures. On a change with schedule impact, we give the owner a potential range and then make sure we revisit that with a regular dialogue with the owner while constantly looking for ways to mitigate the impact."

• George Furnanz with Stacy and Witbeck adds, "We keep our own running sheet and discuss it monthly with the owner and, of course, document the potential impacts. We also continue to try to come up with solutions to reduce the impact and cost to the owner."

The commonalities are important: Talk (don't write) and attempt to mitigate as a team. Be willing, as we have seen, to mutually acknowledge uncertainty. Also, come up with a mutually agreed-upon process in advance for dealing with schedule impact.

Did you also note the differences about how and when to come up with an estimated schedule impact? Remember, there is no One Best Way, and good, experienced professionals will disagree on what they view as the best way. The only way I know of to resolve this is through an open, verbal, and sometimes difficult dialogue. The project team needs to talk and surface their different suggested approaches and mutually agree on a team approach to time impact of changes on *this* job. Again, World Class teams do this *before* the first change order.

Dealing with Late Owner Changes

Late owner changes can be a slow death for projects where schedule and budget are critical. Good examples are hospitals, museums/performing arts projects, and transit jobs, where technology is changing so fast that what was originally specified is no longer state of the art. How does a World Class team manage these without just saying no to the end users?

On the Exploratorium project in San Francisco, the team agreed that it would be useful if the GC, Nibbi Brothers, and the CM, KPM Consulting, drilled down into the schedule to identify potential drop-dead dates for owner changes relative to trade specialties and areas. Meanwhile he set up a team with the designer, GC, and his organization to develop an approach to working with the owner. The consequence? The team, including the end user, has an increased confidence that schedule, budget, and end user intent will all be met.

A Legal Perspective on Collaboration and World Class Teamwork

When I was working on the San Francisco Federal Courthouse back in the early 1990s, there was a Federal Appeals Court judge in the partnering workshop who happened to specialize in construction litigation. (Note: Judges take a very personal interest in the fit and finish of their chambers!) At one point in the workshop when the partners were arguing over a somewhat contentious change order, he intervened. He admonished the team by saying, "Let me tell you all something. Unless you resolve this issue among yourselves soon, I will guarantee you that if it ends up in my courtroom, you will all end up losers." The team applied themselves a little more diligently to the issue.

Most stakeholders, at least on larger jobs, are well aware of the lose-lose consequences of a project going into litigation. Wayne Lindholm with Hensel Phelps comments, "I've been on a combative, litigious job and know how bad it hurts. I do not ever want to do that again." Who wins if you end up in litigation? The question is not really necessary with 98 percent of folks in construction, but I ask it anyway just in case. And, clearly, with more public jobs being bid on the basis of best value and selective/subjective criteria, a contractor, designer, or owner with an adversarial reputation does not have a very bright future.

> Discourage litigation. Persuade your neighbors to compromise
> whenever you can. Point out to them how the nominal winner
> is often a real loser—in fees, expenses, and waste of time.
> —ABRAHAM LINCOLN—

Again, World Class teamwork does not and should not call for blind trust. All stakeholders continue to be obligated to uphold their legal and contractual obligations. As one of our clients put it, "You need to do the minimal level of documentation required by the contract even if it is done after the verbal agreements. Anything beyond the minimal level is unproductive and a waste of time and effort."

> Trust but verify.
> —RONALD REAGAN—

What do attorneys think about engaging on the basis of World Class behaviors such as common goals, teamwork, trust, and personal commitments? My experience is that it comes down to this: If they view their job as keeping you, their client, out of litigation, they will endorse a collaborative process—with the understanding that it will not compromise your legal and contractual rights. As Phillip Howard says in *The Death of Common Sense*, "Modern law is unknowable. It is too detailed."[18] He goes on to reference OSHA's four thousand rules and the notion that no one, not even the OSHA inspectors, can possibly know all the OSHA regulations.

Lee Evey with PENREN flipped traditional contracting on the Pentagon Renovation program. As he describes it, "Traditional contracts assume that design and construction are going to fail. As a result of this assumption, contracts are all about punishment, assessments, fees, fines, and so forth. The vast majority of owners can tell you with great assurance and detail what they will do if their project runs into trouble. But when I ask them, 'What do you do when you have an extraordinarily successful design and construction project?' they become confused. At PENREN we set about to write contracts that could deal with failure but could also deal with and promote success, with an emphasis on people getting rewarded for excellence and exceeding expectations. This validates the notion that you can have a World Class team regardless of your selected project delivery method."

Again, World Class teams are willing to openly and transparently discuss their *personal* interpretations of contract meaning and intent. They focus not on winning but on creating a mutual understanding that supports their ability to work together as a team to achieve their common goals which speak to the owner's real intent.

Bob Finney of Caltrans explains: "Construction contracts, or parts of contracts, can be perceived to favor one side or the other. Strong project teams understand this and find a commonsense middle ground, using flexibility within the contract and acknowledging their project's needs. This often starts with the small things."

Investing in Developing a Project Culture of Shared Risk and Transparency

Developing a project culture of shared risk and transparency which, in turn, can deepen trust, performance, and personal well-being is an ongoing process on a project and does not often occur naturally. If a process of talking openly about potential risks, costs, and profits does not occur on a project the team will talk about it obliquely and non-verbally in the form of letters, e-mails, games, and posturing with a Business as Usual culture with its predictable consequences.

As we'll see in chapter 14, this process rarely realizes its full potential on a project in the first forty-five to ninety days. It takes time, experience, and mutual learning by the project team to explore, test, and validate the value and limits of openness and transparency on their project. Having, talking about, and committing to a project protocol that makes it not only OK but imperative that team members engage on this basis can both ensure and accelerate this process.

AN EXERCISE: THE BOMS BOARD™: TOOL FOR MUTUAL RISK ANALYSIS

Here's a tool and an exercise a project team can utilize that both identifies and seeks to prevent or at least mitigate potential project risks. I use the term BOMS as an acronym for Breakdowns, Obstacles, Mistakes, and Screw-ups—anything, internal or external to the team that could hinder their ability to achieve their goals.

How to implement: Ask each individual to identify what to them would be the top three BOMS that could hinder the success of this project. Then have them meet in multifunctional subgroups of at least three but no more than seven individuals. Have them agree as a subgroup on the top three BOMS and rank them. Number 1 should be the most probable and/or the most catastrophic, and so on.

Go around the room and have each team share their top BOMS. If another team has taken their top BOMS, have them share their second.

Then introduce the BOMS Board and have each team mutually agree on where on the Board their BOMS would fall and plot it.

What you now have is a two-dimensional assessment of risk. You can continue with this exercise and have each team answer three questions about their BOMS:

1. How would we react if we were in Business as Usual? You can bet it will be some form of game playing, case building, letter writing, etc.

2. How can we prevent the BOMS as a World Class team?

3. If we cannot prevent it, how can we minimize its impact on our team goals?

BOMS Board

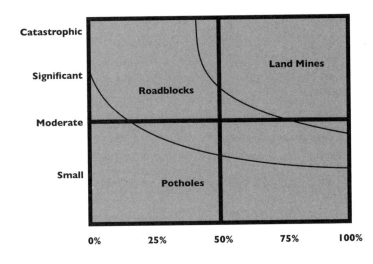

9

WORLD CLASS TEAM BEHAVIOR #5

Own Project Success as a Team with No Excuses

It is exciting to watch a team take possession of an issue—
and not just our design-build team and the owner,
but also the third parties, the utilities, and even the neighbors.
World Class teamwork harnesses people's passion to be part of a team.
You have to be excited and have the confidence that we, as a team,
won't let anything trip us up.
—MIKE APARICIO, VICE PRESIDENT, SKANSKA—

Business as Usual: Team members blame failures on one another and/or outside circumstances. Victim mentality.

Good Teams: Can be limited by circumstances seemingly beyond the team's control.

WORLD CLASS TEAMS: The project team and individuals hold themselves responsible for project success regardless of the circumstances. A no-excuses mentality. Adversity strengthens the team.

If you've done an effective job of goal setting and risk analysis coupled with open, verbal communication, you will have left your fellow team members in a place of owning project success as a team. What is the value of a project team owning overall project success? The project team is enabled—they no longer are a victim of their circumstances but rather a master of them. With this can come true commitment and passion.

Perry Dealy of Dealy Development, who was the owner's rep on the second tower project for San Diego's Grand Hyatt Hotel, explains: "When 9/11 hit, we were 20 percent underway. The uncertainty around that event and its implications for the hospitality industry had created a lot of pressure to stop the job. We sat down together as a team, weighed our options, and kept working while we were figuring it out. Everyone left their egos at the door, and with that we overcame all of the seemingly tremendous adversity and skepticism. And all of us left that job with long-term friendships."

On the City of Phoenix's Valley Metro Rail's Line Section #3 project, the team began brainstorming project goals. Early in this process, Senior Project Manager Bob Fouty of general contractor Archer Western asserted, "We can complete this job four months early." A number of the other participants rolled their eyes and started asking questions about permits. Bob replied, "No problem—we can do this with some help from the owner." Someone asked, "Well, how are we going to ensure that the design is completed in time?" Bob answered, "We can deal with that. Here's what we'll do, and I'll need this from the designer." And so on.

As it happened, the initial $95 million scope was increased by an additional $43 million in owner changes. The team met the original contract date *even with* the changes, and Bob Fouty earned the nickname "No-Excuses Fouty." Here's Bob's take on what happened: "It's all about attitude and someone having to step up and set the pace and do whatever it takes to bring the team along. On jobs that fail, there's no shortage of blame, and as the PM you can be sure that you'll get more than your share if not be crucified. Why not be bold and recognize that some people may initially be skeptical or critical of what you see as possible. But when the team starts to see the very real possibility of achieving those goals, those same individuals will be much more inclined to forgive you for bruising their egos."

In *Happiness Is a Serious Problem*, Dennis Prager states, "In general, expectations lead to unhappiness." But he goes on to say: "Where we do not have full control, we should not have expectations. And we do not have full control over most of the important things in life—our health and the health of those we love. We do, however, have control over some other important things. We control whether we expend our best effort; we control whether we act decently or not—we have moral free will; and given health and safety, we also control the quality of our work."[19]

By assuming control over the success of their project, individuals and the team can develop team expectations that acknowledge the reality of what they as a team can genuinely influence. Barry Thalden of Thalden•Boyd•Emery Architects explains: "Everyone creates their own life experience. If you make that assumption and allow a project team to do this, you can ask the people, in effect, 'What kind of life experience do you want to have on this project?'"

A World Class team gets as close as possible to defining and pursuing their own dreams on their own terms while always acknowledging their contract and specifications.

A good test of whether a project team truly owns project success is listening to their conversation. Are they talking about how they will avoid and/or mitigate future and potential challenges and roadblocks as well as seize new opportunities? Or are the majority of their meetings and conversations caught up with fixing current problems, reacting to circumstances, playing games, figuring out who's to blame, telling stories, and complaining? These are two entirely and fundamentally different contexts with which to view the project and the relationship of the team to its circumstances and to one another. Context is everything, especially in how a project team approaches its challenges.

As Alan Bliesmer, Operations Manager with Hensel Phelps, puts it, "A World Class team operates at a level that allows the team to overcome obstacles and challenges, ultimately attacking a project with a solution-oriented approach. A World Class team recognizes that each member relies on and supports the success of all team members."

Owning project success can also mean that the team changes the definition of the game or project and sometimes even the contract. Here is an example where the team had a mutually agreed-upon imperative to expedite completion: On a $100 million learning center, the project team—with the support of their senior management—so owned the game that they offered to pay for the salary of a state regulatory staffer and to house him or her on site in order to help expedite their project. Without this arrangement, the state agency could not have supported their aggressive schedule.

On this World Class team, both the owner's and general contractor's senior management had to be highly reassured that everything was being done that could be done within the current contractual relationship and with current resources. In other words, there had to be fundamental trust. But again, it was up to the project team to assure senior management that the change would enhance overall project results for the owner and all stakeholders. The team at the project level still owned overall project success.

Enabling a Project Team to Own Project Success

They are, in effect, redefining project success in a manner that allows them, as a team, to truly own it. By coupling the goal setting process with an open verbal discussion of potential risks (remember our 85/85 Rule), the team is now left with a very real sense that "yes, we can overcome most, if not all, obstacles and win this game as a team."

Start by giving your team a choice between all playing the new game or each playing their own game (Business as Usual). Then inquire who wins with each method. They soon begin to see the value to them personally in playing and winning as a team. In my experience, once this ownership begins to take hold, executing the game merely becomes a matter of identifying key goals and processes, having them make personal commitments to action that support those, and getting out of their way.

When we commit ourselves, we're "all in."
—PETE DAVOS, VICE PRESIDENT WITH DESILVA GATES CONSTRUCTION,
USING A POKER METAPHOR—

Simplify and Create a Compelling Definition of the End Result or Game

A key aspect of owning project success and a no-excuses mentality is mutually agreeing on the limits of the playing field. How you define the field and the game determines how you will play the game. If the playing field is open-ended or indeterminate, owning the game is meaningless. Dan Gilbert of Kaiser Permanente explains: "Unless you have some metrics or goals, you could be losing as a team and not know it."

Limits are necessary, but project teams have a tendency to underestimate their limits. For example, on school projects—as with most projects—the legal and contractual term is "substantial completion." But that is a rather sterile, uninspiring goal and can be construed as disconnected from the true intent of the project to the end user. Instead, World Class team leaders like Stephen Sharr of the Los Angeles Unified School District simplify the goal and playing field to "kids in seats no later than X date." They acknowledge that they, as a team, need to influence absolutely everything associated with getting the kids in the seats. That means dealing with permit agencies, utilities, facilitating move-in of FF&E, air balancing, etc.

With private projects, the goal can often be simplified to "able to initiate revenue operations." On bridge and highway projects, it is often "open to traffic." On water projects, it can be "pumping water." Some might say these goals merely equate to contract documents calling for "substantial completion." Maybe. But stating goals in a clear, powerful manner that speaks to the end user and every team member is much more compelling. President Kennedy certainly realized that when he stated his goal of not only putting a man on the moon but also "bringing him back safely"!

Are There Any Limitations on a Team's Ability to Truly Own Overall Project Success?

Let's consider a circumstance that few project teams purport to influence, let alone control: weather. How can a project team own the game with respect to weather, which most project teams defer to the omnipotent "Weather Gods"?

A good example is the Caltrans 92/880 interchange project with Flatiron Corporation and Granite Construction as joint venture partners. They already had a common stretch goal of completing the three-year project six months early. They were well on track toward this goal eight months into the job. The funding agency representative from the Federal Highway Administration, who was part of the team at this point, said to the team, "If there was some way we could complete this job by the end of next October instead of March in the following year, we'll [FHA] support and fund it." Maurice El Hage, Area Construction Manager for Caltrans, Dave Niese of Flatiron Construction, and Jack Shewmaker of Granite Construction encouraged their team to consider it.

The team initially considered expediting a major interchange during the upcoming rainy season impossible. An analogy would be traveling the Northwest Passage in winter—before global warming. It's a time when on a highway job in northern California, everyone goes into a state of near hibernation and total dependence on the weather, or, more precisely, the rain. Everyone knows "Hey, we can't control the weather!" But this team was up for it, so they started by breaking the challenge into key subcomponents:

1. Working backward from next October, what work do we need to expedite, figure out, and make happen, especially during the upcoming rainy season, to meet our goal? Now let's prioritize these activities and leave ourselves with options relative to what can be done when it's raining and what cannot.

2. Prior to the forecasted rain coming, Jack and Ed will meet and mutually agree on a day-by-day basis on what, if any, work can be done prior to, during, and immediately following the rain.

3. Jack and Ed will periodically meet and mutually agree on where and how much earth to stockpile and how to protect it.

4. Jack and Ed will mutually agree on what operations will pay off the most from working Saturdays and coordinate this verbally with inspection and the FTA—who has given us the tentative OK to consider this.

5. Between now and the next rainy season, we as a team will mutually agree on where and how the cost of double shift work could expedite the job. And again, coordinate our estimated cost with the funding agency—verbally.

6. On a daily basis during rain, Jack and Sue will meet and coordinate truck access and scheduling to minimize mud and inefficiencies.

Notice the common denominator: ____ and ___ will meet and mutually agree—verbally and daily in most cases! As Dave Niese, the Area Manager from Flatiron, put it, "The driving goal on the 92/880 was always 'open to traffic.' That's the critical thing. How soon can we make this project benefit the public through acknowledging, but not being limited by, our circumstances?" So are there really any absolute showstoppers on a construction project?

Did the 92/880 team achieve their goal? No, but they came close and enabled the project to get started well ahead of what might have been expected in the spring. The important thing is that they were willing to test their limits as a team and be the best they could possibly be.

The need for each individual to see what is in it for him or her to play and win toward common goals is a vital prerequisite for World Class teamwork and owning project success. It will also serve as the glue to hold them together. In the 92/880 example, every team member acknowledged that it would be the extraordinary pride in being part of a team that did something that was considered undoable.

Bringing Third Parties into the World Class Team

How about if ancillary and impacted individuals and entities were described not as third parties but as fellow project stakeholders? On the Washington DOT $1.1 billion Alaskan Way Viaduct and Seawall Replacement project with multiple key stakeholders, the team agreed early on not to use the term "third party." Rather, key players like the Port of Seattle, Seattle Dept. of Transportation, as well as a dozen others were to be considered fellow stakeholders along with WSDOT and Tutor-Perini/Dragados, the JV design-build team.

On a recent K–8 school project, the project team prioritized the top three impediments to achieving their team goal of completing the job four months early. Guess what? All three had to do with third-party regulatory and permitting agencies not in the room. These included the state school inspection board, the city relative to street improvements, and the electric utility's ability to provide permanent power.

As we saw in chapter 6, another prerequisite for owning project success is to ensure that the goal-setting process includes all individuals who could potentially ensure the future success of the team. If in doubt, include them. This must include key third parties, such as:

- Permitting agencies
- Utilities
- Specialized regulatory agencies (e.g., state school, health care agencies)
- End users (school administrators, a member of the medical staff, operations and maintenance, etc.)
- Environmental agencies

- Oversight/funding agencies
- Neighbors
- Funding agencies

In twenty years, I have never seen it hurt a project or team to include a third party in a goal-setting process. Worst case? They at least understand the common goals, how the team will support them, and vice versa—and they get a free lunch.

In my experience, however, project teams are not initially inclined to see value in inviting third parties in. Why?

- It would be opening Pandora's Box.
- The third parties will have nothing to contribute.
- They will insist on a more rigid application of the contract documents and specs.

In the majority of cases, third parties are viewed as impediments to be managed and informed only when necessary and someone to whom the team will at best provide timely responses to their complaints.

Owning overall project success means not merely managing and reacting to these third parties but rather acknowledging them as potential assets to the team, if not valuable team members in their own right. This starts with being willing to engage verbally at the project outset with the third parties about what is really, really important to them about this project. The vast majority of the time, their needs and requirements are not expressed to the degree, in the detail, and with the emphasis that the individual representatives of the third-party agencies would like to see. This does not necessarily mean that their personal needs would be more difficult to achieve than those inferred by the contractor from the contract requirements. When the team demonstrates a genuine interest in their personal needs, these often-bureaucratic agencies become true partners and even coaches to the team.

Dennis Mori, Project Executive with LA METRO's Eastside Extension project, invited third parties to quarterly partnering sessions well prior to their active involvement on the job. He notes, "We were able to proactively engage with them not just around the success of our project but also in such a way as to enable them to facilitate their efficiencies and needs."

My experience suggests that it is mutually beneficial to include these third parties in the goal-setting process. The result? Invariably the team ends up with mutually supportive goals involving the third parties, and they can support one another and achieve true win-win outcomes. A good example is including Airport Operations in airport construction team sessions. Air Ops are usually considered to be uncompromising and ultraconservative. Necessarily, I might add. "No D-9s running amok on the runway denting the 'tin,' please." Yet when they see the value of, say, completing a two-and-half-year project six months early—as they are at McCarran Airport's Terminal 3—they are willing to engage with the contractor and airport project management in expediting otherwise seemingly intractable rules without compromising safety.

As Jake Adams, Program Manager for Los Angeles World Airports, said about his Runway 25R project, "By having Airport Operations present in each of the partnering workshops, we were able to proactively and collaboratively manage the interface between them and the contractors."

On longer-term projects such as transit projects, third-party interface changes over the duration of the project. By working backward, a World Class team mutually agrees on a no-later-than date to engage with each third party. When they discuss it as a team, they invariably agree to engage with the third party well in advance of when any individual stakeholder might see the need. For example, the contractor might say, "We're going to be in this area in June, and we'll be doing this type of excavation." The owner will say, "Did you know you needed a permit for that from X agency, and that takes at least six weeks for approval?" and so forth.

A World Class team considers, only as a last resort and judiciously, the use of silver bullets or additional resources. By silver bullets I mean the team's senior managers as individuals who might help expedite a third party's or team member's action. This should be done only if the team agrees that it has exhausted its capabilities and that senior management intervention is crucial to the achievement of their team goals. A team that owns its game will help their senior management with this task. They will not just throw it in their lap but rather facilitate their ability to truly enroll the third

AN EXAMPLE OF WORKING WITH THIRD PARTIES

Here's an example of how a World Class team on Rady Children's Hospital (McCarthy and Anshen+Allen Architects) worked with their California state hospital inspector (OSHPD) to ensure no/minimal delay on their aggressive schedule completion goal:

1. Of Steve (i.e., a request of Steve, who runs the weekly owner's meeting): Have as a STANDING AGENDA ITEM at all owners' meetings = Identify our anticipated (at least 6 weeks out) OSHPD inspections, challenges, and delays and develop mitigation plan as a team specific to each issue. This will be developed within 48 hours with accountability to resolve within 24 hours. Above will done with Dan, Joanne, Sara, and/or Janice.

2. Of Dan (in-house inspector for the hospital): When an issue comes up, convene the team to include the OSHPD inspector on site or after his visit and mutually agree on action items.

3. By Joanne (the architect): I will walk the site with the OSHPD inspector prior to change order review.

4. By Dan: If we have a change order for him/OSHPD inspector, we will do a field walk prior to change order review.

Note what was conspicuously missing from the above: writing letters.

party. In other words, they still own the game by influencing their executives' ability to support their team goals!

Steven Boehm, Los Angeles Unified School District, explains: "We have to recognize third-party issues right from the beginning of the job as challenges and continue pushing them all the way through. And although we at the management level can sometimes help with our counterparts at the agency, it is by far more effective when the project team at the field level takes on the challenge and it becomes a person-to-person relationship thing with the third-party agency's individual reviewers. Sometimes this involves virtually camping at their plan check office."

Dealing with Obstacles—
and Turning Lemons into Lemonade

On the Caltrans Wilfred Ave. Interchange project, the team acknowledged that the new statewide storm water pollution control plan was not only unclear but also had the very real potential of significantly delaying the job over one year. So how did the Ghilotti Brothers/Caltrans team deal with that? They set two goals. Number one, the project would be complete without any delay by the storm water plan. Number two, they would be acknowledged as a model of excellence in interpreting and implementing the new plan.

A World Class team takes obstacles and turns them into opportunities. The leadership of World Class teams recognizes that just complying with a spec or coping with a challenge is not inspiring to team members, nor does it bring forth the true creative potential of the project team. Any challenge can be turned into an opportunity, and the best way is to face or solve or even redefine the problem from a different perspective.

The Undisciplined Pursuit of Needing More—
Resources, Time, Money, Etc.

On Los Angeles Unified School District's South Region Elementary School #9, the team had a big concern. Inspection resources had been severely cut back, putting the project's aggressive schedule goal at risk. When it came to figuring out how to ensure inspection resources adequate to support the contractor's work over a large site, Sundt Construction's superintendent offered to provide the inspector with a golf cart. "That is really thinking outside the box for a solution," acknowledged Steven Boehm, the district's regional manager on the job.

A common construction project phenomenon is requesting additional resources, such as design, inspection, surveying, etc.—preferably on site. Oh, and more money wouldn't hurt either. For example, a contractor might state, "We need the A&E on site five full days a week starting now." Frankly, when you dig into this as a team and challenge the team to ask "What key processes are being hindered relative to our common goal?" additional resources are not always necessary. Let's say the contractor mentions the RFI response time. A better question might be "What do we, as a team, need to do to expedite RFI response to support our common completion goal?" It is rarely just a question of adding more design resources. Here are some options:

- We can meet in the field to mutually agree on conditions and the proposed solution and give verbal authorizations.
- We, the contractors, can prioritize and verbally present these to the design team on some weekly frequency.
- We can conduct meetings two or three times a week with the designer(s) on site to go over prioritized RFIs.
- We, as a team, with the designer can walk the site twice a week. We will let them know in advance what we want them to look at/for and if they need to bring a subconsultant.
- We, as a team, can review upcoming design to anticipate future RFIs. We can conduct conference calls on certain RFIs, especially those involving out-of-the-area vendors or subconsultants.

Barry Thalden of Thalden•Boyd•Emery Architects relates the experience on the award-winning Chukchansi Casino project, where the general contractor requested all RFIs returned within seven days. His response: "Tell me which ones you absolutely need to meet our common completion date goal and when you need them, and I'll get them to you. But also let me know which ones I can defer beyond a week and prioritize these for me. In either case, we will verbally contact you immediately if we cannot meet the date you request and provide you with one we can meet. Is that acceptable?" It was. By the way, this project team was and continues to be the only team that achieved by their own ranking a perfect 10.0 on my teamwork scale. Kudos to Thalden•Boyd•Emery, McCarthy Building Companies, and the Chukchansi Casino.

How else can contractors support designers and vice versa? "The key is the flow of information to the field that supports the contractor's work flow," says Fred Powell of NBBJ. "This requires the contractors to ask the right questions. We can help them do this by earning their respect so they do their analysis before they ask the question." This is another good example of coaching—this time by the architect.

Here's the point: Rarely do project teams make optimal use of the resources they do have. It's all too easy to request more resources, funding, and time. Second, the question should not be approached from the point of view of more resources but rather "What needs to be present in the way of improving our _____ process to achieve our common goal?" If we have truly exhausted that possibility, then and only then as a team we can mutually agree on the specific processes that could be expedited with additional resources. This approval might include the value of having these resources relative to our goal; the projected additional cost; and how we, as a team, can present this request to senior management in a manner that allows them to make a *good business decision.*

Enabling the Field Level to Own Project Success

Where are the lower limits, and how willing and able are lower-level project team players willing to own overall project results and success? On Santa Barbara's Cottage Hospital Phase IV $400 million-plus rebuild, early on the project team seemed to be at an impasse on an issue related to RFI response. The mechanical subcontractor, Steve Murray, President of the Murray Company, stood up and said, "This is not working and is really slowing us down." I asked him what he intended to do about it. He said, "Well, I intend to fix it. Who's with me?" One of the other subs raised his hand, then a subconsultant, a mid-level individual from the owner's team, and so forth. When one of the senior project managers raised his hand, his counterpart said, "No, no, let's keep it at their level."

Steve ended up with a team of about ten individuals from all key subs, the owner's organization, the CM, the designers, and the general contractor, and he promptly set up a meeting. His Task Force for Success is now thirteen months old and is on track for the project schedule goal. Steve sits in on the executive team meetings and reports on the status of his task force. Senior management periodically sits in at the beginning of the task force's meetings and acknowledges their efforts. Steve explains:

The Task Force for Success meets every Thursday with representatives from all stakeholders. I try to start by stimulating a non-technical discussion by raising subjects for discussion relative to working as a team vs. those areas where we may be building walls. A recent weekly topic was "With fourteen months to go, what obstacles exist today that might prevent us from achieving success?" I continue to stress to the team that we are not there to solve problems but rather to ensure that the right people are working and communicating on them. We've also created "can-do" t-shirts showing the three pertinent team goals: $300 million, 187 beds, and 42 months. It is fun for me to do this and see the team succeed.

Unorthodox? Yes, but it worked. The lesson? Give the ball to those players who are committed and have the initiative and willingness to run with it regardless of where they are in the project team. Passionate commitment from individuals or, better yet, a team, will trump formal responsibility every time.

Dan Gilbert of Kaiser Permanente notes, "You need people who are missionaries with an almost evangelical fervor for the team to win. They are willing to go out of their way to support their fellow stakeholders to achieve mutual success."

As Sylvia Botero of RBB Architects, Inc., a Marvin Black Award winner in 2010 for Mission Hospital in 2008, puts it, "The role of senior management is to empower our people at all levels to be the best they can be."

10

Blur Organizational Lines; Everyone Is 100 Percent Accountable for Everything

When everyone on a project team assumes 100 percent accountability
for everything, this becomes the greatest behavioral concept you can have.
It exponentially multiples the number of eyes and minds you have looking out
for project success. And it saves everyone money.
—ROBERT DEVELLE, NASA'S JET PROPULSION LABORATORY—

Business as Usual: Peaceful co-existence, AKA "The Cold War." You do your job, and I'll do mine. Live and let live.

Good Teams: Teamwork within traditional roles. Formal structure adhered to. Each individual and organizational entity responsible only for their scope of work. Help others when asked.

WORLD CLASS TEAMS: Organizational lines are blurred. Everyone 100 percent accountable for everything. Help one another without being asked. The project team as an informal communication network grounded in common goals.

Conventional wisdom says that blurring organizational lines and helping others without being asked requires a crisis.

World Class teams disagree. Yes, individuals and organizations coming into a new project tend to strongly identify with their own jobs and organizations. And this is good. Heaven help us if each of us were willing to compromise our defined roles, responsibilities, and accountabilities to our organizations too easily or quickly.

With time, on most projects, individuals begin to develop positive personal relationships that go much deeper than the initial, arm's-length, stereotypical, and institutional assumptions we hold about one another. And, as we've seen, on projects of any size, there will be a formal construction management protocol that is either part of the contract or the construction manager's process.

But like anything else in life, we are all willing to make exceptions when the situation warrants it. A sports metaphor is apt here. On a seamless basketball team, each player has a position but is truly committed to doing whatever the situation calls for to make the points, assist, or make a defensive stop.

> On our 92/880 Interchange project, we were engaging with one another
> more like fellow employees of an employee-owned company
> than we were as separate stakeholders.
> —MAURICE EL HAGE, AREA CONSTRUCTION MANAGER, CALTRANS—

Indeed, on many World Class teams, the individual team members end up identifying as much with the project team as they do with their own organization. Mike Aparicio, then Project Executive with the Washington Group, recalls, "On our LA METRO Eastside Extension Light Rail project, you could actually walk into meetings and not know who was with the Transit Authority and who was part of the design-build team."

The Problem with Focusing Only on Individual Roles and Responsibilities

A byproduct of the scientific approach to management in the early part of the twentieth century was the division of labor and the notion of specialization within organizations. Like any good idea, this was taken to excess, and in the 1970s, organizations in the U.S. began to realize that overemphasis upon job descriptions and role responsibilities killed flexibility and creativity. We were losing market share to the Japanese, who pushed team decision making down into their organizations. Likewise, overspecialization led to departments within organizations that literally did not talk with one another until very high up their organization ladders.

I was involved in a Navy project where team members felt that it was imperative to focus on defining roles and responsibilities to resolve conflict. I challenged that assumption and asked the team: "What are the consequences of relating exclusively on the basis of individual roles and responsibilities?" Here's what they came up with:

- The team is not focusing on the customer or the actual end user's needs. Roles and responsibilities are internal processes.
- Roles and responsibilities tend to produce a silo effect or an "It's not my job" mentality. They can work against teamwork.
- Written roles and responsibilities can be interpreted different ways by different individuals.
- Roles and responsibilities are not dynamic and do not acknowledge that over the course of a project, roles will need to change to adapt to changing project and site issues and opportunities.
- They do not inspire people. Rather, they reinforce a bureaucratic mindset and culture.

"Just defining individual roles does not help the overall project," says Ash Wason of Carollo Engineers. "There will always be situations that call for group or team interpretation and judgment. Also, individuals, left alone, tend to define their roles in terms of their own self-interests."

Where Role and Responsibility Definitions Can Help a World Class Team

Although an excessive focus on defining roles and responsibilities can be counterproductive, as we have seen, they can be helpful in two situations:

1. Spending authorization. Clearly and openly defining levels of authority relative to spending authorization is imperative to World Class teamwork. Jack Shewmaker of Granite Construction notes, "You need clearly understood levels of signing authority relative to changes, especially when the owner has hired a third-party construction manager."

2. Dispute resolution. Virgil Curtis of Balfour Beatty identifies another facet of construction where individual role definition is useful: "It helps to know what the next level is when elevating disputes and issues."

I'm not advocating avoidance of responsibility. Rather, the team collectively and individually must hold themselves accountable for team and individual performance. This is a completely different mindset.

Creating a Willingness to Cross Over and Help

The challenge of team integration has only increased on construction projects, particularly as they become much larger and more complex. How do you integrate the designer, owner, and contractor who virtually speak different languages and have different agendas? In the late 1980s, professional construction management came into its own, as did project partnering. The 1990s saw the development of new PDMs and construction methodologies that all call for a real-time, integrated approach to decision making at the lowest level possible with the project.

The challenge today remains the same: How do you enable ever more specialized human resources to bring their talents to bear on a construction project and quickly integrate into a team or collaborative effort?

Some examples:

- Contractors who are willing to provide solutions along with their RFI to assist the designers
- Colocation on site of all major stakeholders
- Owners who are willing to work with the design-build team in design development to make design review nothing more than a formality
- Designers who are willing to come out to the site and make judgments *with* their owner and contractor
- Owners and designers who are willing to work with the general contractor in developing a team project schedule that takes significant time off the baseline or contract schedule
- Inspectors who are willing to help contractors do work right the first time

Tom Gusich with University Mechanical subcontractors notes, "On one job due to our past relationships, we were asked to come out and do a constructability review, and we were not even part of the project team at that time."

In my experience, we need not worry much about individuals on a project compromising their loyalty to their parent organization. Nor does blurring of organization lines mean that you will do the other person's job. The challenge is integrating individuals into a team with velocity and in a manner that enables them to be willing, within limitations and subject to ethical and contractual guidelines, to do whatever it takes to make the project successful—to work to meet the team's common goals.

As noted previously, a prerequisite for this is shared goals and trust. If I'm going to step out of my role and do something that you might not expect from me, you would want to know that I am doing this to support *our* common goals. In other words, you have no reason to question my intentions.

Lou Palandrani of Clark Construction Group notes, "All stakeholders need to commit to a platform of goals for the project that will trump any individual agenda. With these goals in place, we can develop 'blended teams' of key stakeholder representatives who can actively come together to anticipate and influence the success of a key element or process of a project."

> If you want to build a ship, don't drum up people together to collect wood,
> and don't assign them tasks and work, but rather
> teach them to long for the endless immensity of the sea.
> —ANTOINE DE SAINT-EXUPÉRY—

Yes, there is an element of risk here, but the benefits far outweigh it. Wayne Lindholm at Hensel Phelps says, "Everyone crosses the line and rallies to takes care of whatever needs to be done to get the job done."

Here's a measure of teamwork that distinguishes Good from World Class project teams: Do individuals help and support their partners *only* when they are asked, or do they offer support and help *without* being asked? Without the mutual understanding of common goals, what can happen on a project if someone offers to help you without being asked? You probably wonder what they are *really* up to and suspect a hidden agenda, or perhaps you believe that you owe them something in return. I call this the "keeping score" game.

Consider the value of helping one another without being asked. It begins to create willingness to respond in kind, which ultimately leads to a project culture of mutual support and coaching. A fundamental assumption comes into play here: 95 percent or more of construction project players want to be in a relationship with their colleagues that is characterized by dynamic mutual support. Jim Linthicum with SANDAG describes it as "where they begin to look out for one another."

Another indication of organization lines being blurred is whether problems, issues, or disputes are seen as team challenges or solely the responsibility or fault of one team player. With very few key exceptions, the best solution will come *only* from a collaborative effort, which starts by defining the problem as a *team* challenge or a *team* opportunity.

Everyone 100 Percent Accountable for Everything

Hold each individual on the project team accountable for everything? "You've got to be crazy!" a contractor told me. "No one on a project will be willing to do that." Yet if you assume that individuals want to assume accountability, you get comments like this, from Dave Cavecche, Suffolk Construction Company: "Seeing a team really taking ownership of and accountability for a project, and not just for accountability's sake but because they are truly excited about it, is very satisfying. With that also comes a sense of pride for them and myself."

If you start with common goals and the team truly owning overall project success, it's only a small step to expecting that each team member, in turn, is 100 percent accountable for total team success. Yes, conventional wisdom, or Business as Usual, dictates that I'm accountable for what is in my scope of work and you for what is in yours. On a World Class team, all members of the project team are accountable for total team performance to their agreed-upon team goals. Furthermore, they hold each other accountable for that performance. To enable individuals to freely take this responsibility requires the presence of five World Class team behaviors: common goals; the team truly taking responsibility for overal project success; open discussion of potential risks; organization lines blurred; and open, direct, verbal communication.

Joanne McAllister of Anshen + Allen, Architects says, "When we are all held accountable for the final result, we are all a part of its success or failure. Failure to meet the goal is a failure of the team and the individuals."

This level of commitment starts with the development of common team goals which each partner has a vested stake (both business and personal) in achieving. You cannot have 100 percent joint accountability without common goals. Tim Jacoby, Vice President of Facilities with Rady Children's Hospital, explains: "World Class teamwork is holding one another accountable and executing what you said you will execute so that the team can achieve its goals."

Without common goals, what are you *both* accountable to other than your individual contract requirements? In other words, with common goals we are all playing the same game.

As Wylie Bearup of the city of Phoenix states, "It is truly rare on a project that on any one issue, only one individual or organization is responsible for the fix or the solution. Furthermore, on any issue it is likewise true that all partners can potentially contribute to the solution."

In his best seller, *Teams at the Top*, Jon Katzenbach speaks of "mutual accountability wherein no member can fail; only the team fails."[20]

Bob Finney with Caltrans notes, "Sometimes folks on partnered jobs are getting along so well they are reluctant to bring a problem up for fear of offending the other party. On World Class teams, everyone recognizes it is their responsibility to speak up if something is not working, and no offense is taken. The best teams will raise an issue together even if they disagree." A good example is an inspector working with a contractor to ensure that work is done right the first time. In other words, both inspector and contractor are assuming joint accountability for quality.

Ken Schacherbauer of Perini Building adds, "If a craftsperson is working on a project with common goals shared by the other subcontractors and inspectors, everyone is looking out for one another. An example would be an electrical sub calling the HVAC sub and coordinating which side of the panel the starter needs to be on. On Business as Usual projects, subcontractors just do their scope of work even if they know it is wrong."

Daniel Pink writes, "Encouraging autonomy doesn't mean discouraging accountability. Whatever operating system is in place, people must be accountable for their work. But there are different ways to achieve this end, each built on different assumptions about who we are deep down. Motivation 2.0 (control, carrot & stick) assumed that if people had freedom, they would shirk—and that autonomy was a way to bypass accountability. Motivation 3.0 (intrinsic satisfaction) begins with a different assumption. It presumes that people want to be accountable—and that making sure they have control over their task, their time, their technique, and their team is a pathway to that destination."[21]

This is the premise underlying World Class teamwork. With that premise, traditional notions of control kind of go away.

A currently well-accepted view of team accountability on most construction projects today is that *everyone* is responsible for safety. In other words, no one should walk past an unsafe condition or act but instead should say something or stop the unsafe act. Why can't this level of accountability exist over all domains of project success?

Pat Shafter of Swinerton Builders explains: "On a Business as Usual team, you are focused just on your task. On a World Class team, you are marrying into everyone else's task. As a project manager, I am always looking forward and supporting and building up others. If someone else is weak, I look for ways to support them."

One hundred percent joint accountability goes hand in glove with proactive meetings and collaborative problem solving and coaching. Surprises, mistakes, and day-to-day problems will still exist, yet it is the context in which they are dealt with which is important. As will be pointed out in chapter 13, the first response on a World Class team is not to assess blame or accountability but rather to address and resolve the issue relative to its impact on our common goals.

In the proactive meetings of World Class teams, participants keep the end result in sight as a team. Mike Ghilotti of Ghilotti Brothers says, "A proactive meeting process is of value where you can say 'Now what happens if this does not happen?' or 'What happens if this does happen?' Meetings become more like war gaming or scenario planning. Likewise, when it is a 'we' game, the optimal solution is invariably a collaborative one which can either be dealt with in the meeting or delegated to a team or task group to resolve outside the meeting."

The World Class Project Team as an
Informal Network of Communication

A World Class project team ultimately takes on aspects of a network or a community of shared interests rather than a formal organization structure. U.S. Army General Stanley McChrystal (retired) has explained how he successfully adapted the traditional Army structure to fighting an unconventional war in Afghanistan. "Though we got our message out differently than did our enemies, both organizations increasingly shared basic attributes that define an effective network. Decisions were decentralized and cut laterally across the organization. Traditional institutional boundaries fell away and diverse cultures meshed [architects/GCs/owners—author's note]. The network expanded to include more groups, including unconventional actors [third parties—author's note]. It valued competency above all else—including rank. It sought a clear and evolving definition of the problem and constantly self analyzed revisiting its structure, aims and processes."[22] I can't think of a better definition of a World Class team.

A project team culture of mutual accountability demonstrates a high level of mutual respect which significantly enhances teamwork. Such respect communicates that "I value our relationship and your commitment and contribution to our team to such an extent that I know you would want me to say something should you not be performing per our mutual goals, commitments, and agreed-upon standards of behavior." This can be challenging when close personal relationships are involved. Yet, as we ask World Class teams, what are the consequences to the team if an individual fails to hold their fellow teammates accountable? Here is where it is useful to have a conversation among project team members to make it OK and even imperative to be willing to hold your partners accountable. This behavior rarely comes naturally even to a high-performance project team.

11

WORLD CLASS TEAM BEHAVIOR #7

Think Outside the Box as a Team

If it's not laughably impossible, hopelessly impractical,
preposterously insurmountable, start over. You're not doing it right.
—UMAIR HAQUE, *THE NEW CAPITALIST MANIFESTO*—

Business as Usual: Everyone defaults to doing things as they have done them on previous jobs. Engaging with other stakeholders with different ideas would just waste a lot of time and either slow things down or involve more effort.

Good Teams: Innovative approach to work processes, means, and methods by contractor/design-build team only.

WORLD CLASS TEAMS: True, outside-the-box thinking by the entire team, as a team, over the duration of the job on all facets of the project. Develop the schedule as a team.

On the Cherokee Hard Rock Casino project in Tulsa, the general contractor and owner had a big, although transparent problem: The window glass supplier was unable able to meet the stretch/team goal for opening to enable revenue operations. The approach initially offered by the GC was to take the curtain wall glass out altogether, which would be cheaper. The owner and architect were aghast: this would compromise the aesthetics of the structure significantly. The architect, Barry Thalden of Thalden•Boyd•Emery Architects, then proposed an alternative solution which was not even a compromise: "We suggested that if they constructed floors one through eight without the curtain wall, these floors would be obscured by the existing building. They then could build floors nine and up with the curtain wall, since by the time we were ready to build them, the availability of the curtain wall could be assured by the vendor. Not only would this support the schedule goal, but it would also be significantly less costly to both the general contractor and the owner."

Collaboration causes innovation.

—IBM—

True outside-the-box thinking, by definition, challenges conventional wisdom about what is possible on a construction project. It cannot be taught, and very few organizations have been able to institutionalize it. How many Apples and Steve Jobs are there? Construction projects, by their nature, do not encourage project team outside-the-box thinking unless there's a major crisis. Note the previous reference to the Northridge earthquake and the repair of the Santa Monica Freeway in Los Angeles. Why is this?

- It is safe and predictable to conform to past means and methods.
- It is assumed that new ideas will require more work to implement.
- It is assumed that a new idea will never work due to . . .
- It might be perceived as "directing" the contractor or design-build team.
- It can create conflict and issues over established roles and responsibilities.
- It can result in bruised egos and questioning of the intentions/motives of those who would propose truly radical approaches.

So how does a construction team overcome this inertia?

Let's start by hearing from Gary Janco, Executive Vice President of CC Myers Inc., perhaps the most innovative and resourceful senior bridge construction manager I know. Gary, by the way, is a winner of 2011 Supervision Award given out by the Golden Beavers and the 2011 Contractor Achievement Award given by the Associated General Contractors of California. He was also the "boots on the ground" guy with the Santa Monica Freeway earthquake rehabilitation in 1994.

To get a job these days, let alone to execute it safely and profitably, you need not only to get your employees to come up with new ideas but also the entire project team.

And you've got to get everyone on board with the ideas. The best way I've found to do this is to earn their trust by doing what you say you're going to do. Explain the how and the why. If they understand that it is for the good of the project and the industry, they'll support it and help make it work.

Four Ways to Stimulate Outside-the-Box Thinking

There are four effective ways to stimulate a construction project team to think outside the box:

1. Have the team set and commit to truly stretch goals beyond the edge of what they currently see as possible before they talk about the "how-to."
2. Have project team members work in multi-organization task teams on key processes.
3. Keep the team's conversation focused on future success, not the past.
4. Have them acknowledge the assumptions that are limiting outside-the-box thinking on key processes.

1. Have the team set and commit to truly stretch goals beyond the edge of what they currently see as possible before they talk about the "how-to."

We have explored this in chapter 6 on goal setting, but it is worth reinforcing here in the context of enabling innovative thinking. Remember that the only way to achieve truly stretch goals or BHAGs is by doing things completely differently, not just by incremental improvement.

Mike Ghilotti, CEO of Ghilotti Brothers Construction, says, "When a team sets measurable goals well beyond what is expected or their contractual obligations, it draws the people together in a way that enables true creativity and innovation."

Dave Mallik of Whiting Turner Construction adds, "Meeting the contract requirements usually just gives you an OK project, not a great one. When a team sets goals beyond those requirements, that is the beginning of the process to become a World Class team."

Committing to truly stretch goals creates the opening or space for a team to engage in outside-the-box thinking. Without this space, people can question the intentions of those who would suggest such ideas. What's their agenda? Are they out to compromise my design?

On construction projects, goal setting, as noted, should include all domains—schedule, quality, cost, community impact, LEED status, and profitability, as well as safety.

2. Have project team members work in multi-organization task teams on key processes.

Mix up team members from different organizations. Cohabitation or sharing of trailers is always good. Our tribal bonds are strong, and we're comfortable working with people who speak the same language and think the way we do. Indeed in just about all partnering meetings individuals tend sit with their own flock.

Some pundits argue that there can be no true innovation without discomfort or disrupting the status quo or what is comfortable. Taking this a step further, an innovative leader's role is to create what I term "managed project dissonance."

> **TIP:** The next time one of your subordinates comes to you with a challenge, problem, or issue, request that they meet with their counterparts and then come back and present a team solution.

3. Keep the team's conversation focused on future success, not the past.

Build on those individuals who think it's possible—not on the naysayers. I'm not talking Pollyanna optimism here but rather distinguishing between communication that creates the potential for future action and communication that does not. The latter includes:

- "We've never completed MEP concurrently like that before."
- "It always takes 90 days to close out a project in this agency."
- "We tried expediting that and it didn't work."
- "We've never done that before."

Ask those who see possibility to expand on their idea and invite the team's participation in making it work:

- "Jack, say some more. If we did that, what would be the benefit to the project?"
- "Beth, what would we have to have figured out to achieve that goal?"
- "Fred, how might we make Jack's idea of a zero punch list at substantial completion work from your perspective?"
- "I understand your skepticism Mike, but assume for the moment we found a way to do that. Now what's possible? What does the rest of the team think?"

4. Have them acknowledge the assumptions that are limiting outside-the-box thinking on key processes.

This by definition is not easy or comfortable. Nor is there one best way. Surfacing the unspoken assumptions and different assessments and testing the supposed limits can only come through face-to-face, verbal give-and-take with your project team members. On World Class teams, this is an ongoing process as opposed to a one-time thing.

In the balance of this chapter, we will explore some of those assumptions that limit teams from true outside-the-box thinking related to key construction processes.

Stimulating Outside-the-Box Thinking: The Eight-Foot Bar Metaphor

Trivia test: Do you know what the current men's world record for the high jump is? For the past several years, it has stood at 8 feet ⅜ inches and has been held by Javier Sotomayor of Cuba. When I ask project teams what the record was back in the 1960s, a few people can recollect that it was in the mid-to-upper-six-foot range. And what was the accepted "truth" about humans' ability to jump over seven feet? Physiologically impossible, said the kinesiologists and other fitness experts.

The breakthrough? The Fosbury Flop (and foam to land on!)—going over the bar backwards. By challenging teams to set goals that equate to eight feet, you're in effect saying that this job needs to generate the equivalent of a Fosbury Flop.

Dan Gilbert of Kaiser Permanente explains: "Ultimately the value of this metaphor comes from understanding under what conditions we as a team

The Fosbury Flop

could achieve the eight-foot bar on this project. All project team members need to be willing to take themselves away from what they might normally expect of themselves and one another."

As one general contractor told us, "If you don't set the bar high, how do you achieve great things?"

On the other hand, I ask, "What happens when the judges set the bar at nine feet?" A few wags say, "You get a pole." Well, of course, the jumpers don't even take off their warm-up suits, let alone try. So we are not looking for a nine-foot bar.

The challenge that World Class teams constantly ask themselves: "Is our goal truly an eight-foot bar today?"

An Outside-the-Box Approach to Expediting Schedule

THE BOX

(THE ASSUMPTIONS THAT LIMIT OUTSIDE-THE-BOX THINKING)

From the contractor's point of view:

The baseline schedule is the schedule, and I assume this is what the owner really wants today. There's no point in trying any harder. Oh, and involving the designer, owner, or CM in developing the schedule with us would just be a committee that would slow us down. Thanks, but no thanks.

From the owner's point of view:

The contractual schedule is the best we can hope for. It's totally up to the contractor/DBT how fast they (the contractor) want to proceed, and their choice of means and methods, etc. We'll tell them what they can't do or expedite. Oh, and giving them advice or direction would open ourselves up to a potential claim.

From the designer's point of view:

We've done our part. Now it's up to them to build it the way we designed it. We don't have the time to spend getting involved in their schedule. And the contractual times for document turnaround are what we'll comply with.

From the CM's point of view:

We're there to monitor their (contractor's) performance to the baseline schedule.

How do World Class teams approach a project's baseline or contractual schedule? They start by validating one fundamental assumption: *that the contractual schedule is just that*—a contractual date.

It's a date that someone, or multiple persons, somewhere, at some time in the past came up with based on certain assumptions about what was possible at the time they put it together. It is amazing how often many project players view the contractual completion date as a something that God has handed down from above and is therefore sacrosanct. No, it is just a date—albeit one that needs to be acknowledged as a contractual one.

Dave Niese of Flatiron urges, "Don't let the contractual schedule limit the team. That schedule was developed by an engineer at one point in time. If I ask him now about it, he's often willing to acknowledge, 'I didn't contemplate this at the time.' He made that decision based upon what he had on hand at that time."

The team must ask: Where are we *today* with regard to the schedule with the people/team here? What do we all know about site conditions, drawings, key impediments/opportunities, owner desires, seasonal weather conditions, etc.? Acknowledge these openly and verbally as a team.

Acknowledge uncertainties as key processes that the project team, as a team, will need to figure out. President Kennedy's moon BHAG is a good example. If we had had to wait to figure out how to do all the things we did not know how to do in 1961 before he set the goal, he never would have set the goal, and we would have gotten to the moon in two or possibly three decades.

> You have to set goals that are almost out of reach.
> If you set a goal that is attainable without much work or thought,
> you are stuck with something below your true talent and potential.
> —STEVE GARVEY, FORMER MAJOR LEAGUE BASEBALL ALL-STAR—

Involving All Stakeholders in Schedule Development

Here's a great opportunity that few projects capitalize upon: developing the schedule *as a team* with contribution and commitment from all stakeholders.

If you make the assumption that *everyone* has committed to the team/ stretch goal, how might that alter the contractor's/DBT's willingness to involve the owner, CM, and designer? The contractor/DBT might realize they share the same goals and sense of urgency and invite them to help. I have yet to see a schedule that could not be improved by the committed involvement of the owner, CM, designer, and third parties. Vitas Rugienius of Hensel Phelps urges, "Develop your project's goals with your subcontractors and other key stakeholders. A World Class team is open to accessing all entities. This has the effect of bringing out the best of all of us and is infectious."

It is useful to remind owners and designers that expediting the schedule is often the most effective process to reduce costs, both direct and indirect.

> Involve everyone and welcome ideas from everywhere.
> Anyone can be a leader or contributor just so long as they contribute,
> and the most meaningful way for anyone to contribute
> is to come up with a good idea. New ideas are the lifeblood of the
> organization [project], the fuel that makes it run.
> —JACK WELCH, FORMER CEO, GENERAL ELECTRIC CORPORATION—

Get the subcontractors and subconsultants involved. I was facilitating on a K–12 school project, and the owner broached the idea of completing the job six months early. The general contractor's project manager and superintendent said, "No way." I asked the subcontractors "Could each of you possibly expedite your work to support six months early?" All said yes, albeit with some conditions that we were able to address later. The general contractor and the rest of the team enthusiastically agreed to pursue a goal of six months early. Another benefit of having subcontractors and subconsultants involved? They not only understand but also see how they actually contribute to the big picture. They are no longer ancillary or second-string players but are truly on the team. Let's hear from two.

Tom Gusich with University Mechanical & Engineering subcontractors explains, "On World Class teams, they will ask us what we really need and listen to us. And we need to really understand how we interface with others and not just to throw more men at the project but to consider changing the logic. We want to be part of the solution. For example, on the Phoenix Downtown Sheraton, we did a lot of prefabrication in our shop utilizing BIM."

Peter Mondery with Southern Contracting adds, "As subcontractors, we're typically considered bottom feeders to be used and abused. Involving us in the process of developing the schedule gives us a level playing field to contribute on. We're relating to the others now as key partners and on the basis of what we can contribute to the overall project success. Also, I have ownership in the success of the job and am not dictated to. On Business as Usual teams, we're an afterthought."

A World Class team also openly acknowledges the value of new ideas is to everyone's benefit and agrees that the rewards need to be shared much as the risks. For example, any saving in time due to beating the contract completion dates becomes "project float."

Jack Shewmaker of Granite Construction notes, "There needs to be a level of trust that the benefits will be for everyone's mutual success and not taken advantage of by any one stakeholder. An example might be if we find a time saving, and the owner now expects a cost savings to him." A World Class team talks about this process before the contractor finds that first time saving.

Get a team together to brainstorm ideas. The contractor/DB team may want come up with a draft schedule involving key subs prior to the brainstorming session and distribute it to the attendees, but that's OK. Remember that creativity in any endeavor is maximized when participants are living in the moment, with no stories and no "what might have beens."

Dennis Turchon of Caltrans explains: "A World Class team is constantly brainstorming ideas. There is a huge benefit to the job when the entire team is involved in how to do it better. It leads to much better efficiency. Especially on our jobs involving piles—with all the inherent uncertainty—when you can ask the general contractor 'What do you think?' you get much better results, especially on our larger jobs with multiple staging."

Get Everyone Engaged

The other benefit of developing the schedule as a team? It gets everyone on the field with the contractor and not on the sidelines as a passive onlooker, let alone critic. They begin to own schedule completion along with the contractor/DB team. This is critical to owning the game, as we saw in chapter 9.

An owner, CM, or designer on a World Class team will certainly express concerns about ideas the contractor is offering. The difference is that on a World Class team, they look for ways of making them work and not rejecting them out of hand. For example, someone might say, "I've got a concern with the sequencing you're showing here. But what if you tried this?"

Brian Cahill of Barnhart Balfour Beatty notes, "In construction if some people aren't genuinely involved in the goal-setting process, they can sometimes be inclined to prove you wrong. And this does not work to anyone's advantage."

"This process can be messy," says John Jansen with Kiewit, "and it is often not very clinical, but it definitely brings forth a much more creative environment."

Distinguish between expediting and accelerating. Start with not considering acceleration. Then, and only then, when the team has determined how far they can go without acceleration, consider acceleration on some aspects of the project if that is something all parties would be open to entertaining. Teams are inevitably surprised that by truly collaborating, they can often achieve a stretch schedule goal without the acceleration they believed would be mandatory.

Here's another benefit of developing the schedule as a team. Schedule ownership by all stakeholders ensures that adequate human resources, material, and equipment will be there when needed to support the schedule. Contractors often ask me, "How will we know if the owner/CM/designer will have adequate resources to support our work?" If individuals from these entities are truly involved in developing the stretch/BHAG schedule with the contractor/DB team and commit to that date, you can be reasonably sure they will have their resources there when the schedule calls for them.

Lastly, remember that schedule development on a World Class team is a dynamic process as circumstances, stakeholders, priorities, and technologies change.

EXERCISE: A BRAINSTORMING PROCESS
FOR YOUR NEXT WORLD CLASS PROJECT

A tool I've found very effective is to group owners, contractors, designers, and CMs into small, mixed-discipline, four-to-six-person teams after they've set their schedule completion goal. Challenge each team to come up with at least two really good outside-the-box ideas within ten minutes. During the same time, they need to prioritize them, with #1 being their best idea to achieve the schedule goal. In the full group setting, each team then shares their best idea, followed by a second round with their second best idea. Emphasize that anything goes. They can talk about resequencing, staging, altering the project delivery method (one team came up with and subsequently opted to implement LEAN), phased/partial acceptance, acceleration of a particular phase of the work, and so forth.

Give each individual two points. They can allocate them both to one of the ideas or one each to two ideas, etc.

After this exercise, it is rare to see a team not come up with viable ideas to shave at least 10 percent off a project's projected completion date. At the conclusion of the ranking of ideas, get teams in place with champions and a deliverable for each idea.

On the Phoenix Westin project, Tom Gusich with University Mechanical came up to me at the outset of the session and asked how he could give away three tickets to the Lakers–Suns NBA playoff game that night. You guessed it: They went to the team who was judged by the whole partnership as having brought forth the best overall schedule reduction idea. You should have seen the passion that the teams applied to their brainstorming when the award was announced at the outset of the exercise! When the time was up, there was a chorus of "No, no, we need more time!" from all of the teams. The end result? Six specific ideas that, in the opinion of the team, would significantly impact schedule and cost with task forces dedicated to each idea for follow-up and development.

Gary Janco of CC Myers talks about how his projects implement a similar process on a weekly basis: "We have a suggestion box on our jobs and we pull out the ideas weekly. Project management then reviews and rates the ideas on a scale of 1–5. Individuals with the best idea can win up to $125."

Here are two examples of the kinds of ideas this exercise can generate:

A. Naval Hospital Camp Pendleton with Clark Construction Group and McCarthy Construction as JV design-build team:

1. Modular construction (ORs, patient rooms, bathrooms) enabling prefab (43 votes)
2. Take one day off each activity on each quadrant. (10 votes)
3. First floor approval faster than whole hospital to expedite foundation and underground (28 votes)
4. Mechanical/overhead coordination in layers (17 votes)
5. Delete green roof (4 votes)

B. Elementary School #9 with Los Angeles Unified School District and Sundt Construction:

1. Temporary waterproofing system re: roof to expedite drywall (11 votes)
2. Start on utilities/scheduling and sequencing. Break up ties between activities that don't need to be tied together. (9 votes)
3. Provide golf cart for inspector to drive around sites so he can help us drill down on pre-inspection. (4 votes)
4. Go to city and release utility tie-ins. (3 votes)
5. Open up 2 CP activities with drywall, CP on ground floor and first elevator deck. (2 votes)

An Outside-the-Box Approach to Quality

THE BOX

From the contractor's/DBT's point of view:

The spec is what they want. No point in questioning that. If I do start to question it or offer suggestions for improvement, the owner's going to think I'm fishing for change orders, and the designer will get defensive.

From the owner's point of view:

The spec is what the designer came up with and is what we think is best given our budget, etc. To involve the contractor about the level of quality would be counterproductive. All they will be looking for is shortcuts and lesser substitutions.

From the designer's point of view:

Talking with the contractor about quality will just compromise the integrity and aesthetics of my design. Just build it per my specs.

This book is not intended to be a primer on construction quality—a topic which merits volumes on its own. It is well known that there are plenty of viable quality models out there, from LEAN to the U.S. Navy's now-widespread three phases of inspection. Yet having said that, it's important to acknowledge that project teams do not seem to be taking advantage of that knowledge.

I'll focus on how a World Class team can approach collaborating on quality to achieve outside-the-box results. Start by emphasizing that you are not in any way going to compromise or shortcut the existing plans/specs. On a design-build project, emphasize that existing schematics are a just a baseline or minimum threshold. Again, World Class teams acknowledge existing assumptions, concerns, and expectations about quality and ask, "What now would be a level of quality that would truly meet the intent of the owner and end user?" As Kathy Mayo of AECOM puts it, "Building what is spec'd is not always the best solution for the client."

Issam Khalaf of Jacobs notes, "Buildings today are smarter and built to last longer. LEED and sustainability are important. The best way to realize this on a project is through true outside-the-box thinking by the whole project team."

This can be facilitated by direct, open interaction between designers and contractors. Fred Powell of NBBJ Architects on Stanford University's Li Kai Sheng Center for Knowledge and Learning says, "We had a very personal relationship with the ornamental sheet workers. They came up to me and pointed out that the continuation of column detailing from the interior to the exterior was not consistent. They felt we needed to have the same detail throughout the column and offered to do it at no cost."

Don Wright, now with Bechtel, speaks of a project with a previous employer: "I got a letter from a vendor stating that he couldn't/wouldn't meet the owner's specs because it would not give the owner what they really needed. We took the vendor's idea and presented it to the owner and within a half a day got the go-ahead to proceed with this new approach."

Having the End Users Stimulate
Getting Outside the Box on Project Quality

Getting outside the box with quality can be stimulated by directly involving the end users. It is relatively common for project teams to interface with school principals, medical staff, or operations staff on water and public works projects. But how about on justice facilities? That's right—involving the inmates! Talk about "inviting the fox into the henhouse," as one doubtful designer put it.

On the Alameda County Justice Facility, a project with Vanir Constructon Management and Hensel Phelps as design-build team leader, the Chief Probation Officer of the facility challenged the design-build team to really take into account the kids who would be living in the facility. So she brought three of them to one of the partnering workshops. Two boys and one girl in baggy pants, t-shirts, and backward baseball caps stood awkwardly in front of thirty-five owners, architects, construction managers, and contractors who, in turn, viewed them with jaundiced eyes.

The chief probation officer gently coaxed the kids into sharing what they would like to see in the new facility. One of the boys began, "Well, we really like to draw pictures, but we can't all the time 'cause there's no place to do it." One of the architects asked, "What if we were to make some of the walls like big white boards where you could use colored erasable markers?" "Yeah," said the kid, "that would be way cool." The conversation continued for another forty-five minutes with the designers rapidly writing notes and asking questions until the manager said the kids needed to get back to their classes.

Andy Morgan, Vice President of Vanir Construction Management, describes the experience: "The focus of the team clearly changed as a result of those presentations. The project was about the kids from that point. The presentations put a face on the end users and gave us all a better understanding of who they are and how they got there. That more enlightened view of our 'clients' clearly had an impact on the outcome of the design for the project. Everything from the color selections and art work to the floor plan was better as a result."

Here again, a goal-setting process is critical. How would we know, as a team, that we truly achieved extraordinary quality given the processes, resources, and abilities that we have on this job? What would be an extraordinary end game? This is a tough question to ask and especially to quantify, particularly with designers in the same room with owners and contractors. But it is an extraordinary opportunity for World Class teamwork.

Here are some examples of goals for achieving extraordinary quality:

- Be sought out as a model of excellence for _____ projects by having _____ owners/designers visit our facility NLT _____.
- Meet or exceed the quality finish of the Disney Center or the luxury of the Club Seats at the Dallas Cowboys Stadium.
- Award winner (specify awards).
- No punch list at project completion; or complete within 30 days of substantial completion; or no more than 250 items on punch list at substantial completion. No punch list items that delay project or increase cost.
- Design review/approval achieved in ____ days or within ___ of completion of design development or at the completion of design development on a design-build project.
- Zero rework.

An Outside-the-Box Approach to Minimizing Environmental Impact

```
┌──────────────── THE BOX ────────────────┐

  From the contractor's point of view:

  It's all about "not walking on the grass." Avoid Notices of Violation; they'll stop
  my work. Compliance with the environmental monitors/inspectors is going to
  be hard enough—all of them have a personal, tree-hugging agenda and no
  understanding of construction.

  From the owner's point of view:

  The contractor/DBT has to be watched. They have no incentive to do anything
  other than the minimum to get by, which is to say, their interpretation of the
  contract requirements.

  From the environmental monitor's/inspector's point of view:

  I'm the traffic cop. But contractors will just avoid, tolerate, or pay lip service
  to us. They will also complain "it's not in my scope."

└──────────────────────────────────────────┘
```

On a recent project in the Presidio of San Francisco, the project team was challenged by significant environmental regulations and constraints. The project involved the National Park Service and the Presidio Trust, which has the stewardship over one of the most hallowed landmarks in the Bay area. It would have been easy—no, make that hard—for the team to just comply with the environmental documents or avoid complaints and notices of violation.

But the team went well beyond this and set a stretch goal for themselves of "cultural and natural resources at the Presidio *enhanced* during construction and exceeds mitigation measures." They then developed a process where the environmental monitor, Margaret, would participate in the weekly meetings. A standing agenda item at these meetings was "work coming up in the next three weeks that could have environmental impact or the opportunity to enhance the environment." Margaret was also committed to the team's goal of expediting the project schedule by three months, which meant that if an issue or opportunity came up, she would work with the contractor and owner to ensure that its resolution did not slow down the project team. A win-win outcome.

Here's what Nabil Hissen with Zoon Engineering, Inc. and consultant to the San Francisco Presidio Trust says about the team's efforts on one challenge: "A lot of the slopes we're building will have to be reforested. The problem is that the trees won't grow at the required level of compaction. So we brought it up to our contractor, CC Myers, and, working together, we are trying to make reforestation work. Another contractor would have told us 'the heck with it—get out of our way and allow us to build it per specs.' This was a true paradigm shift."

How about this for a team goal? 'Net energy zero' in the first year after the owner takes occupancy. This was the team goal for the Exploratorium in San Francisco. The team came up with this independently of specifications and contract requirements.

Making the Project a Positive Experience for Third Parties, the Public and Facility Occupants

THE BOX

From the contractor's point of view:

Third parties and the public are a nuisance to be kept at arm's length. Let sleeping dogs lie, and if they yelp, respond to their complaints or, better yet, have the owner deal with it all.

From the owner's point of view:

I've got to keep the contractors from doing things that will generate complaints. I've got to run interference for the contractor with the major public stakeholders.

From the public's point of view:

They're all the same—owners, contractors, and designers. They don't give a hoot about me and the impact this project is going to have on me during construction. I've got to yell loud and frequently just to get heard.

The above assumptions lead to a reactive mode of relating with third parties, which, in turn, can preclude proactive or outreach possibilities.

The Rancho Los Amigos Hospital (Los Angeles County) project in 1993 was a major addition to an existing, operating hospital. The County/Hensel Phelps Construction team was brainstorming stretch goals when the hospital administrator spoke about minimizing the impact of construction (noise, dust, traffic, etc.) on hospital operations, patients, and staff. I challenged this as a "don't walk on the grass" sort of goal which limited the project team to a reactive role—not very empowering, very Business as Usual, and very subjective.

Someone suggested, "What if this project were to be a *positive* experience for the patients and staff during construction?" Someone else replied, "Get real. This is a major addition to an operating hospital; it is not going to be a positive experience." In spite of widespread skepticism, the team kept the goal, and later in the workshop they brainstormed and subsequently implemented the following ideas:

• Viewing ports in the fence at wheelchair height (This was an orthopedic hospital with lots of patients in wheelchairs.)
• A fence-painting contest for the patients and staff
• A monthly contest for patients and staff to, for example, guess the amount of concrete poured, with the closest answer winning a free lunch
• Placing a model of the new hospital wing in the lobby of the existing hospital and giving a talk once a week for patients and staff on progress, etc.
• Conducting tours once a week for interested staff
• Reporting on project progress and fielding questions at the monthly medical staff meeting
• The contractor going door to door prior to Thanksgiving and handing out turkeys to some thirty homeowners along an access route
• At Christmas, everyone on the project team down to the individual craftsperson "adopted" a kid in the hospital. They collected $5,000 and bought gifts for the kids.

This Hensel Phelps project was completed five months early and won one of six Marvin Black Awards for partnering excellence given out that year by the Association of General Contractors of America.

Minimizing Costs through Outside-the-Box Thinking

THE BOX

From the contractor's point of view:

The owner, designer, and CM are all "off the clock." They have no incentive to make timely decisions with me or by themselves that maximize my efficiencies and minimize my costs. The owner and designer will assume any suggestions we have for cost savings are cutting corners.

From the owner's point of view:

The contractor is in a "blow and go" mode. Don't rush me. I need time to make sure I'm making the right decision and it's supported by my seniors and other project stakeholders. The contractor/DBT are only interested in cutting their costs, not mine.

From the designer's point of view:

What's the hurry? And besides, I've got limited resources. We can't do everything in a hurry-up mode just to please the contractor. The contractor is looking to poke holes in my design.

On the $350 million Naval Hospital at Camp Pendleton, the joint venture design-build team of Clark/McCarthy came up with numerous ideas to reduce costs to meet an audacious team goal of completing their project at contract value with any costs due to unforeseen conditions or owner adds offset by true value engineering. The ideas were discussed with the design-build team seeking to understand the assumptions and intent the owner had in their schematic drawings that led them to choose the product or material they selected. With this understanding, they could jointly make a good business decision on the value of any options the design-build team might bring forth. One specific idea that came up in the partnering session by a subcontractor involved replacing the called-for roof waterproofing with an alternative material. The idea was openly and, albeit initially, tentatively accepted by the owner. The estimated savings? About $800,000 to $900,000.

In addition to expediting the schedule and managing change orders, there is another side to minimizing project cost which is not as measurable but can be considerably more costly. And that is the cost of time or, more precisely, untimely decisions. And yes, World Class teamwork requires more conversations with more people up front. But consider two things:

1. These conversations are with individuals who share your passion and commitment to reducing costs without compromising quality.

2. A one-hour meeting with all the individuals who have something to contribute to expediting a key electrical submittal will save ten times the time in back-and-forth tennis, let alone potential conflict and schedule delay.

Stephen Sharr of LAUSD explains: "A World Class team can optimize decisions relative to cost over the course of their project by making them timely, collaborative, and proactive. This eliminates time, friction, and angst among team members. This, in turn, can create big savings, especially at the field level, as well as avoid future claims."

Vitas Rugienius of Hensel Phelps echoes Stephen's remarks: "On a World Class team with common goals, you are always able to limit the impact and mitigate cost impacts by talking about them openly with your team members."

"People tend to underestimate the cost of time on a construction project," says Dave Niese of Flatiron. "There's a lot of time spent trying to make the right decision. It is often better to go forward with an imperfect decision and handle the imperfections after the fact."

> Be quick but don't hurry.
> —COACH JOHN WOODEN, UCLA—

Another contractor adds, "It's often difficult to explain to an owner the cost of time due to delay. For example, a loss of one day paving really took two days from us, and then we also lost the opportunity to pave another job. On World Class teams, you communicate very clear time expectations with the client, which enables you to reduce costs by early clarification of potential cost impacts."

How about costs from a designer's perspective? Fred Powell from NBBJ explains: "When everyone on the team understands the big picture and project goals from each stakeholder's point of view, you optimize efficiencies. For example, if I discuss the design goals of the project with a craftsperson and he shares his construction concerns, we can both come up with a solution that best addresses cost as well as quality."

An Outside-the-Box Approach to Value Engineering

THE BOX

From the contractor's point of view:

Getting the owner and designer to consider value engineering is swimming upstream. They've got a "not invented here" mentality and will assume all my suggestions are cheap substitutes. Also, any VE idea I or my subcontractors put forth would take a lot of time and effort to document and sell, and the final decision, if favorable, would be made too late. Besides, there's no clear understanding as to how the savings would be divided up. So why bother?

From the owner's point of view:

We've pretty much VE'd this project out. Any solutions the contractor might come up with would be compromising quality and functionality.

From the designer's point of view:

Just build it per plans and specs. And besides, I don't have the time or money to spend analyzing ideas from the contractor.

There is a lot of talk about value engineering on construction projects, but results rarely measure up to much. Why? Clients tell me that it is due to assumptions above that project stakeholders have about the value engineering process—or lack thereof on a Business as Usual team.

As Frank Miller, Vice President for subcontractor DynaElectric, says, "On a World Class team, I can come up with credits and savings that I can offer to the owner. You can talk about what is really important to the owner—and it is not just cost. This enables us to give them a project that they really want."

There is also one limiting assumption that may exist with the designer: "Will I get fairly compensated for my time and effort spent in both considering and approving any value engineering ideas?"

How do World Class teams look at value engineering? Fred Powell with NBBJ Architects says, "Invest everyone on the team with enough mutual respect and knowledge that they feel entitled to bring forth ideas and make suggestions. Ideas are the commodity we deal in, and the more we get on a project, the better the project." "If you really want value engineering to happen, you need to set a goal as a team," adds Perry Petersen of Petersen Construction Services.

Dave Niese with Flatiron says, "World Class teams never respond with an easy 'no' to their colleagues ideas' about cost or schedule savings. All on a World Class team are never satisfied with just what is spec'd."

World Class teams also address up front the question of how the savings from successfully implemented value engineering will be divided up. My experience is that on few (less than 25 percent) projects does this formula exist, or, if it does, it is not clear to all stakeholders. Again, a project team can create a team or *partnership* understanding of value engineering formula if it is not in the contract. Typically the split is 50/50 net design review costs.

But achieving this understanding too can be dicey. Paul Ligocki of Hensel Phelps explains: "On a World Class team, there's a level of trust that what I'm giving the owner is fair. On other teams, the owner may question our 'give back' even if I'm giving them one dollar back for every dollar I save them."

The question then becomes: How do we as a team facilitate the consideration of ideas to best reach our goal? A World Class team starts by assuming the following:

1. The more ideas we get, the more the possibility of good ones that could help us achieve our cost goal.

2. The easier and less disruptive to their work that contractors perceive the value engineering process to be, the more ideas they will bring forth.

3. To the extent there is both an expeditious and fair way for the designer to be compensated to consider and redesign, if necessary, the value engineering idea, the more open they will be to considering them.

The WCT approach: Verbally float the value engineering idea to the owner and designer. Get a preliminary "go" or "no go" response from the owner and/or designer. If "no go," thanks, but no thanks. You as a contractor need not waste any more time or effort developing the idea, but we, as the owner and designer, appreciate your coming forward with this idea.

Perry Petersen of Petersen Construction Services notes, "You need to get the idea discussed and worked out in principle by all parties before any detailed costing is done. Then, as a team, agree on how much detail is needed. Invariably, you don't need as much as you think."

If the preliminary response is "go," then the team mutually and verbally agrees on:

- ROM of savings
- Next steps to consider the idea: What does the owner/designer need to see or hear? In what format? Can we do some of this as a team?
- ROM of potential design review and revision costs. I have seen this to be a deal killer on its own.
- How soon does the idea need to be implemented so as not to adversely impact our team schedule and other potential costs?

Bob Finney of Caltrans adds, "The key is getting all sides to develop the idea together. When an idea becomes 'our plan,' you have the benefit of everyone working together to make it work. The team won't let it fail."

An Outside-the-Box Approach to Safety

```
┌──────────────────  THE BOX  ──────────────────┐
│                                                │
│  From the contractor's point of view:          │
│  We've got a great safety program if everyone would comply with it. We'll do │
│  what we did successfully on the last job.      │
│                                                │
│  From the designer's, CM's, and owner's point of view:  │
│  Safety is entirely up to the contractor or design-build team. We will comply │
│  with their program.                           │
│                                                │
└────────────────────────────────────────────────┘
```

Question: If you'd asked the senior executives of British Petroleum five seconds before the explosion on their Deepwater Horizon rig if they had a "world class" safety program, what would they sincerely have told you? You might have asked the same question of the executives at Tokyo Power prior to the March 2011 tsunami.

My point here is not to disparage the intentions or abilities of these individuals but to illustrate the very subtle yet compelling influence of hubris on our attitudes toward safety. Nor is the intent of this book to be a primer on construction safety but rather to speak to the opportunity that having a World Class team can bring to construction project safety.

If safety is seen as a project-wide culture as opposed to a contractor-imposed set of rules and procedures—or program—with opportunity for all to contribute, you get a whole new set of creative possibilities: inspectors attending contractors' safety briefings, owners and designers being empowered to stop work if an incident has potential for immediate harm, and any individual stakeholder who may have something to contribute being involved in job hazard safety analysis. The difference between having just a great safety program and a project-wide safety culture is commitment, not merely compliance, by all the project stakeholders to mutually agreed-upon safety standards and actions. Project safety is one of those phenomena that no matter how sophisticated and comprehensive your safety program is, at some point it becomes Business as Usual and loses its edge.

Alix O'Brien with URS Construction Management explains: "When you have a really high-performance team, they can sometimes become too relaxed and dismissive of confronting one another on potential safety hazards. On World Class teams, you have an ongoing enthusiasm and constant energy that constantly challenges what you're currently doing. Without this there can be complacency."

On the LA METRO's Eastside Extension, the team executed a phenomenal 4.25 million man hours with zero lost-time accidents. Dennis Mori, METRO's Project Executive, explains: "The partnering and World Class teamwork process allowed everyone to look ahead toward high mutual expectations. This energized individuals to be extraordinarily safety conscious."

Similarly, Les Osterberger, Vice President with A. O. Reed, the mechanical/plumbing subcontractor on Rady Children's Hospital, says, "On World Class teams, you create a culture of safety which translates into a strong, ongoing awareness and learning. On other jobs, there's a tendency to look at it from a scorecard point of view. On this job, safety was pushed down to second- and third-tier subs. The GC, McCarthy, had a full-time safety guy on site, and we didn't fear him. Issues like using a box cutter to open a box were brought up in safety meetings in a way that didn't fix blame but stressed learning. It also created a peer pressure from us subs. We didn't want to let the team down." The Dupont Corporation, for example, has conducted an empirical study and created a process that establishes a measurable correlation between having a strong safety culture on a project and the predictability of safety incidents. The processes exist. What's missing? A project team having the commitment to execute them as a team.

Here's another example of an outside-the-box approach to safety. On a Suffolk Construction school project, the safety manager suggested setting up a Safety Committee (no big deal here) but with participation *only* from tradespeople—no foremen or even lead persons. The participants would be rotated every sixty days and, while they served, would be conduits back to everyone else on their scope of work.

The lesson? You need to be more than a little unorthodox to break up the Business as Usual mentality to safety that even comes from experienced, professional craftspeople who have a great safety track record.

Figuring Out the How-To by Working Backward from the Goal

According to consultant Jim Selman, author of *Coaching: Beyond Management,* personal requests and commitments create a future and leave people in action toward that future. It's important to be very specific here. As we saw in chapter 7, World Class team members make requests of individuals, not institutions. We've found it useful to make these very specific and clear and to document them. The result? It's like priming a pump. If you leave people in action over the next month with a comprehensive list of requests and commitments that support their common goals, it establishes a precedent for the balance of the job.

Furthermore, if your team has set project goals that they as a team truly own and are committed to, figuring out the how-to is just a question of applying themselves and aligning their actions. They've done the hard part—creating meaningful, measurable goals to which they're all committed. The horses are harnessed and they can smell the barn, as an old cowboy put it; now let them run.

Now have the team work backward to figure out the how-to—reverse engineering. What are the key processes that we, *as a team*, are going to have to invent, figure out, make happen to realize our schedule goal? This process is similar to what many people refer to as pull-planning.

Back to President Kennedy's statement of putting a man on the moon. If you were part of NASA in 1961 and asked yourself the question above, you might have come up with the following:

- We need to develop a propulsion system that will enable the capsule to escape the earth's atmosphere.
- We need a life-support process/system to keep these guys alive.
- We need to create a lunar landing module.
- We need to select and train astronauts.
- We need to find a way to communicate with these astronauts.
- We need to come up with a way to get them back through the earth's atmosphere without burning up.
- We need, of course, to invent Tang and Velcro.

Now let's talk construction. If you have developed a true stretch goal, there will be processes that the team has yet to figure out or create. If they are not able to come up with any, have them reset their stretch goal until it is truly a stretch goal. Here's a great opportunity for outside-the-box thinking.

Some examples on a design, bid, build project include:

- We need to expedite critical submittals to support our schedule goal.
- We need to expedite change orders.
- We need to find a way to expedite RFIs to support our schedule.
- We need to expedite critical permits.
- We need a clear, mutual definition of "substantial completion."
- We need to develop a schedule that supports our stretch goal.
- We need to ensure inspection is timely.

How about a design-build project?
- We need to find a way to expedite design development with the end user = "over the shoulder reviews"? Result? The formal design review is just a formality, and we truly meet end user intent.
- We need to expedite owner-approved submittals.
- We need to expedite and minimize owner scope adds.

How about a project involving IPD/BIM/PMIS?
- What are the overarching project goals that we want our IPD/BIM process to help us achieve?
- Given the above, we need to establish a clear understanding of an IPD/DB process as a team on this project that enrolls all stakeholders.
- We need to develop a schedule for implementing IPD that will support our overall schedule goal on this project.
- We need to find a way to implement a BIM process with all subcontractors and subconsultants.
- We need to develop a Project Management Information System (PMIS) as a team that supports our goals.

Likewise, design-assist gives everyone a head start on a collaborative effort:
- We need a way to work together between owner, GC, and designer to

meet and incorporate owner needs to support our schedule completion goal.

- We need to develop a means of establishing a optimal GMP no later than May 1.

Press for Individual/Team Commitments to Action with Names and Dates

Once the team has a list, validate that it is truly comprehensive by asking, "If we found a way to do all of these processes with a velocity that supports our stretch goal, would we have a good shot at achieving it?" If the answer is yes, the team now needs to get into action via requests and promises relative to each of the key processes that the team has identified as critical to achieving their goals. For example, determine "OK, who needs to do what, when, to expedite the curtain wall submittal in a velocity that supports our substantial completion goal of September 30?"

For example, if you're talking about expediting submittals, you might ask which submittals are critical. Let's say they come up with fire, life, and safety. You might now ask, "Who would have something to contribute to finding a way of expediting this submittal with a velocity that supports substantial completion NLT April 15, 2013?"

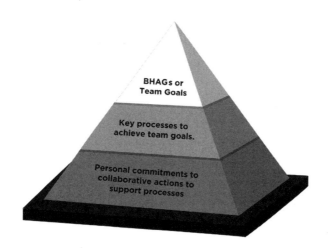

From Team Goals to Personal and Team Action

TIP: If the urgency (to achieve the schedule goal) requires action within the next two weeks, have the team identify names, date, and deliverable. If the action is beyond two weeks, identify names, champion, and a no-later-than date for the meeting or deliverable.

Once the players are identified, push for accountability as a team/task force. When can you all come up with a process for expediting this submittal (if not today)? Who's going to lead/champion this team?

True outside-the-box thinking acknowledges that no matter how confident you and your teammates are of your leading-edge processes, abilities, and resources on a project, there is always an opportunity for implementing them better, safer, and/or faster as a true World Class team. Outside the box thinking also can be a key bridge or bond between all project stakeholders. As we saw in chapter 6, all of us share fundamental human needs of pride, enjoying our work, recognition, and a sense of fulfillment from our work efforts. But consider also that the opportunity to express genuine creativity is something we also all share and value. To the extent this creativity is allowed to fully express itself and becomes integral to our day-to-day working relationships, each of us and, of course, the project significantly benefits.

12

WORLD CLASS TEAM BEHAVIOR #8

Transform the Project Delivery Method into an Informal Communication Network

Business as Usual: Project delivery method gamed by each stakeholder to take advantage of self-serving opportunities, such as cutting corners on quality in design-build. Lip service paid to construction process, e.g., BIM.

Good Teams: Project delivery method executed inflexibly and as end in itself. BIM application limited and uncreative.

WORLD CLASS TEAMS: Project delivery method and construction processes/ BIM do not limit team from doing what is best for the project. They are creatively modified, adapted and optimized by the team. Result: an informal communication network with passion and committed action.

World Class Teamwork Works with All Project Delivery Methods

It really doesn't matter what delivery method you are using. That's right— whether you're using design-build, CM at Risk, or it's a straight hard-bid job, World Class teamwork significantly enhances and optimizes all project delivery methods and construction processes (e.g., BIM, Last Planner™ System, etc.). How? It enables the project team to modify and adapt their PDM or construction process to what is truly best for their job. The result? An informal network of communication grounded in common goals backed up by personal commitments that does what is best for the project.

With common goals, open, direct verbal communication, the team truly taking overall responsibility for project success, proactively managing risk, organization lines blurred, and 100 percent accountability by all for everything, it should be apparent that on a World Class team the formal structure and PDM at some point become, in a sense, irrelevant. Don't get me wrong. Lest I sound like a heretic, you need to start all jobs with a clear PDM, procedures, and a formal contract which continues to stay in force.

All major projects are obligated (out of legal or business necessity or invariably both) to start with procedures and prescribed processes relative to the contract and project delivery method. But it does not end there. As with coaches of great sports teams, all stakeholders invariably start a game with a detailed game plan built upon certain assumptions. But the really good ones have an uncanny ability to take their initial game plan and adapt and change it relative to what's happening on the field. They do not let their initial assumptions limit their ability to do what is necessary to win.

Dave Niese with Flatiron Construction explains: "A World Class team does not let the PDM control what is right for the job. It acknowledges that the PDM is what the owner thought was best when they were writing the specs. The question should be 'Given what we know today, what's right for this project?'"

Again, the definition of what is right or best comes from a project team acknowledging the contract, specs, PDM, and their current circumstances, and then freely defining and committing to, as a team, common goals for their project. These goals should also speak to the end user's intent, which may or may not be expressed well in the contract documents or specifications. With that approach, World Class teamwork allows a project team to truly optimize its PDM and construction processes. It also leaves the team members in committed action.

Having personally worked with project teams utilizing all major PDMs on over five hundred construction processes worldwide, including negotiated private-sector jobs, I can discern absolutely no difference in the level of teamwork and performance between World Class teams utilizing any of these PDMs. At some point all World Class construction teams behave essentially the same—evidencing all ten World Class team behaviors and with their team members in committed action.

It is not my purpose in this book to judge the relative merits of project delivery methods. A World Class team deals with the hand it is dealt relative to circumstances, its chosen PDM, and its people and their expressed

Formal Hierarchal Project Structure

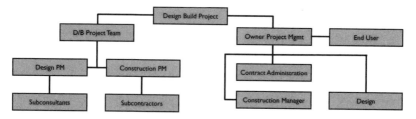

Informal Communication Network

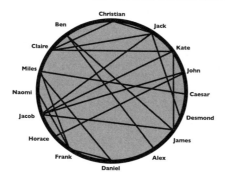

Formal PDM to Informal Communication Network

needs and wants. I acknowledge that using newer alternate PDMs enhances a team's ability to achieve WCT relative to, say, a straight hard-bid job. But they certainly do not ensure, let alone guarantee, it.

Tim Jacoby of Rady Children's Hospital notes, "When Integrated Project Delivery began, there was the expectation that it would solve everything. Well, what we learned was that a delivery method is a tool that may or may not work. It's not about the delivery method; rather, it is about the people and their ability to work together." Despite my reluctance to judge PDMs, I believe that IPD comes as close as contractually possible to enabling World Class teamwork.

Chet Widom, FAIA, consultant to the Los Angeles City College system, seems to agree when speaking about BIM: "BIM is an important tool. It is not the solution, but it is a tool to help your team get to the solution." I might add, it is how the project team chooses to utilize the tool that enables them to get to the solution. You can have great tools and processes on a construction project, but without the committed action to execute them, they are for naught.

Managing the Three Key Challenges of Working with PDMs and Construction Processes

A World Class team faces three primary challenges when working with PDMs and construction process:

1. The uncertainties and assumptions in a world of multiple PDMs and processes
2. The need for committed action—not just theory and organization charts
3. Enabling the formal PDM to evolve into an informal network of communication that does what is best for the job

1. The Uncertainties and Assumptions in a World of Multiple PDMs and Processes

As previously pointed out, in today's and tomorrow's world of multiple PDMs and construction processes, an absence of clear, mutual expectations can suboptimize project performance.

Doug Duplisea with the Kiewit Companies cautions, "With a new and different delivery method, there can be a lot of understandable uneasiness on the part of the owner and other stakeholders. They're asking themselves, 'How do we know if we're going to get the best product with this process? How do we manage our risk?'" These questions can get obscured by the jargon and language of a new, alternate project delivery method.

These are some additional assumptions and expectations that individuals beginning a construction project might have:

- The PDM and contract will/will not manage or eliminate my risk.
- The PDM and contract will/will not enable us to work together as a good or high-performance team.

- The PDM and contract will/will not eliminate conflict.
- There is a best way to implement a PDM or contract.
- We do not need to ask hard questions of one another because the PDM and contract will take care of them.

Indeed, I've seen numerous project teams where these assumptions were not adequately addressed and individuals operated on the basis of altogether different assumptions. This creates a fertile ground for misunderstanding, uncertainty, stress, and conflict. "Oh, I thought the design-build team should be responsible for that." Likewise, debating the merits of the PDM or process is academic and putting the cart before the horse. PDMs and construction processes are tools, not solutions, that should support a common purpose and the owner's true intent. They need to be used, modified, adapted, and sometimes changed in a way that is best for the individual project and team. In other words, a project team starts with addressing the fundamental question of "What is our common purpose?" and then asks themselves, "How do we get there from here as a team, acknowledging but not limited by our formal relationships in, for example, a CM at Risk contract?" In other words, do not be a slave to your project delivery method or construction process. Be willing to risk letting the team develop informal relationships that do what is best for the project. And then have them hold themselves accountable for their commitments to one another.

WCT teams are in the driver's seat together, and together they determine where they want to go and, given their PDM, what is the best way to reach their common definitions of project success. The question should not be "How do we best execute design-build (or BIM, etc.) on this job?" Rather, the question should be "Given our common goal of completing this job three months early, how can we best optimize BIM (or execute design-build) to support that goal?"

Several years ago I was called in to help on a major hospital renovation well underway. They were utilizing a LEAN project delivery method, and they rated themselves a 4.6 on my 1–10 scale: on the downside of Business as Usual. What were some of their issues? They could not agree on a means of fully implementing LEAN at the project field level. Ongoing and numerous owner changes, a lack of alignment between different owner functions and departments, and a very uneven, unaligned understanding of and commitment to LEAN had put the project well behind schedule and over budget.

The solution? Have them set team goals for the balance of the job; identify key processes to achieve those goals, utilizing and modifying LEAN where the team believes it can help; and then gain personal commitments to execute those processes.

With any new model, process, or theory, there are often heady initial expectations. The business world is strewn with great concepts, theories, and business models that have fallen well short of expectations when faced with reality—Management by Objectives, Total Quality Management, and Strategic Planning, to name a few. All were, and are, great concepts with potential value, and they seemingly made unequivocal sense. But none were or are now a panacea. This is the trap Jim Collins speaks of in *How the Mighty Fall* when he talks about searching for a silver bullet. We can become so seduced by the process and how it may have worked successfully on a previous job that we assume the same will apply to our new project. This, as we saw on the health-care project using LEAN, can lead to a single stakeholder attempting to control the application of the process rather than the team doing what they believe is best. We've spoken previously about the fallacy of control.

Even supposedly well-known models, concepts, or theories offer no assurance of common interpretation and successful implementation. Take design-build, for example, which has been out there for a while. There are still no universal best ways or industry-wide guidelines how on to best execute it. Thomas Davenport and Jeanne G. Harris explain in *Competing on Analytics: The New Science of Winning*, "The more an organization knows about a term or concept, the more widely disparate are the definitions."[23] And this, somewhat paradoxically, can be good. As we will see, it offers the opportunity for a project team to take that concept or PDM and creatively adapt it to their circumstances in a way that best meets their common goals.

With IPD, contractors, owners, and designers are encouraged to make decisions as a team and assume risk together. Then they are rewarded for achieving predetermined goals from an identified pool of incentives. This sets the stage for true collaboration and trust at an early stage. Yet as Eric Long, Executive Vice President of DPR Construction, puts it in the January 2010 edition of *Executive Construction*, "The challenge is when people retain their old behaviors and operate within their own silos rather than the interests of the entire team. You can't have individuals withholding information from their budgets or scopes of work. You need to strip away that fear and work openly."[24]

2. The Need for Committed Action—Not Just Theory and Organization Charts

Alternative PDMs, concept models, role definitions, and flow charts are great, but they no more predict how individuals will actually behave and interact with one another on a project than do the Ten Commandments. What a specific project requires is committed action or, better yet, leaving the team in committed action toward a common purpose.

Chad Olson, Senior Project Manager with Suffolk Construction (not involved in the above LEAN project) notes, "LEAN is great but needs to be complemented by overall project goals and personal commitments that the team and individuals are held accountable to. With World Class teamwork, there is committed action, and you need this regardless of the PDM or construction process you employ."

This reinforces the adage that "you can contract for a project delivery method but not for human behavior." The latter can only come from freely made, personal commitments.

Sue Stewart, formerly Senior Vice President with McCarthy Building Companies, seems to echo Chad's observations: "To reach an owner's objectives in this environment, there should be an investment in aligning all members of the team to make sure they thoroughly understand the desired outcomes (goals), challenge the standard operating procedures, and define a process they all believe will truly support those desired outcomes. The key is to gain commitment. Only then do team members know where they are going and together have a determined and completely customized process they are sure will get them there."

3. Enabling the Formal PDM to Evolve into an Informal Network of Communication that Does What Is Best for the Job

If you look at a case study of a successful application of any PDM or construction process, the project team has taken it and internalized it or, as Sue Stewart says, "customized" it. They have adapted it to the unique project circumstances and nuances and the wants, needs, and understandings of the team members. In other words, they created "the best way" to execute the PDM on their project, backed up with personal commitments to implement it.

That is why on World Class teams we are seeing hybrids of project delivery methods develop not only at the start of a job but over the duration of the job as well. Jim Link of Skanska explains: "When you have a World Class team built upon trust, it allows the team to push the envelope further than they ordinarily would with the PDM. It allows them to experiment more and come up with creative applications that best suit their project."

Optimizing BIM as a Team

BIM is a game-changing tool that truly enables a project team to collaborate on a real-time basis at the field level. Yet it too is not a panacea. No technology, by itself, will change the way people work together.

Alix O'Brien, URS Construction Management, explains, "BIM is great, but it is not a replacement for old-school coordination in the field between superintendents."

Patrick Peterson, Project Director with McCarthy and winner of a BIM Modeling Award in 2009, notes, "On one project we had budget problems early on. The key in these situations is being able to modify your delivery techniques and processes to support overall project success and the team goals. In BIM, World Class communication is critical, as is having a common goal that everyone has bought into—inside and outside the team."

Halfway through the Grand Canyon University's Events Center project, the project team enhanced their BIM modeling effectiveness by recognizing the need of having the full team, including active subcontractors and subconsultants, either present or on the phone during all BIM review meetings.

World Class Teamwork with a Completely Unconventional and Unprecedented Delivery Method

In chapter 4 we considered the North Island Naval Base Coronado Bachelor Enlisted Quarters and the truly unique approach to design-build that the Navy and Hensel Phelps entered into. The goal of early completion drove the project. Even implementing a conventional design-build project would have been too late.

When the team met for the first time at their partnering meeting, the design-build team had very little idea of what the Navy was expecting. There were no schematics or even a design concept. "We were starting with an almost blank sheet of paper," as Hensel Phelps' Project Manager Bill Welch put it. One project stakeholder said, "This was a setting for what could be a massive train wreck or an extraordinary opportunity for a truly innovative and highly collaborative approach."

The opportunity was a process that allowed the owner and design-build team members to work together, with little other than a lump sum and the requirement that the facility house some seven hundred sailors, to optimize creativity and innovation from the get-go. In other words, they started with few assumptions, constraints, or limitations. On a Business as Usual job, the design-build contractor would have viewed this situation as a mouth-watering opportunity to shortcut functionality, aesthetics, and quality and take full advantage of the lack of limits. But Hensel Phelps viewed their risk and opportunity differently; they saw that the real risk, or opportunity lost, would be not being selected for future jobs of this sort from the Navy or any other public agency. They're betting on the very real probability that more and more public jobs will be awarded on this basis.

In this setting, the team-building process (which really ended up being more of a concept design workshop) initially just focused on developing specific, measurable design criteria which met, or exceeded, the needs of all project stakeholders and was buildable well within the timeline and lump sum. These criteria became partnership goals or standards with no contractual obligation. Again, they were going forward on trust and specific personal commitments.

Here are the project team's stretch goals:

1. Achieve LEED Gold.
2. Flexible layout that enables a percentage of rooms to economically be convertible to future privatization.

3. Rooftop lounge; tennis courts; survey scores of residents = 7+. BEQ sought out as a place to hang out by the sailors.

4. Reduce maintenance costs by at least 25 percent relative to comparable buildings.

5. Parking near facility with bike access and/or ability of residents to walk to all recreational facilities on and off base.

6. Win nationwide award(s)—to be determined.

7. Final design approval no later than September 30, 2010.

8. At completion of design, estimated cost of total project = contract value.

They went on to invent and commit to a very specific approach from that day forward that would produce the design concept collaboratively as well as partner during the subsequent design development process. With this foundation, they believed, design approval and review would be merely a formal acknowledgment of what they had done together. The design was, from the very beginning, a team design, not just the DBT's design. Paul Ligocki, HPCC's Operations Manager, said this process "would be totally transparent with regard to costs." In other words, both the DBT and owner would be making decisions regarding all facets of design and the trade-offs relative to cost and quality.

Let's look at how specific and collaborative they were in establishing their initial commitments towards the goals:

Developed joint design concept with buy-in and contribution by all partners no later than April 26, 2010. Note: date of workshop was March 17, 2010.

1. Of Sam (request of); Bobby; Ed; Terrence; Patricia: meet on 3/19 at JWDA (the architect's office) at 10:00 + Mike S+. Purpose: give HPCC input on priorities, likes, and dislikes.

2. By Mike S: after the above meeting, we will call/meet Navy partners to help us put together collaborative vision.

3. Of Sam+; Ed; Bobby; Terrence; Mike S+: will meet on 3/25 at 1:00 for a "What do you think about our concept?" session; By Terrence: I will input to CDR Bergen and Capt. Lindsey.

4. Of Dan/Terrence: be a liaison with senior management to and from the partnership during design phase.

5. Of Sam; Todd: develop survey/access current data of Housing and get to Mike S NLT 3/19.

6. Of all project stakeholders and all disciplines: meet on 3/31 through 4/2 to enhance design and gain total buy-in to concept and basis of design.

NOTE: Whatever assumptions individuals may have had about the design of this facility now become a "partnership concept."

The lesson from the above? If you bring together project team members committed to World Class teamwork, you can optimize project results even without a formal project delivery method. The Coronado BEQ, once awarded, resembled more of a private, negotiated job.

The Future

Fifteen years ago or so, the notion of World Class or high-performance teamwork was relatively rare in construction, particularly in public construction. It was, as one general contractor told me, a "serendipitous circumstance." In a public and private construction world of nothing other than design, bid, build projects, Good was about as good as it got. But now a wealth of alternative project delivery methods and collaborative construction processes (Last Planner™ System, BIM, VB, PMIS, etc.) plus higher owner, contractor, and designer needs and expectations make World Class teamwork a viable and necessary standard of excellence for a project team to strive to achieve. In other words, while having an alternative project delivery method on your project does not ensure World Class teamwork, it now makes it more possible.

One final point: Construction project delivery methods and processes can be expected to be in a continual state of flux and improvement. Likewise, construction projects will continue to become more and more complex. The need for creativity, speed, focus, and adaptability will only increase.

Obviously change and innovation can be good, healthy, and necessary. Imagine how dull and uncreative construction would be if project stakeholders had only one choice or One Best Way when it came to selecting and executing a PDM, construction methodology, or process. Yet even if there were one, clear, accepted PDM or construction process, that would by no means ensure committed action.

World Class teamwork offers a universal, dynamic protocol for enabling individual and team behavior to support any PDM in a manner that supports overall project excellence, even on design, bid, build projects. The result is teamwork that resembles that of an informal network of relationships rather than a textbook model of a PDM. On World Class teams, or networks, individuals are bound together by common goals and facilitated by both formal and informal communication processes.

A bit presumptuous? Maybe. But as our design and construction tools and methods become more sophisticated and complex, there's an increasing need to ensure that their potential gets fully optimized and results in committed action toward a common purpose.

13

WORLD CLASS TEAM BEHAVIOR #9

Deal Openly and Verbally with Issues and Conflicts

Sometimes it takes a few, nasty disputes for individuals
on a project team to get confidence in themselves.
—JIM LINTHICUM OF SAN DIEGO ASSOCIATION OF GOVERNMENTS—

Business as Usual: Disputes linger and fester. Unwilling to acknowledge mistakes or errors. Issues default to potential claims.

Good Teams: No claims. Conflicts can be resolved, but process can be painful. Job can become stalled. Egos bruised and intentions questioned.

WORLD CLASS TEAMS: Conflicts resolved or, if not, quickly elevated to the next level without ill will or personal rancor. Still trust your partner, and the job is not stopped nor delayed.

With virtually any project, let alone those that are particularly challenging from a design and constructability point of view, will come differences of opinion, alternative perspectives, varying interpretations, and even conflicts. Yet of this all can be good. A certain amount of open tension on a project is useful. It candidly acknowledges the reality that on a construction project we all, individually and collectively, face competing demands, needs, goals, and pressures.

Gentlemen, you can't fight in here! This is the War Room!
—PRESIDENT MERKIN MUFFLEY, *DR. STRANGELOVE*—

There's a trap here, however, and herein lies one of the subtle differences between Good and World Class teams. Let's look at the different assumptions:

- Combat teams, of course, are in full body armor. Claims consultants and attorneys are on retainer from the beginning, leading to a self-fulfilling prophecy.

- Business as Usual teams tend to operate in avoidance of blame, responsibility, and risk. The initial reaction is to find the guilty party or avoid being labeled the guilty party. The result? CYA, letter writing, game playing, case building, and posturing.

- Good teams acknowledge the reality that on construction projects there will be conflicts and they may be messy. That messiness unfortunately can stall or stop the job and bruise egos. Open confrontation is avoided. There is also a tendency to shove problems under the rug and write letters/ e-mails in lieu of verbal discussion.

- World Class teams assume that we are all playing the same game (common goals) and that although we may have disagreements, misunderstandings, and conflicts, team members do not question others' intentions or personal integrity. There is also the confidence that any issue will ultimately get reasonably resolved and not necessarily stop the job. Jim Linthicum of SANDAG emphasizes, "On our projects, people have an expectation. And that is that all issues will be worked out—regardless of with or by whom. It may involve a third party, but that's OK too."

There is a danger in each of the three lower modes of Combat, Business as Usual, and Good. I call it the difference between playing to win and playing not to lose.

Playing to Win versus Playing Not to Lose

Good and Business as Usual project teams all too often play merely to avoid losing. Why? They look at disputes/issues as standalone events to be managed for their individual self-interests to minimize or transfer risk, retain control, dominate, and/or satisfy their personal egos. A good metaphor here is a football team sitting on what may seem to be a comfortable lead.

It is all too tempting to just sit back and play safe, defend, and avoid any offensive risks. As we've seen, on construction projects, in the absence of clear, measurable and compelling common goals, this is the default game. In this context, issues or conflicts tend to be dealt with on a short-term, autonomous basis. The consequences? Time is wasted, the job might even stop, stakeholders tend to polarize, and individuals start to question one another's intentions.

> In order to succeed, your desire for success should be
> greater than your fear of failure.
> —BILL COSBY—

But what if you and your World Class team are operating on the assumption that you all are playing to win and delight the client and you have clear, compelling team goals toward that end? First of all, an issue or dispute is considered just a impediment to be better understood, managed, overcome, or mitigated as the team continues to pursue its common goals. It may even be considered a sign of a dynamic, positive relationship, whether it is merely a rock in the road or maybe even a boulder.

Whatever the challenge, have this attitude: "We, as a team, will do our best to deal with it." A key assumption of World Class teams is that by virtue of having common goals, we can usually find common ground. Vitas Rugienius of Hensel Phelps says, "On a World Class team, issues and disputes can help us understand where the other person is coming from and can help us help them to achieve our common goal."

Secondly, when there is an issue on a World Class team, team members do not question others' intentions but continue to trust them. The issue may involve a difference of opinion, different assumptions, a mistake, miscommunication, or even incompetence. But with this perspective, the question of intentions does not even come into play. There is no need to raise voices, get personal, or lose tempers.

Jim Houchins, Vice President with JE Dunn Construction, explains: "On World Class teams, you air it out without being personal. When a project team can do this, they can overcome the vast majority of issues and conflicts." As we'll see, sometimes airing it out can result in agreeing to disagree, in which case you elevate the issue to the next level while continuing to trust your partner.

On World Class teams, you assume trust unless and until someone does something blatantly obvious that tells you that the trust is broken. In this case, it may or may not be game over, back to Business as Usual. More about this in chapter 15.

Virgil Curtis of Balfour Beatty explains: "On World Class teams, I do not believe the other individual is lying or intentionally misrepresenting things. I expect a high level of honesty and personal integrity. Jobs run a lot more smoothly when you don't have to worry about underhanded, hidden agendas."

Understanding that intentions are not the issue enables a World Class team to approach the issue or dispute from the perspective of seeking mutual understanding of what really happened and, given that, asking "How do we go forward?" When you ask, "How can we best resolve this issue today on a go-forward basis as a team to continue to support our effort to achieve our common goals?" the solution becomes one of realigning the team's future actions with its current goals and circumstances. Invariably, on World Class teams the issue is a lack of understanding or alignment around goals, priorities, and responsibilities. This is a relatively easy fix when you are not worrying about your fellow stakeholders' intentions. Getting bogged down in questioning intentions and placing blame involves negative defensive energy, stress, and dwelling on the past, while a go-forward approach involves an opportunity to come together as a team to possibly create an innovative, breakthrough solution. Which game do you want to play?

Robert Develle of Jet Propulsion Laboratory says, "In the old days, I felt as if I had to be the 800-pound gorilla in the room. And I didn't like playing that role. On World Class teams, you resolve issues by listening and to some degree empathizing with your partners. It validates the notion that nice guys don't always finish last."

On World Class teams, there still may be accountability for an issue, mistake, or problem. The attitude should be, "Yes, we acknowledge there is a design deficiency here, but we're going to solve it first as a team and then deal with accountability, not blame, later."

Issam Khalaf of Jacobs CM notes, "There is no point in being confrontational—be a team member. Excluding gross negligence, I put the contract 'on the shelf,' lend my ear to all, and refuse to take sides. I actually enjoy that role, and that may include leaning on parties—including the owner or my client—if need be, for the good of the overall project."

Three Guidelines for Conflict Resolution on World Class Teams

Conflict resolution on World Class teams not only is much more expedient, but it also avoids personal stress and unresolved issues as well as strengthening the team. A project team becomes stronger from the personal understanding and confidence that comes from individuals resolving issues where there was previously no protocol or prescribed solution. They learn, in other words, that they can overcome obstacles and differences together. Disputes can also be a source of personal growth. In fact, some experts assert that without a certain level of tension and stress, true personal growth cannot occur. They learn that, as one client put it, "We can count on one another when things get difficult."

A crisis is a terrible thing to waste.
—PAUL ROMER, STANFORD UNIVERSITY ECONOMIST—

Here are some guidelines within which to make that happen.

1. Resolve it verbally at the lowest possible level by attempting to achieve mutual understanding of what actually happened.

Clients tell me that the more complex the issue, the greater the imperative to attempt to understand the issue verbally. "If I can sit in the contractor's chair and try to understand where they're coming from, then we can possibly find common ground and resolve an issue where both parties respect the decision," says Richard Welsh of the Bureau of Reclamation. Written communication can never communicate the nuances, degree of difficulty, and understanding of a situation that a verbal, back-and-forth dialogue can.

Letters and e-mails almost never resolve issues on construction projects.
People verbally communicating do.

The longer an issue is left unresolved or unspoken, the longer it remains damaging and uncomfortable, and the job stalls. Peter Mondery of Southern Contracting explains: "On World Class teams, we work hard at resolving the issues quickly in the field. But if we can't, we can at least usually agree on constructability and keep the job moving while we elevate the dollar issues."

Tony Ferruccio of Mactec adds, "Through presenting each other's views, you have the opportunity to find common ground and the mutual recognition of the impact of what you agree on relative to overall project success. With that, you can concentrate on trying to find a compromise if not a solution."

When discussing problems, use terms like "From my perspective ..." or "The way I view this . . ." This phrasing acknowledges that your understanding represents your perspective and allows room for other individuals' perspectives on the situation. Also, express your concerns without placing blame. For example, you might say, "I have a concern: This submittal may be late, which will in turn impact our schedule goal. What should we do?"

TIPS: Be modest and be willing to acknowledge uncertainty.
- Ask "What have I misunderstood?"
- "This is unclear to me."
- "What might I have done differently?"
- "Can you show me where I might have missed something in the specs?"

Striving to seek mutual understanding of what happened and what assumptions people hold behind their assessments can often unlock a seemingly deadlocked issue. Boone Hellmann of the University of California, San Diego, observes, "When hard lines are set, there are invariably some assumptions *behind* those positions. It's important to try to surface these verbally. These can often be very mundane and easily resolved issues. For example, a contractor might really desire more timely payment. For us it might involve what is really a low-cost solution. It's important to talk about and uncover the true drivers, which can often be bollixed up in contract language."

On World Class teams, very little time is spent justifying or defending oneself. Nor is much time spent complaining about or criticizing others. All of these involve a negative, toxic energy that stop a project from moving forward. Likewise, do you enjoy spending time around individuals who do so? Indeed, these behaviors are essentially irrelevant on World Class teams. On WCTs you are not questioning one another's intentions. Yes, you might be sharing different opinions, but the emphasis again is always upon reaching understanding to keep the job moving forward.

2. Declare it quickly and seek to resolve it verbally, face to face, and at the site if possible.

I was recently involved in a dam project with a substantial backlog of unresolved or approved change orders, all well documented by both contractor and owner. At one point a senior manager for the owner said, "Well, I suggest that each side document their understanding and position and then elevate these documents to the next level so that they can resolve them. The issues and disputes on this project are so complex that they need to be written."

Absolutely not! If two parties in the field agree to disagree and the contractor wants to proceed with the work, the contractor might say to the other party, "I'm going to send you a letter, per the contract, indicating that we had this discussion, and I am proceeding at my own risk. OK?" Again, use written correspondence to memorialize a verbal understanding.

Face-to-face dialogue at the site is important. Written correspondence is woefully inadequate at explaining circumstance in a manner that assures clear mutual understanding, such as the need for additional shoring or storm water protection. Include all who might be involved in the decision, such as the owner's estimator.

3. If you cannot agree, verbally agree to disagree and elevate the issue and keep the job, and your mutual respect and common goals, intact and moving.

On the McCarran Airport Terminal 3 project in Las Vegas, a subcontractor said he might feel a little awkward "just going behind someone's back and taking the issue up to the next level of management." Don Wright, Bechtel's Program Manager on the job, put him at ease by telling him to verbally assert to his counterpart, "Hey, we obviously don't see eye to eye on this. How about if we just kick it up to our bosses and let them deal with it and we just move on?" Don adds, "The value of a conflict resolution ladder comes from team players realizing that asking for help is not a sign of weakness but is key to World Class teamwork. They need to know that there will always be a backstop."

The Value and Use of a Conflict Resolution Ladder

A conflict resolution ladder and dispute/issue resolution protocol are almost mandatory. Having them in place and understood makes it OK for lower levels to agree to disagree, keep the job moving, and still trust one another.

It is not unusual to hear project management-level personnel assert that they will be able, or should be able, to resolve *all* conflicts and issues at their level—particularly early on in the honeymoon stage of the project and that therefore there really is no need for a resolution ladder. They believe that to elevate an issue would imply failure or ineptitude on their part. This attitude can inadvertently work against them later in the job when they feel compelled to resolve an issue among themselves which could be more quickly and appropriately resolved at a senior level.

With the understanding that all issues do not need to be resolved at the field level, I have seen mature World Class teams state issue resolution goals along the lines of "95 percent of issues resolved at the Fred, Janice, and Mark level; the remaining 5 percent at the Mike, Terry, and Marilyn level." As one client put it, keeping 5 percent at the management level takes "some of the pressure off the field level to resolve everything."

Some World Class teams specify time frames after which if a level of management or supervision cannot agree, they must elevate it to the next level. This is a good idea with teams new to the notion of agreeing to disagree. On more mature project teams, it may be fine to let each level determine when elevation is necessary. For example, the issue may involve acquiring some data from a third party that might take several days. But even in those circumstances, it is discussed quickly and the time frame for resolution is mutually agreed upon.

As Perry Petersen of Petersen Construction Services adds, "The resolution ladder must have a timetable for each level to ensure that the team does not lose momentum."

Sample Conflict Resolution Ladder

NOTE: This project was the Texas Department of Transportation project with Williams Brothers Construction.

TXDOT	Decide or Elevate within	Williams Brothers
Inspectors	2 hours	Supervisors
Jacob	1 day	Glenn
Kirk/John	1 day	Jesse
John/Duane	1 day	Bob/Randy
Duane/Richard	--	Doug

The worst thing a team can do with a dispute? Do nothing, sit on it and let it fester. Instead, acknowledge it, and kick it up after you've made a good collaborative effort to resolve it. Let it go. Keep the job moving.

Sue Dyer, CEO of the International Partnering Institute, explains: "Confusion always creates chaos. When there is an issue, and the field team disagrees, and they don't know where to take the issue for resolution, they get stuck. It does not take too long for the working relationships to get strained."

Senior management should not be too quick to solve issues for subordinates but at the same time should always be available to intervene if necessary. There is a delicate balance here. As Mike Aparicio, then of the Washington Group, says of his counterpart, Dennis Mori, Project Executive for LA METRO on the Eastside Extension: "Dennis always had his hand on the tiller, albeit sometimes lightly. He was even-keeled, available, and always was open for a pragmatic, practical solution. He had the big picture in mind. We had two issues go to the DRB, and we were able to defuse them with humor."

Here's another creative, positive, and very personal way of resolving issues. Wayne Lindholm with Hensel Phelps has had a long-lasting relationship with Rebekah Gladstone, campus architect for the University of California, Irvine, over several projects. Wayne and Rebekah would have what he termed "Starbucks Breaks" if something was bothering either of them.

> My idea of the successful life is to move from failure to failure with enthusiasm.
> —WINSTON CHURCHILL—

In *How The Mighty Fall*, Jim Collins says of teams on the way up: "Team members argue and debate, not to improve their personal position but to find the best answers to support the overall cause."[25] For teams on the way down, "Team members argue to look smart or to improve their own interests rather than argue to find the best answers to support the overall cause."

Using Alternative Dispute Resolution (ADR) on a World Class Team

Utilizing a third-party resource does not preclude a team from being considered World Class. In fact, teams that do so and continue to trust one another and work collaboratively are what I term very mature WCTs. In other words, they can agree to disagree all the way up to the very top of their internal resolution ladders, involve a third party, still trust one another, and keep moving forward as a team toward common goals.

A note of caution, however. Putting an issue into a third party's hands can be risky. As SANDAG's Jim Linthicum, a professional mediator, says, "It is a gamble that an independent third party will side with them. No third party can fully understand specific project issues as well as you and your counterparts do. You might as well take your money to a casino."

14

WORLD CLASS TEAM BEHAVIOR #10

Initiate and Sustain Continuous Review and Improvement

Continuous improvement is not just a goal; it is a mindset.
It is the belief that you can never be good enough and having the heart
to push yourself to limits that seem impossible to achieve.
—LONNIE MORELOCK, THE KIEWIT COMPANIES—

Business as Usual: Enforced compliance at best. Old stereotypes adhered to and past behaviors repeated.

Good Teams: Just meeting the specs is good enough. Why try any harder? No need for formal review or assessment as a team.

WORLD CLASS TEAMS: Continuous, formal review and improvement of all facets of the project over duration of job that is measured. All team members learn and are able to grow professionally.

On a construction team, the notion of continuous improvement, let alone TQM (Total Quality Management), does not typically carry with it the resonance and impact the term gets in the manufacturing or service sectors. The key challenge is measurement—or the inability to effectively measure team performance. Construction projects are a one-time, relatively short-term process.

Most jobs do measure performance to schedule, outstanding change orders, submittal status, RFIs, and so forth. Contractors can and do measure their efficiencies in terms of man hours associated with the implementation of a process such as concrete pours or activities such as rework. Larry Cochran, Vice President of Kiewit, says, "We are constantly striving to improve our quality programs on every front and, although we have made significant progress, we must always be committed to continuous improvement." For example, Kiewit crews are trained to build work to the project requirements and meet or exceed the owner's expectations, perform work right the first time, and monitor performance against requirements to ensure quality is always improving.[26]

Likewise, owners find the notion of continuous improvement of high potential value but nevertheless elusive. Steve Iselin with the U.S. Navy asks, "NAVFAC executes much of its work in teams. How should/could we go about assessing team performance, and ultimately how can we improve performance at large across the very many NAVFAC teams we have?"

I assert that it can be done, and it is of extraordinary value. Additionally, a project team can adopt a process of continuous team improvement regardless of their chosen project delivery method.

The Value of Continuous Project Team Review and Improvement

In the two years I've had project teams (approximately seventy projects) assess themselves in workshops against my ten best team practices, *never* has a construction team started higher than a 7.1. Only about 4 percent of these teams rated themselves 7.0 (middle of Good) or higher coming into the partnering activity. My point? It is very improbable that a project team will start off a project with World Class teamwork (8.0 or greater). What does this mean? On virtually all projects there is always is an opportunity to improve teamwork not only at the outset of the job but over its full duration.

Captain Mike Williamson of the U.S. Navy says, "Everything that crosses your plate on a construction project is an opportunity to get better. If you do not see every job as an opportunity to improve, both at the outset and over its duration, you are stuck in an old rut."

1. What gets measured gets improved.

It is also relatively rare for a construction project team to ultimately achieve World Class teamwork without mutually agreed-upon standards and a process for continuous improvement and review. As you'll recall from page 12, in my informal survey of project and conference participants, the consensus is that no more than 8 percent of construction projects nationwide ultimately achieve and sustain my definition of World Class teamwork. And this comes from people whose organizations have committed to a formal partnering process.

Bay Bridge - West Bay Approach
San Francisco, CA - 2003 to 2008

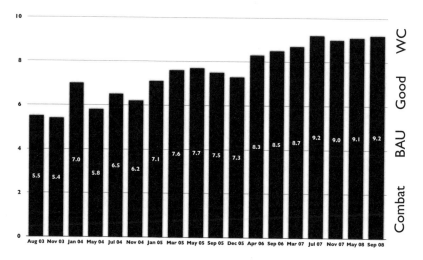

This is a compendium of quarterly survey results of partnering workshop attendees over the five-year duration of the West Bay Approach Project, San Francisco, CA.

It is like expecting that a group of kids, or adults for that matter, who start a pick-up game of football or basketball will immediately work together as a high-performance team. Developing teamwork in any endeavor is like baking a cake: It takes time—but also a recipe or agreed-upon protocol for success. To the extent that a project team truly commits to striving toward clear behavioral and quantitative standards or goals, has a regular and valid means of measuring their performance against those criteria, and establishes meaningful and open understanding and exchange of the data/feedback during this process, they can and will improve their performance.

"Metrics, metrics, metrics," say some consultants, suggesting that quantitative criteria are the answer. "But don't make it too metric," cautions Stephen Sharr of the Los Angeles Unified School District. As one sports commentator put it, "The statistics only tell part of the story." How, for example, do you measure a construction project team's ability to overcome adversity or deal with a totally unpredictable circumstance?

With just hard metrics, "you can end up getting gamed," says Lee Evey, former PENREN Program Manager. "We had a goal at the Pentagon Renovation Program project that said all phone calls needed to be answered within five rings. Well, a contractor went out and hired $5-an-hour kids who just picked up the phone and had no idea of how to handle the caller's request. We subsequently evaluated our contractors subjectively but based on facts and data. We also did monthly reviews of ourselves. For example, how quickly did we pay our contractors?"

In a recent study, the International Partnering Institute (IPI) found that project teams that measure their progress, make adjustments, and hold one another accountable to live up to their commitments tend to improve over time. The study was based on the analysis of thirteen projects over a two-year time period using a standardized survey of construction team effectiveness.[27]

My experience is that on construction projects, a combination of both hard (schedule, safety, etc.) and soft metrics provides the best value. See my sample score sheet on pages 226–228.

2. Rarely, if ever, does a project team get World Class teamwork or their stretch goals completely figured out in the first 60–100 days of a project.

Continuous review and improvement are necessary because it's so rare to get it right in the early innings. This applies both to construction processes such as schedule, expediting change orders, and RFIs and to team behaviors (the ten WCT Behaviors). If a project team has set goals and they get it figured out in the first thirty days or so, they did not set the goals high enough. They did not really challenge themselves, or perhaps favorable circumstances came into play. Either way, the goals need to be reset.

Also, it is not unusual for a job to be underway for six months or so before a team is truly tested. Prior to this, a false sense of security can set in—much as a sports team can assume after a couple of winning games, they've got it all figured out.

I've seen more than a few project teams raise the bar, particularly for schedule completion, a few months into a project when they began to realize their full potential as a World Class team. In other words, "Hey, we have been able to identify and implement some truly outside-the-box ideas that have significantly enhanced our ability to achieve our audacious goal."

3. Different individuals will have different assessments of what is going well and what is not at any one point in time over the duration of the job.

Differing assessments can create fertile ground for misunderstanding, inefficiency, and conflict. You think the submittals are being turned around well, but he thinks otherwise. A process of continuous review and improvement provides the opportunity to mutually agree or, in some cases, respectfully disagree and come to a mutual understanding.

Kathy Mayo with AECOM explains: "The important thing is to have an open conversation around what the team is doing well and not well so that the individuals participating are not threatened." It is useful to have the team focus on measurable goals, processes, or team behaviors. This way the focus is on "our" behavior and not any one individual's behavior.

Construction projects are dynamic human enterprises. As you can see with the West Bay Approach score sheet on page 219, a project team's effectiveness can ebb and flow over the duration of a job. This is not unusual and affords the opportunity for learning. For example, a team might need to ask, "Why did our score for expediting changes drop two points in the past three months?"

4. What may have been seen as significant at the outset of a job may be quite different than what is significant at a later date.

Owner priorities will shift, resource availability will change, and weather will have its unpredictable impact. The focus of the job will change as well. For example, it might evolve from substructure to MEP to finish trades to close-out. Every member of the project team must know exactly where things stand at all times.

Jim Cowell of Caltech notes, "It is important to continually review team performance and goals. Construction projects are of a long duration, and what seemed really important at the beginning of the job is rarely important later on."

Steve van Dyke with McCarthy Building Companies says, "You have to consistently adjust your goals throughout the project because things change due to the dynamics of the job. It's important to keep focused on the overall goal but to 'up the ante' or change a goal as required at different states."

5. People and organizations will continually cycle in and out of your project.

How do you integrate newcomers in a way that quickly assimilates them into a World Class team and maximizes their contribution to the team? For example, a key subcontractor may be there for only a third of the duration of the job. How can they be brought into the team in a way that both supports the team's goals and deals with the subcontractor's priorities and needs?

A periodic review of overall team goals and processes can facilitate the transition of individuals and organizations into your World Class team.

Robert Develle at JPL notes, "As subcontractors come in and come out, it is important to have a process that brings them onto the team. By doing so you keep the team relevant to its current challenges."

On a large transit or airport project lasting four-plus years, it is not unusual to have only 35 percent of the key project personnel who started the job there at its conclusion.

6. It's important to have a day of reckoning as a team.

Individuals and organization stakeholders appreciate the value of an objective assessment of themselves as a team once they've begun to identify as a team, own the game, and are willing to hold themselves 100 percent accountable for everything. Writing down the goals and commitments and having all stakeholders know that they will be holding themselves accountable on ____ date for reviewing their performance gives everyone a sense of focus and mutual accountability.

This should include "putting the moose on the table" if things are really as bad as they may be. But again, the challenge becomes "Given our assessments today, how do we go forward as a team?"

222

> Face reality, then act decisively. Most mistakes that leaders make arise
> from not being willing to face reality and then acting on it. Facing reality
> often means saying and doing things that are not popular, but
> only by coming to grips with reality would things get better.
> —JACK WELCH, FORMER CEO, GENERAL ELECTRIC CORPORATION—

In my experience, WCTs actually look forward to their review sessions much in the same way that a sports team with a commitment to excellence relishes playing challenging opponents. They're an opportunity to test and validate a project team's effectiveness as a team.

7. A review allows senior management to communicate their ongoing commitment to World Class teamwork.

Another value of having a formal process for team performance review and improvement is that it is one of the best tools for senior management to show the team their commitment to World Class teamwork. If senior management is willing to take twenty-five to fifty key project personnel offsite with them for a half-day review workshop once a quarter, the project team gets the message: This is important.

Bob Finney of Caltrans explains, "Review workshops provide the framework for understanding how a team will work together. This is particularly important if team members are new to partnering or are not familiar with each other. When the project team sees senior managers making time for project partnering and talking openly and personally about it, they are motivated to engage each other on a similar basis."

8. Continuous review and improvement are both an attitude and a process.

Dave Mallik of Whiting Turner Construction notes, "There needs to be a process. And while data and metrics are good, sometimes it's just going for a walk together, talking and looking at things. I had a subcontractor tell me that the job was 'killing him.' I said, 'Let's go for a walk.' While looking at his site, I asked him, 'What would maximize your productivity?' and I just listened."

Virgil Curtis of Balfour Beatty adds, "At least once a quarter, semiformally, we sit down at the project level and one level above to mutually review team and project performance."

Refocusing a Challenging Job to Delight Owner

A project can be contractually late and or over budget and still exceed the end user's expectations. How can this be?

Mike Llamas, Vice President of Operations for Ghilotti Brothers, explains: "In the past two weeks I've been involved in two projects which had been substantially delayed by an extremely wet winter and changed conditions. Yet when the teams met to reassess their goals, they modified them to give the ultimate end users what was really important to them *earlier* than what the contract called for. This was accomplished even though our new completion date goal for the overall job went beyond the original contract completion dates. The team achieved this through a candid assessment of where we were as a team; what was really, really important to the ultimate end users; and some innovative, outside-the-box thinking by the whole team." One of these projects was a road rehabilitation for the National Park Service in the Marin Headlands above San Francisco. In the case Mike was referring to, what was really, really important to the end user was access to a specific stretch of one of the roads being rehabilitated.

A similar experience occurred on the Salinas Valley Memorial Hospital project, which was a retrofit/upgrade of an operating hospital. These are about the most challenging project types I know. The team was late due to multiple unforeseen conditions and owner changes. Owners, designers, and contractors were all equally frustrated. So I asked the hospital representative, Michelle Keith, "Given where we are today, what is really, really important to your doctors and staff relative to completion?" She responded, "Getting the operating rooms back in operation with supporting mechanical and electrical equipment by year's end." The team came up with a measurable goal and action plan with the critical involvement of key subcontractors and subconsultants to achieve that critical milestone and keep the client happy.

A cautionary note: Don't make changing or abandoning your team goals too easy, but only do so after careful deliberation by the whole team.

Using the Review Process to Look at the Job from the Subcontractor's Point of View

Here's a different approach to project evaluation: flip it. That's right—look at it from the subcontractor's perspective.

On McCarran International Airport's Terminal 3 project in Las Vegas, the team recognized that although the opinions of the managers, owner, general contractor, construction manager, and designer were significant, what was really important to their ability to meet their aggressive schedule goal was the assessment of their subcontractors. So they started by having the subcontractors assess the team's ability to meet their schedule goal and teamwork.

The team then went about removing obstacles that the subcontractors saw. The result? The subcontractors left with the confidence that the entire team was supporting their ability to successfully build the project. It also reinforced to the subcontractors how critical their performance was to the overall success of the project. They are the ones who ultimately suffer or flourish as a consequence of a World Class team.

But Don Wright with Bechtel didn't stop there. "Based upon our discussion, said Don, we aligned our CM services to assure that we supported subcontractor needs." In doing so, Don was, in effect, positioning his organization to coach the subcontractors—something subcontractors did not normally expect from a construction manager. The lesson? Different perspectives on project performance invariably produce different opportunities for improvement and can revitalize a project team.

AN EXAMPLE OF A TEAM DASHBOARD OR SCORECARD

Review performance against not only project team goals but also the key processes identified as needing to be expedited or figured out relative to meeting the schedule goal. As you'll recall from chapter 6, there are typically no more than a dozen key processes.

The project was a facility for the U.S. Bureau of Reclamation Lower Colorado Region and Whiting Turner Construction as the design-build contractor. The e-mail survey was sent to all project stakeholders (approximately 12) during the months of July, September, and October. The scores represent their collated response which was, in turn, sent back to all stakeholders.

Good to World Class™

September Performance Results

Boulder City Green Building Partnership

1	2	3	4	5	6	7	8	9	10
No Way				Iffy				Dialed In	

	BHAGs or Big, Hairy, Audacious Goals	July	Sep.	Oct.
1	Move in 2 months early or NLT July 17, 2011.	6.7	4.0	4.8
a	Expedited submittals.	5.7	7.9	7.7
b	Expedited design review at 30%, 60%, and 100%.	5.3	7.6	7.3
c	Facilitated quality compliance.	5.7	8.1	8.0
d	Developed BHAG schedule that we're all committed to.	6.7	7.6	7.3
e	Defined scope of work for mods and expedited.		8.1	7.8
2	LEED Platinum. 7.3	7.3	9.1	9.4
3	All physical reconfiguration/modification of building done in-house for 10 years after completion of construction.	7.3	6.9	6.4
4	Zero recordables.	6.8	7.9	7.9

5	Residents involved, informed, excited about new campus & improved main street entrance.	8.0	8.1	8.0
6	Zero rework. Only minor punch items at SC and fixed within 5 days.	6.0	7.3	7.9
7	Project complete at CV + variance mods + maximum 7%.		7.8	7.9
8	No dispute goes to Bev/Meagan or Paul.	6.4	7.9	7.8
9	Wins an award.	6.8	8.3	9.0
10	Zero ARA compliances.		8.0	7.9

- We highlight any score that is below a 4.5, as these are areas that should be discussed with the team and could benefit from some rework, as well as scores 7.5 and higher to draw attention to the strengths within the project.

- Are we expediting the above Key Processes in a manner and with a velocity that supports the achievement of our BHAGs?

- Are these still valid key processes or have we moved past the process?

- Are there new key processes that we should be tracking or monitoring that will support the achievement of the BHAGs?

1	2	3	4	5	6	7	8	9	10
Combat			Business As Usual			Good		World Class	

Boulder City Green Building Team's Working Relationship on a Scale from 1 to 10

Good to World Class™ Team Ratings

See Grid Above

July	8	Good/World Class
September	8.5	World Class
October	8.6	World Class

What World Class behaviors do we do well?

(Group discussion: How does this strength help us as a team? How can we capitalize on it in the future?)

- Organization lines blurred
- Proactive team meetings (2 votes)
- Measurable team goals
- Team owns the game (3 votes)
- Trusted business advisor
- Issues resolved (2 votes)

The team then went on to identify those World Class team behaviors they do well and those, if improved, that would positively impact the success of the project.

What World Class behaviors can we improve on? Where and how and what would be the impact on our goals?

- Team owns the game (2 votes)
- Proactive team meetings (3 votes)
- Issues resolved (2 votes)
- Outside-the-box thinking (2 votes)
- Open, direct verbal communication
- Measurable goals that all commit to
- Organization lines blurred
- Continuous improvement

(Group discussion: How does this behavior hinder our ability to achieve our goals? How can we improve it?)

Using Project Data Effectively to Enhance World Class Teamwork

On Business as Usual teams, survey data gets ignored—if it even exists. On Good teams, it is reviewed with little or no action. So how do World Class teams handle surveys and project metrics?

Project performance data can be just data or a powerful tool for management to use to monitor and actively encourage collaborative improvement. Here's a sample of an e-mail Mike Ghilotti, CEO of Ghilotti Brothers, sent to *all* team members following a monthly project survey:

From Mike to project team,

Excellent work, Team Wilfred!!
Most all of the ratings were up and some significantly. As well as an increase in the percentage of responses. However, let's set a goal of 70% (up from 56%) responses (or purge the list so that only relevant candidates are included). And an average rating of 4.3 (up from 4.05) next survey. We can do it!
Thanks,
Mike Ghilotti

Over the past six years, twelve Ghilotti Brothers projects have ended up as World Class teams. I attribute this to a very strong commitment to nothing less than World Class teamwork from their senior management. Again, what gets measured and what senior management takes an active interest in gets improved. This can be done creatively as the following example from Kiewit illustrates.

Kiewit's Doug Duplisea explains their "Raving Fan" survey: "We send out three surveys. We do one at the beginning to identify what's important to them. We then do one every 3–4 months to see how we're doing against their initial expectations. And then we send one out at the end to ask them if they can honestly say, 'We are a Raving Fan of Kiewit.'"

The above comments and resultant actions by the respective project teams validate the age-old truism that what gets continually measured, actively monitored, and reinforced by senior management invariably gets improved.

Everyone Learns and Is Able to Assume Greater Responsibility on the Next Job

With open, frequent, objective and subjective team review comes the opportunity for learning. Learning is especially enhanced when a team can compare its performance over time. For example, a team might notice that their rating of the submittal process improved from a November score of 7.1 to an 8.4 in January and ask, "What are we doing better as a team with respect to this process?" This does not apply only to junior team members. If a project team is striving toward World Class teamwork and has stretch goals, everyone will come away with something they did not know before.

Keep in mind that generation "Y" or what the *Engineering News Record* refers to as the Millennium generation values freedom and growth and are not afraid to "jump ship" if they are not finding it with their current employer. Professor William W. Badger at Arizona State University states in the article, "The Gen Y people have a different value system and way of communicating."[28] He goes on to state, "They want fewer rules and more freedom."[29]

Some project teams actually set a team goal that as a consequence of achieving their team goals and World Class teamwork, "Everyone would be able to take the next step professionally."

Dennis Mori with LA METRO says, "If you're fortunate to hook up with a World Class team early in your career, it becomes a confidence builder and makes you want to set the bar higher for yourself on future projects."

The Importance of Celebrating Team Success

With continuous improvement and learning comes the opportunity for acknowledgment, celebration, and joint social events. It's important to reward and celebrate *team* success—and not just that of your own organization. When a project team first achieves World Class status, hits a major milestone, or overcomes a major obstacle, host a barbecue, take them to a ball game, or bring in a keg of beer on Friday.

Jeff Lage of Skanska observes, "On a World Class team, you cannot get them together enough. They truly enjoy one another's company."

My favorite example is the Federal Correctional Institution project in Victorville, California. With all due respect to the good citizens of Victorville, there was not a lot to do out there on the fringe of the Mojave Desert. So the team took things into their own hands. Their list of social activities outdid the event calendar on a respectable cruise ship. They had a weekly golf game, Friday night beer bust, safety barbecues, Wednesday night spaghetti dinners, off-road truck rallies, a bowling league, Monday night football get-togethers, and more. To what extent these activities contributed to the team winning a Marvin Black Award in 2005 is hard to say. But I do not believe they hurt.

On the subject of award fees, it has been validated that trust-based awards and fees result in better performance than purely quantitative fees. See Lee Evey's comments on page 138. Why? Quantitative awards based upon measurable results lead to a minimum-to-get-by attitude and the fear that you can get gamed. They rarely reflect and can often obscure the owner's real intent. Trust-based award fees, on the other hand, because they are not easily measurable, often result in the contractor making an extra effort to ensure an award.

Perry Dealy, CEO of Dealy Development, shares an example of celebration: "Upon the successful completion of the San Diego Grand Hyatt's second tower, the owner, Doug Manchester, had a plaque placed conspicuously in the hotel lobby with names of each of the project stakeholders on it." When I visit San Diego, even if I'm not staying at the Hyatt, I'll often take my guests and friends over to the Hyatt to show them the Ventura Consulting Group's name on the plaque!

We at Ventura Consulting have since 2009 hosted barbecues on site for project partners once they realize the 8.0 World Class threshold. Another idea—where you have multiple projects that report to a single owner, contractor, or CM, consolidate the monthly surveys and workshop results to that individual to provide comparative data on their projects. This works if you are utilizing a common standard of measurement, such as the ten WCT behaviors or something similar. This process has the effect of institutionalizing the World Class team process and language throughout the organization and providing senior management with means of evaluating teamwork. See Steve Iselin, Executive Director of NAVFAC's, comment on page 11.

The rule? If the team is winning and functioning as a World Class team, they will enjoy almost any activity that allows them to socialize together. That's right—you cannot have too many barbecues.

Be Willing to Periodically Review and Revise Your Metrics, Your Criteria, and the Review Process

As the job changes, the team should ask themselves, "Do we have a process in place on a go-forward basis that will accurately and meaningfully measure our success?" I've seen some World Class teams come together every two weeks on super-critical jobs involving intense coordination and unpredictability, where the team needed to involve every player. On other jobs, they may elect to utilize survey data monthly and conduct review sessions every four to five months once they've achieved World Class teamwork.

Jack Shewmaker with Granite Construction says, "We're metric'd out as a society. A World Class team needs to be constantly asking themselves, 'Do our metrics and criteria provide value and enable us to learn and progress towards our goals?'"

Continuous Review as an Integral Part of a World Class Team

As we have seen in this chapter, there is significant value in a meaningful process for continuous team review and improvement. Once the team has established their goals, ask them how and when they would like to be measured. If a project team truly owns the game, they will welcome coming up with a meaningful review process.

Continuous improvement is just that. Regardless of where you are, how well you are doing and have done on a project, and the project delivery model you are executing, there is always an opportunity for improvement. It is, as are all change processes, both an attitude and a explicit process.

Lessons Learned from a World Class Team

Jet Propulsion Laboratory Flight Projects Center

To give you the idea of the scope of what can be learned on a World Class team, here are the results of a "lessons learned" workshop on NASA's Jet Propulsion Laboratory's Flight Projects Center project in Pasadena, California, with Swinerton Builders, LPA Architects, and Vanir Construction Management. They won a Marvin Black "Special Recognition" Award in 2010 for partnering excellence. This is in their own words of what they believed they did well relative to the key processes and goals on that job.

Access/laydown areas:

- Being creative and flexible
- Team effort
- Subs understanding parameters
- Started process early and asked for it
- Open communication

Expedited submittals:

- Good, open communication between design team and subcontractors from the get-go
- At weekly meeting, the general contractor identified what was "hot."
- Resolution during the review process

Developed a partnership schedule for our stretch schedule goal that we all committed to and contributed to:

- Collaborative effort on schedule development
- Subcontractors' honesty to the general contractor
- Schedule = high-priority agenda item in weekly progress meetings
- Did not use schedule as a weapon—rather as a proactive team tool

Expedited Request for Information = RFIs:

- If subs had a question, Swinerton put in a suggested solution with RFI.
- Implementation of web-based program
- Discussed and resolved in field
- As much as applicable, they are written as confirming RFIs following the initial review and discussion amongst the project team.
- Well written, clear RFIs
- Did not abuse the process—they were genuinely necessary

Facilitated personnel access (Note: this was a high-security facility):

- Swinerton limited who has privileges to access site = one vehicle per trade in contract
- Was in bid documents
- Created a model

Expedited inspections:

- Subs signed inspection request form
- Swinerton holding subs to task
- Had a defined process as a team
- JPL inspectors accessible and available for questions in field
- Willingness of JPL to change inspection protocol
- Co-existed

Expedited change orders:

- Subs willing to proceed with work without a signed change order
- Expedited the change order review process as a team = mutually and verbally agreed on scope/time impact prior to developing independent written estimates
- Willingness to give and take if close
- Subs can talk to construction manager directly to clarify.

Expedited procurement:

- Awareness of lead times
- Prioritizing submittals and their review
- Early submission
- Monitored status weekly

Expedited commissioning, testing, and early start-up:

- Commissioning start-up status begun early as a team and documented weekly
- If an issue arose, we addressed it immediately and within 24 hours.
- Started early with time to react to problems
- Maintenance staff involved early in process
- Did weekly walk-throughs as team

Cost goal = Project complete at contract value + maximum of 7½% additive change orders minus 1% deductive changes = net 6.5% cost to owner excluding soils remediation costs:

- Owner willingness up front to acknowledge changes

Safety goal = Zero recordables/zero incident rate on a go-forward basis:

- Inclusion of safety personnel in meetings and early

- Swinerton quick to react to and address issues

- High staff awareness at all times

- Safety embedded across the board

- Upper management commitment

- JPL set criteria in the bid documents for EMR of less than 1%

Quality goal = Zero rework. Zero punch list at substantial completion:

- Early identification

- Making QC known every week by QC foremen that "right the first time" is expected

- Joint walk-through with A/E + written A/E site report

- Swinerton Builders checking in field

LEED goal = LEED Gold:

- Design team implemented design strategies to ensure LEED Gold Certification

- Commitment and buy-in to LEED Gold by the entire project team

- Follow through on our commitments

- Helpful and competent LEED consultant

- Active participation by Swinerton Builders to get stuff done up front

Third-party impact goal = Zero unplanned business interruptions to the Jet Propulsion Laboratories operations during construction:

- JPL involved and aware of project status and upcoming activities
- Both JPL and Swinerton identified needs and made adjustments.

Conflict resolution goal = 90% of issues resolved at the Pat, Sam, Tony, Craig, and Scott level. No claims:

- Agreed to agree to disagree and elevate issues and keep job moving
- No ulterior motives/intentions
- Honored our word
- Professional
- Open communication of potential issues early and verbally

What worked in moving from Good to World Class teamwork on this project?

- Open communication
- Facilitated communication
- Honest communication
- Continuity of personnel
- Neutral, fair, and good outside facilitator

What could have been improved in the teamwork process?

- Involved other entities sooner/more proactively in partnering sessions
- Included field trade superintendents in partnering workshops
- More social get-togethers (BBQs, etc.)
- More offsite field trips

What experiences are each of us taking away from this project?

- Good safety
- Great teamwork

PART THREE

Special Cases

15 Fix the Problem Project with Immediate, Positive, and Sustained Results

Business as Usual Teams: Argue, case build, tennis, and escalate while the job stops.

Good Teams: Tolerate it = do nothing, put it off, while case building to bring out issues at conclusion of job.

World Class Teams: Declare the conflict or issue verbally without blame; hit the reset button; and start over on the basis of common goals, teamwork, and personal commitments.

We've all been there. Projects that began with good intentions by all and still went south. What do you do when a team is stuck in Business as Usual, let alone Combat? What works?

Have the team hit their project reset button. You don't have one? Create one. On a construction project, you cannot just walk away from the other party as you can when trust is lost in many commercial relationships. You have an obligation—often contractual—to continue and complete the project.

But prior to even considering a reset button, project stakeholders need to see where they have a choice on a go-forward basis. If there's one thing I've learned, it is that you cannot mandate or force change. You can, however, give project team choices that they can consider as a team. "As a team" is important. Most individual stakeholders on a problem project do not view themselves as having a choice as a team. Nor, for that matter, do they even consider themselves a team. On a problem project, behavior and decisions are invariably unilateral and not collaborative.

Give the Project Team Three Choices

When a project becomes a problem, offer the team three choices: argue, do nothing, or reset.

Choice #1: Argue about who's right or wrong about why this project and team are screwed up and who's to blame.

They reject this quickly. All stakeholders will, albeit reluctantly, concede that each of the other stakeholders has a lot of evidence, at least in their own minds, to argue their case. The end result of these debates would be at best a reinforcement of each stakeholder's original convictions. Case closed.

Some project stakeholders insist that if we "understood the root causes" of our disagreement, as one owner put it, that would help us resolve it. That might not hurt, but it would take a lot of time, and mutual understanding of what happened in the past—even if it were to occur—offers no guarantee of future success.

Brian Cahill of Barnhart Balfour Beatty comments, "I do not want to hear about anything that happened in the past. I want to talk about how do we get from where we are today to where we need to be. Box the history in a lockbox and set it aside. When a team is not working well and there's a lot of bitching and crying, they've got to realize there's nothing they can do about the past. Isolate it and move on."

Choice #2: Do nothing—let it ride.

Of course, I do not literally mean do nothing at all, but rather let the status quo play itself out. Extrapolate the current game by having the team actually project and quantify their expectations.

> Another one of the few absolutes in construction: If you ever want to get an adversarial team to agree on something, ask them what would be the consequences of continuing to be adversarial.

Almost invariably, they agree that it would certainly not get any better and that there's a better than 50/50 chance that it will get worse. Then have them talk about the *personal* consequences of a job continuing to be

Business as Usual or Combat. I'll bet the word *stress* comes out in one form or another from virtually everyone.

On a problem project, there's a strong, compelling tendency to respond reactively and reflexively to your counterpart's actions or words. In these circumstances, our survival instinct can take over and actually hasten the spiral of decline. For example, you get a letter from a fellow team member stating you are to blame for a faulty installation. Your instinctive reaction is to respond in kind—with a letter asserting your innocence and that the blame lies elsewhere.

The appeal of a major fine against the contractor in a large public works project in southern California is just now coming to trial over *fourteen years* after the project was supposedly completed. Now who would enjoy that experience? As we've noted, once a job is in a Combat or Business as Usual mode, this mode becomes self-perpetuating and self-fulfilling and infects any and all. Everyone is in the CYA mode and hunkering down in their foxholes.

Somewhat paradoxically, without being given a choice, many people accept Choice #2 as tolerable. Why? "Hey, the job will eventually get built. Yeah, it's no fun, but the outcome is predictable even though it may not be desirable. And I don't have to change my behavior. I can deal with it, and this too shall eventually pass." It's important here for the change agent to keep in mind that everyone is afraid of something when it comes to change, even if what they've got is not very satisfying.

Choice #3: Hit the project reset button.

To reset a project, all the team members must agree to set aside all of their baggage, stories, reasons, and assessments of one another—in other words, wipe the board clean. Next, and quickly, create a common set of goals for the balance of the project—from this day forward—that would equate to an extraordinary success and could *only* be accomplished through World Class teamwork. Then create a very specific way of working together toward those goals based upon teamwork and backed up by specific individual commitments to action, grounded in trust and personal integrity.

This last bit is important. In other words, each of you is no longer going to be relating to your counterpart on the basis of past experience, but now you are going to be relating to one another on the basis of common goals and personal commitments for future action that you make together here today.

Richard Welsh with the Bureau of Reclamation says, "The third option is definitely the way to get a project back on track, and senior management must definitely take the leadership in making that choice and executing it with their counterparts."

Guess what? I have *rarely* seen a team reject the third choice. Most construction professionals are intelligent enough to perceive the utter bankruptcy and futility of the first two choices, yet at some point, the costs and benefits of this choice need to be considered. It involves hard work, effort, time, and commitment from all stakeholders—including those who may believe they are the victims. Jim Cowell of Caltech explains: "When you have a problem job, you have to decide if the juice is worth the squeeze. If you're halfway done, it may take more energy than it's worth to resolve the disagreement. The best solution? Partner early and often."

Then begin setting goals and get the team quickly into action toward those goals with personal commitments. Avoid too much debate about why it can't work.

> Doubt can only be removed by action.
> —JOHANN WOLFGANG VON GOETHE—

In his bestselling book *The Tipping Point*, Malcolm Gladwell suggests that little changes can have big effects. When small numbers of people start behaving differently, that behavior can ripple outward until a critical mass or tipping point is reached, changing the world—or in this case, the project.

Do not tolerate any talking about the past. Emphasize that this is a strictly go-forward process from today. You are not interested in what did or did not happen in the past. That is history, and it makes no difference if everyone collectively agrees to let it go. Sometimes I've been told that I am quite ruthless in stopping individuals from going backward and telling stories from the past. But they soon get the message and once individuals begin to engage with one another on the basis of future commitments, that too becomes self sustaining.

Paradoxically, the more adversarial the team, the easier it is to effect an immediate, positive, and sustained shift in teamwork. I could not figure this out for a while until a veteran construction professional told me, "Jim, if the job is just in Business as Usual, there's no real pain. But if the job is in the full-on Combat mode, everyone is hurtin' and sufferin', and and we're all looking for a way out without being the first to drop our shield or give in."

What is the prerequisite for project resetting to succeed? Senior management of all the major stakeholders must, by both words and deed, be committed to going forward on the basis of common goals, teamwork, and trust. And they must be willing to articulate this powerfully and consistently to the team.

What do you do about past disputes, open issues, and claims or potential claims? Have the team agree to set them aside for the day. Put them on a separate track or the lockbox, as Brian Cahill calls it. At the end of the day, once a team that has established that they truly can work together, it is not uncommon for them to be willing and able to revisit and resolve some of the old issues with a fresh perspective, trust, and resolve.

TIP: Never start by dealing with past issues first. This will quickly polarize the team and mire them in finger-pointing and arguing about "who shot John."

Can Lost Trust Be Restored?

Once trust is lost on a project, can it be restored? As we know, trust takes time to be earned. The best way to sustain trust is never to violate it. In today's, and likely tomorrow's, best-value construction climate, all project stakeholders have much more at stake in sustaining an organizational reputation for trust and integrity.

Wayne Lindholm at Hensel Phelps relies on having his people meet monthly among themselves to ensure that they agree on their data, which they then are willing share on no less than a monthly basis with their owner.

Taking the initiative in keeping one another mutually informed on project status with hard data and face-to-face meetings around that data is a good strategy to ensure that you are committed to preventing misunderstanding and ultimately distrust.

As we have seen, World Class teams can work through misunderstandings, different interpretations, mistakes, and even incompetence. As Jim Linthicum of SANDAG says, "There is always more than one engineering solution to a problem." World Class teams also acknowledge that distrust can occur even when individuals' behaviors are well intended. What separates World Class teams from Good teams is how they deal with the perception of lost trust. World Class teams confront it verbally, with the individual assuming it is a misunderstanding, oversight, or mistake, and they put the issue on the table to seek mutual understanding. Good teams continue to speculate on one another's intentions and case-build just in case. On Business as Usual projects, they are reasonably sure of one another's intentions and play games, case-build, and play tennis for the inevitable day of reckoning at the end of the job.

But how about projects characterized by deceit, overt misrepresentation, and not being true to one's word? Jack Shewmaker of Granite comments, "If the issue is a loss of business trust—which is to say a misunderstanding, different interpretation, forgetfulness, or unintentional lack of performance— the trust can be recovered, assuming it does not happen again. But if the loss of trust involves personal trust, then it may be a showstopper."

John Jansen of Kiewit agrees: "If trust is lost, sometimes I can help mediate or facilitate reestablishing it by rolling up my sleeves and helping them work collaboratively. But this also takes a mutual effort by my fellow stakeholders' senior managers. If senior management from all the major stakeholders are not willing to commit to this, then it probably will not work."

Issam Khalaf of Jacobs adds: "Senior managers set the tone to build trust and the confidence of team members. Once confidence is lost, it is incumbent upon senior management to step in and lead by example."

There may be situations on projects where the hurt or damage is so deep that nothing can repair the lost trust. If this exists at lower levels of the project team, senior management can intervene and mutually agree to remove the individual(s) involved and/or manage the issue. But what if the issue involves senior management?

Stephen M.R. Covey writes in *The Speed of Trust*: "Through my work, community service, and personal and family life over the past 20 years, I have seen enough to convince me that on every level—societal, market, organizational, relationship and personal—people often have the ability to restore at least some measure of trust when they have lost it . . . *if* they are really serious about doing it."[30]

So what does it take to get really serious about trust on a construction project? It starts with acknowledging that restoring lost institutional trust on a construction project is *nothing less* than a senior management responsibility, challenge, or even opportunity. Perspective and context are important here. What is it that you and your fellow stakeholders have a stake in being able to resolve or not resolve this issue in the longer term and big picture? Rarely does just one perceived instance of individual mistrust warrant a complete breakdown of institutional trust. Remember the old adage: "You may win the battle [on this dispute], but lose the war [on the overall project, long-term business success, and your reputation]."

Seeking mutual understanding about what actually happened and how the loss of trust may have occurred is a good first step. Doing this without attaching blame, making assumptions about intentions, or getting emotional is challenging. It also requires being willing to acknowledge that in many circumstances, the data/facts are unclear and that even you might be uncertain.

TIPS

- Be willing to acknowledge uncertainty. Doing so makes yourself vulnerable and leaves open the very real possibility of compromise.

- Be modest/humble: "Is there something here we/I may have done wrong?"

- Ask the others for help: "Could you explain to me how you saw this situation?"

- Make concessions only if they are for clear, measurable, and mutually agreed-upon losses that the other stakeholder may have suffered due to your nonperformance or errors.

- Above all, avoid trying to just appease the other project stakeholder through just making concessions. I call this the "buying yourself out" game. This often just merely masks the real conflict and does not get at the fundamental issue of reestablishing trust. It also sets up the precedent that it may well happen again "if you get caught."

Mike Scott of Parsons Brinckerhoff says, "On a World Class team, I'm willing to acknowledge that I might have returned that submittal sooner and even apologize. On a Business as Usual team, let alone Combat, neither of us is willing to admit to any wrongdoing whatsoever. And if you want to talk, they tell you to 'pound sand.'"

Sharing on a personal basis what is truly important to you about this job being successful is another way of reestablishing trust.

On most projects, the only way senior managers will *really* know one another and establish genuine trust is through how they deal with adversity. Trust, like perceived risk, is really a very personal thing, and although we extrapolate it to organizations, nations, and institutions, it basically comes down to you and me.

Unfortunately there will always be those who view construction as one giant conspiracy. This belief puts them in a constant defensive mode and precludes the possibility of Good, let alone World Class, teamwork. If this is truly the attitude of senior management, then all hope for World Class teamwork is lost. Better to acknowledge it early as a team, accept Business as Usual as the inevitable outcome, and take necessary measures to protect your self-interests. Again, there are plenty of third-party resources who can help mediate, arbitrate, or facilitate the resolution of unresolved disputes.

The Imperative of Senior Management Commitment to Change

Changing and, what is often more challenging, sustaining the change in mindsets on a problem project is hard, demanding work requiring vulnerability, commitment, and perseverance. Letting go of the old baggage is the first step. The next step of moving on can be helped if there is a high standard of behavioral excellence which senior management of all major stakeholders is committed to adhere to. Our set of World Class team behaviors offers such a standard.

To end this chapter on a positive note, let us not forget forgiveness. Mahatma Ghandi said, "The weak can never forgive. Forgiveness is the attribute of the strong."

16 Employ World Class Teamwork on the Larger, Complex Project and Program

In the winter of 2010–11, McCarran International Airport's Terminal 3 (Las Vegas) at $1.4 billion contract value was generally acknowledged to be the largest public construction contract in the United States. It involved the construction of a new, major terminal coordinated with parking and major landside improvements. It impacted a major operating airport, involved dozens of trades, required the coordination with multiple concurrent projects, had high-level interface with the city of Las Vegas and the FAA, and had high public visibility. In other words, it was a potentially fertile ground for misunderstanding, lack of coordination, and conflict.

How does a World Class team deal with these challenges? How do you quickly establish and sustain a high-performance team in these circumstances? We'll examine five major challenges of large, complex projects and programs:

- Greater risk
- Greater visibility
- More and more vocal stakeholders
- Longer duration = how do you sustain continuity?
- Larger, more complex organizations

Greater Risk

There is obviously more at risk in all domains—financial, political, social, and personal. A major risk to all stakeholders is the cost of delay, let alone work stoppage. As we have seen, with increased risk comes pressure to defend/transfer risk; this activity can consume a lot of time.

Mike Aparicio with Skanska explains: "On a larger design-build transit job, speed of delivery is the single most important thing you have to achieve. On larger ($500 million-plus) jobs, the fixed cost of our time is enormous and on the order of $3–4 million a month. They have to be productive, and the best way to be productive is through teamwork. Jobs are getting bigger and far more complex as we rebuild our infrastructure. If you fail to nurture and build a World Class team on these jobs, you seriously risk and jeopardize your financial position as a contractor."

Greater Visibility

The larger, complex job—especially in the public sector—is invariably under constant public and media scrutiny. With greater visibility can come pressure to defer decisions and play lots of tennis, with the consequence that the job gets stalled or stopped.

The Pentagon renovation initiated in the late nineties was a $2 billion-plus multiproject program with its own organization, PENREN. It was further challenged by the 9/11 catastrophe, which occurred roughly a third of the way into construction. Lee Evey, former Pentagon Renovation Program Director, says, "If I flubbed up, it could ruin my whole career and that of a lot of other people. We were under twenty-four-hour congressional surveillance."

More and More Vocal Stakeholders

As one participant in a large transit project put it, "We had a cast of thousands on my project." When Caltrans began its Toll Bridge Rebuilding and Retrofit program back at the turn of the century, they held a separate orientation session for all the organizations who had something to say about the San Francisco Bay. Environmentalism is big business in San Francisco. Over seventy-five people from twenty-five organizations attended, including the Coast Guard, the Army Corps of Engineers, Federal Fish and Wildlife Service, the Save the Bay Association, California Fish and Game, the state Coastal Commission, local utilities, and so forth. Bob Finney of Caltrans advises, "On our larger jobs, the team needs to find ways and people in their organizations and those of the other project stakeholders to keep the job moving."

Michael Abeln with the U.S. Army Corps of Engineers in Mobile says, "On our $268 million SOUTHCOM headquarters project in Miami, having World Class teamwork is so much more important because there are so many moving parts. And we had a four-star general watching us every step of the way."

Here's an interesting take from Mike Kerchner, Tutor Perini Corporation's Project Executive on McCarran Terminal 3: "Aside from the dollar value of the work, this project is really not that much more challenging than a $50 or $100 million project; there is simply more of it. The uniqueness of McCarran as in any major terminal is the inclusion of miles of conveyors and equipment supporting the baggage handling system. What is important on these projects is developing a plan and a strategy prior to the work and implementing it. You need to include your key supervision, subcontractors, designers, owners, and CMs from the very beginning to enlist their support. The administrative requirements of working with an active facility and dealing with the countless requirements of the agencies can be burdensome. We have a staff of 50-plus people handling required documentation that involves literally hundreds of others. All these individuals contribute to and benefit from our World Class teamwork."

Longer Duration

McCarran Terminal 3 has a team goal of finishing six months early, with an overall duration of three-and-a-half years. Transit projects in particular are not infrequently of four to five years duration. This lengthy duration manifests itself in several ways. First, there are challenges associated with scheduling and coordination over the span of the project. How do you keep the team focused on the end game throughout the project? Second, these jobs can involve discrete phases of construction wherein different players are involved. Third, there is the issue of turnover of project personnel. How do you sustain relationships when at the end of a four-year project you have maybe 35 percent of the original cast?

Patrick Peterson of McCarthy Building Companies says, "The value of having a World Class team is a long-term positive relationship which, in turn, gives us a platform to work through increasingly larger, long-duration, complicated projects involving ongoing changes. World Class teamwork enables a flexibility within the project team and establishes the environment to complete these jobs and make the right decision for the job and not the individual or organization at the time."

And yet the lengthy duration of the larger, complex job can be an asset if the team practices continuous improvement. Thomas Fodor, Project Manager, Granite Construction, explains: "Long-duration jobs give the team the opportunity to build confidence through previous accomplishments. This, in turn, leads to greater trust and confidence, which can enable a team to take on greater challenges."

Larger, More Complex Organizations

As one experienced contractor told me, "The team-building process frankly had more value in getting the various owner functions and departments working together than it did in getting us working with the owner." Owners' organizations can appear multi-headed and self-contradictory even to individuals within them. Contract administration, project management, and the ultimate end user are often intentionally set up as countervailing departments within a public entity. How does a contractor or design-build team work collaboratively with organizations that do not collaborate with one another and often have decidedly contradictory expectations about the project?

Large airport terminal projects, for example, involve the airport's project management organization, maybe a third-party program/project CM, airport operations, the airlines, concessionaires, the FAA, airport security/TSA, and so forth.

Having an Internal Coach and Being a Trusted Business Advisor

These two reciprocal behaviors are even more imperative on the larger, complex job. As mentioned in chapter 4, how else do you navigate through muddy waters where the organization chart and formal decision-making hierarchy bear no relationship to reality?

Paul Ligocki of Hensel Phelps explains: "On these jobs you almost always have to identify a champion or coach within the owner's organization who is dedicated and motivated to help you navigate. Then you have to find out what they really want and how to best get it for them."

TIP: As a contractor/design-build team leader, get a coach or, better yet, multiple coaches. Recall that a coach is an individual who shares a common purpose with you and a bond of mutual trust or, to use my term from chapter 3, who views you as a trusted business advisor.

TIP: As an owner or CM, once you've established common goals, let your contractor or design-build team counterpart know that you'd welcome being a coach.

Having a coach who is committed to helping you and the project suc-ceed enables you not only to understand the decision-making process but also to expedite timely decisions through that process.

The Increased Utilization of Joint Ventures and Teaming on Large, Complex Jobs

Whether they are design-build or just a joint venture to ensure surety cov-erage or combined construction expertise and sufficient resources, large jobs are increasingly joint ventures. What is the opportunity as well as challenge of these jobs? Creating a World Class joint venture team that is aligned and that truly capitalizes on the resources and capabilities of all team members. Perhaps even more fundamentally, leading construction and design firms value the creation of an organization culture that makes their organization attractive on the basis of its collaborative skills to poten-tial JV or design-build partners. Yes, it's a bit of a beauty contest out there, and firms that have proven ability to work together with other firms have a distinct business and competitive edge.

Len Vetrone of Webcor Builders explains: "Who do we want to team up with? It is firms we have had positive relationships with. This creates an extraordinary opportunity to collaborate."

The Imperative of Executive Commitment and Sustained Involvement

World Class teamwork on larger, complex projects mandates executive involvement and participation from the get-go through project comple-tion. All too often, however, the initial get-together of senior management on larger jobs is limited to the unspoken purpose of establishing personal relationships. I do not argue with the value of these conversations, but it should not end there.

On World Class teams, senior management needs to be able to ask and confront hard questions and "what if's?" relative to risk and potential conflicts. They also need to be able to press for specific commitments from their peers relative to how they will work together to prevent or, if not, mitigate these risks and conflicts.

On the LA METRO's Eastside Extension, a $900 million project, the executive team included the General Manager of LA METRO and the CEO of the joint venture—Washington Group/Obayashi. They met in a facilitated three-hour session every three months over the duration of the project to mutually assess project progress against the team goals, identify potential risks, and communicate the commitment of both senior executives to a collaborative process. Dennis Mori, Project Executive for LA METRO, explains: "Once the design-build contract was awarded, there was no guarantee we would get what we wanted, so we needed clear, ongoing communication at the executive level."

On McCarran International Airport Terminal 3 (Las Vegas), Tutor-Perini Corporation CEO Ron Tutor, Bechtel Program Manager Don Wright, PGAL Architect's CEO Ken Brown, McCarran International Airport Director Randy Walker, and other senior executives met in a 2½-hour session at the outset of the project with their top managers. It is important in these sessions to openly ask some hard questions of one another—such as the ten tough questions listed in the sidebar—and reach a mutual and very personal understanding on those.

Summary

The larger, complex job can be truly a showcase for World Class teamwork. Organizations—public and private—who develop the skills to manage these well reap the rewards of repeat business with individuals and teams they have succeeded with in the past. These relationships make navigating through the larger, complex project infinitely more successful, rewarding, and personally satisfying.

The Ten Tough Questions Business as Usual Project Executives Do Not Ask One Another at the Outset of a Project

Business as Usual project executives don't ask these questions . . . but World Class teams do.

1. What do each of us see as the major risks on this project? What is their potential impact to each of us?

2. What can we and our organizations do to either prevent them or mitigate that impact?

3. What does an extraordinary success on this project look like to each of us? What is really important to each of us? What do each of us personally have at stake in this success?

4. How should we deal with instances where one of us perceives the other's organization (or an individual) as not being a team player or as acting without integrity?

5. What can each of us (the two CEOs) do to promote and sustain a collaborative relationship between our organizations on this job?

6. How will each of us jointly monitor and assess project success over the course of the job?

7. What does our conflict resolution ladder look like—and when and how might we be involved in it? What if we executives agree to disagree? What third-party resolution process would we employ?

8. Which key third-party stakeholders should be involved in the team-building and partnering process? What can either or both of us do to ensure their participation and the support of their organizations?

9. In what areas would it make little or no difference if performance were not extraordinary?

10. What happens if one of us leaves the project?

17 The Role of Senior Management on World Class Teams

As we've noted, World Class teams call for and, at the same time, bring forth different kinds of behaviors from management relative to Good or Business as Usual teams. Consider that a true World Class team is energized by the shared commitment and mutual accountability of its team members more than by its senior managers. Senior management, to be sure, creates the opportunity for team members to express this commitment and the opening for mutual accountability. They are enablers, visionaries, and coaches as opposed to traditional directors and motivators, let alone controllers. In this chapter, we'll explore six ways they can be the former.

Establish and Reinforce Their Personal Commitment to World Class Teamwork

We explored this idea in chapter 8 on risk. The best way senior management can begin this is by acknowledging vulnerability and being willing to be transparent and open. This sets the stage for subordinates to be trusting and collaborative with one another.

Stephen Sharr of LAUSD explains: "It is important that they see management leading by example and from the front. Demonstrating or modeling congruency in my/our trusted behaviors with my counterparts and the other project stakeholders is vital to developing World Class teamwork."

Dave Cavecche of Suffolk Construction Company adds, "It starts at the top. If senior management is not vested in World Class teamwork, people at the project level will get mixed messages. I first have to be committed and to demonstrate this in a way that people can see, which, at the very least, involves me checking in and seeing how things are progressing. I'll also cherry-pick an issue out of one of the meetings now and then and look to see if there's something I can contribute. I'll say, 'I'll take care of that.'"

Keep the Team Focused on the Big Picture and the End Game

This is imperative when the field level is knee-deep in the mud or wrapped up around a minor, albeit potentially divisive, problem or challenge.

Captain Mike Williamson of the U.S. Navy describes the executive's role: "Communicating the commander's intent of what we are trying to do. This needs to be done early. Also, my being available to nurture the team and, at the same time, allowing the team to take its own form. And, if someone or something is off track, to help set it right."

Don Eng of the City and County of San Francisco says, "On World Class teams, less oversight than usual is required. On these jobs I have a confidence level that we have a proven method of solving problems and moving on. Also, I find myself on the sidelines encouraging the staff to act in support of the overall team goals and to try to make decisions at the lowest level as a team and come to me only if necessary."

Encourage Collaborative Solutions and Recommendations

When one or more of your players comes to you with an issue, dispute, or challenge, ask, "Have you checked in with your teammates on this?" or "Can you get back to me with some options that the team at the field level recommends?"

Reinforce the importance of a team or collaborative approach to specific problems and opportunities. Senior managers who are committed to World Class teamwork challenge the project team as a team. For example, you might ask, "Is this issue something that a joint task team might look into?" or "What if the subconsultant, project architect, our superintendent, and owner's rep met to resolve this?"

Jack Shewmaker of Granite Construction says, "My role is best being an advocate for a collaborative process. I do this by providing support and encouragement. Also by trying to get my team to understand why the other side is saying what they're saying. For example, 'Did you think of it this way?' The devil's advocate, so to speak."

Kathy Mayo with AECOM adds, "World Class teamwork has to be filtered from the organization's culture. There cannot just be lip service. I try to work with my people who are preoccupied with the owner's problems and put them in the other person's shoes rather than have them fighting it. And above all, let them know that they should not take it personally."

Give the Project Team the Ability and Freedom to Truly Own the Game

This can involve walking a narrow line. At what point or on what type of issues should senior management intervene with a project team? When is doing nothing perhaps the best approach? Recall our discussion in chapter 9 about enabling the team to own the game. Owning the game can also mean reinforcing or reminding the team that utilizing their conflict resolution ladder does not mean they no longer own the game.

Experienced World Class team senior managers err on the side of not intervening too quickly, even with a highly charged, emotional dispute. Intervening can breed a dependence upon senior management which can contravene an owning-the-game mentality at the field level. Let them have at it, make mistakes, even fail and agree to disagree. If they're reminded of their common goals, in the vast majority of instances they'll reach resolution or agree, perhaps with some nudging by senior management, to elevate the issue.

Leadership: seeing possibility where there is none.

Don Wright with Bechtel says: "Senior management sets the boundaries and gives the team the freedom to work within those boundaries. Even with those perceived limitations, issues can always be escalated and resolved."

Bob Finney of Caltrans cautions, "Don't screw up things that are working. Let the good guys and ladies run. Let them do their own thing."

Wayne Lindholm of Hensel Phelps says, "My job is growing and selecting project managers who can get the job done and then letting them run with it. I try to get stuff out of their way that may keep them from being successful, but they also genuinely need to feel that they own the game. But we do encourage them to ask for help and emphasize that is not a sign of weakness or inability. It is still their project."

Betsey Dougherty of Dougherty + Dougherty Architects adds: "I try to help our new generation take full advantage of the opportunity World Class teamwork affords. They don't have the baggage that some of us still carry and will seize it (opportunity) once they realize the critical role they are playing as a team player on a project. My advice to interns is to learn from their mistakes and, as a result, to strive to be the best they can be and take responsibility for their actions. They also learn that as a designer on a project team, it is all about relationships and mutual respect."

Reaffirm the Importance of Sustaining the Collaborative Process through Monitoring and Participating in the Team's Activities

An example of this is senior management personally taking the time to attend review sessions. This can be a challenge given the time commitment. Joe Brown, former Deputy Director of Construction, Caltrans District #4 (San Francisco), says, "The best use of my time is attending partnering meetings. I learn more there about how the job and team are really functioning than at any other activity."

Also, senior management can reinforce the importance of adhering to scheduled project team review sessions. Yes, even if it falls on a bid date. As one senior manager told me, "I believe it is also important for me to periodically check in on how things are going and to put myself in a position to get open feedback from my team and the other stakeholders."

Create a Collaborative Culture in Your Organization

If World Class teamwork is not to be just a one-time occurrence, it needs to be institutionalized or ingrained in the way the organization does its day-to-day business. This, as we have seen, starts with senior management. If senior management's commitment is to truly execute World Class teamwork with consistency, the collaborative process needs to be integral to all aspects of organizational performance. This can include:

• Management selection: Are we promoting and selecting managers on the basis of their ability to work with clients, customers, and colleagues?

• Management development: Are we training managers in team behaviors?

- Performance reviews and recognition: Do we review and recognize individual and team performance on the basis of how they work with others?
- Celebrations: Do we celebrate collaborative success? Do we actively pursue awards for project teamwork excellence, such as Marvin Black Awards or those from the International Partnering Institute?
- Contract and project delivery method selection: Do we opt for contracts and project delivery methods that encourage collaborative behavior or those that only penalize for nonperformance?

Senior managers who are truly committed to World Class teamwork seek to create a culture wherein collaboration is expected, trained for, and reinforced. The consequence of doing this? World Class teamwork that happens with consistency and velocity. "It's part of our firm's culture to execute World Class projects," says George Furnanz of Stacy and Witbeck, general engineering contractors. "We are now predominantly bidding negotiated or best value work that draws upon our past relationships and references."

Mark Filanc of Filanc Construction notes, "With World Class project teamwork, I am able to build project teams that run without me. I'm assured that they not only are run well from a business point of view but are also aligned with our company culture and core values. This allows me to leverage myself and apply myself to other areas of growing the firm. And in the best-value environment that is increasingly the basis of selection in our markets, you absolutely have to be World Class."

Having said all of the above, also note, perhaps more importantly, what senior management is *not* doing with World Class project teams. They are not making day-to-day decisions. They are not attempting to direct or control the work. Nor are they mandating teamwork. They are not even attempting to motivate, let alone coerce or manipulate, their people. As John Wooden said, "If they're not motivated, they are not on the team."

18   Partnering and Achieving World Class Teamwork

With the advent of formal partnering on construction projects in the late 1980s, collaboration became more formalized. Partnering's initial intent was to provide a vehicle or process to minimize claims by enabling project stakeholders to come together prior to disputes and issues arising.

At its simplest, partnering is just people working together to achieve mutually agreed-upon outcomes or, better yet, common goals. Ideally, it is a voluntary process that each project stakeholder chooses to participate in. Requiring or forcing it, many argue, contravenes its fundamental intent and would make it just another contract provision or Business as Usual activity. Even so, many public agencies from the U.S. Navy to the California Department of Transportation have made it mandatory, and the Associated General Contractors strongly endorses it.

The U.S. Army Corps of Engineers is generally credited with bringing partnering into play in a major way on construction projects. Their purpose: "Clearly, the best dispute resolution is dispute prevention. By taking the time at the start of the project to identify common goals, common interests, lines of communication, and a commitment to cooperative problem solving, we encourage the will to resolve disputes and achieve project goals."[31]

Partnering is a mindset, a tool, and a process. The process can vary depending on the chosen partnering facilitator and how it is adapted to the specific project by the facilitator and project stakeholders. I would emphasize that much like selecting a project delivery method or a design-build team, there is no best way or approach to partnering. The best way, clients tell me, comes from having a facilitator that delivers a process that produces results that exactly meet the needs of all the project stakeholders.

Back in the early 1990s when I began facilitating partnering workshops, it was more or less accepted that they be at least a couple of days and, in many cases, three days long.

Now, even on projects of well over a billion dollars contract value, I often do them in one day, although these may be preceded by a two-to-three-hour executive pre-partnering session. Why the shortness? First, it seems it is just harder today to get all the key project stakeholders off-site for more than one day. Second, many folks have already been through the process, so they can do without a lot of the generic principles and team-building concepts. Third, many of us facilitators have become more efficient at executing the process.

The International Partnering Institute (IPI) was formed in 1996 with the purpose of "researching and implementing partnering concepts and techniques in construction project settings. We wish to work closely with those organizations who are committed to creating high-trust culture by understanding and implementing partnering on their projects and within their organizations."[32] IPI offers programs on partnering resources, partnering training, partnering certifications, partnering awards, and partnering research.

Sue Dyer, a partnering facilitator and IPI's CEO, explains partnering's role in the world of new project delivery methods: "Partnering is the underpinning for making BIM, IPD, and LEAN construction work. This does not happen by chance or because the stars are aligned for the project team. It happens because the owner integrated partnering into their entire construction program and a partnering culture emerged. The partnering culture naturally supports the collaboration that operates in a high-trust environment."[33]

The Relationship between Partnering and Legal/Contractual Obligations and Project Specifications

The project contract necessarily prescribes boundaries relative to how parties will act in accordance with established legal guidelines, prescribed procedures, and the specifications. This is, of course, necessary and good. Yet leaving a project team with just those boundaries can constrain and limit individual and team performance. True freedom, genuine individual commitment, and the ability to optimize creativity and success also requires another field within which the parties to a construction project can interact. That is the field which partnering and World Class teamwork seek to establish.

At the outset of a partnering workshop, it is necessary to clarify the relationship between the two fields. I articulate this in what I call the Partnering Rule:

1. This process in no way relaxes, compromises, or abrogates anyone's legal or contractual obligations or the specifications.

2. However, if the partnership elects to make commitments to project goals or actions that exceed the specifications or legal requirements, great! Go for it.

3. Furthermore, everything agreed upon in the partnering session carries with it no legal or contractual obligation. It is done on the basis of trust and personal integrity.

Partnering and World Class Teamwork

Can a project team achieve World Class teamwork without a formal partnering process? Yes, of course. It is somewhat analogous to asking whether a group of very talented all-star basketball players can be a great team without a coach. Yes, but. The *but* acknowledges two variables: speed (velocity) and consistency. Having a good coach can get a great group of individuals achieving World Class teamwork faster and with a greater probability of success.

Another challenge, as one of my executive clients put it, is "I can't facilitate *and* participate at the same time."

Here's what construction project team members who have attended my partnering workshops say about the relationship between a formal partnering process and a team's ability to achieve World Class teamwork:

• Scott Ashton, Berg Electric: "It allows us to develop personal relationships more easily and quickly. You try to do this on every job, but partnering expedites it. This, in turn, gives us the ability to pick up the phone and talk to individuals while understanding their challenges and the interdependence between us and their work."

• Robert Develle, NASA's Jet Propulsion Laboratory: "Partnering enables World Class teamwork. You can't get there without it."

- Kirk Hazen, Hensel Phelps: "It comes down to the individuals. If you have the right mix, you may not need a formal partnering process. But you would need project 'champions,' which is to say someone to put forth an agenda and help develop goals. Good facilitators can help people get outside their comfort zones and break down walls."

- Jim Cowell, Caltech: "Partnering is huge. It provide space and opportunity for people to be good, bad, or World Class. Otherwise what happens happens without any conscious decision or choice."

- Vitas Rugienius, Hensel Phelps: "The partnering process is a necessary activity of any team striving to achieve World Class results. The process brings out the best in people because it shows all of what is possible. It also brings out honesty and personal integrity and teaches us what our fellow stakeholders are looking for."

- Ken Schacherbauer, Perini Building Company: "You cannot have a World Class team without some sort of team building/partnering process that allows stakeholders to both break down preconceived barriers and then genuinely engage with one another to define go-forward team goals."

- Dan Gilbert, Kaiser Permanente: "It is the mechanism by which you bring everyone in and break them down, shake them up, and then enable them to enter into a team persona. There's no other way to do it. With a third party leading it, you can take people right to it without offending them along the way. I like getting right down to business."

- Perry Petersen, Petersen Construction Services: "Partnering is the backbone of a World Class team. It is where you formulate your vision, goals, and key team processes to make World Class teamwork possible. But you need a World Class facilitator who can compellingly communicate the protocols and practices to the team in way they can use them."

- Ash Wason of Carollo Engineers: "Teamwork doesn't happen naturally. It requires a leader/facilitator, or it won't happen. The process done well increases the level of importance of setting common goals. I believe that it is best not to put a requirement for partnering in the contract documents. It is important to let everyone freely commit to the process."

Pitfalls of Any Partnering, Team-Building, Trust-Building Process

As with any process, there have been cases where the intent of the partnering process has been abused. Owners, designers, and contractors have used partnering as a self-serving tool or even weapon, as some would contend.

The most common abuse is justifying one's selfish actions on the basis of partnering or teamwork. In these instances, partnering and teamwork quickly become "bad" words, and project stakeholders become very cynical about anything associated with the terms or the process.

Another situation where a collaborative effort can do more harm than good occurs when teammates assume that since they are partners, there is no need for due diligence or to maintain requisite documentation. I call this the "just trust me" game.

As Lee Evey, former DBIA president, states, "Selection of the team members and the business structure to include the contract and reward mechanism you choose to utilize will go a long way toward making the partnering process easier."

The U.S. Army Corps of Engineers statement on partnering notes: "Partnering does not require the elimination of case-building documentation. Such records are still necessary should litigation occur. Even in the absence of litigation, accurate, factual records are one of the best ways to avoid confusion and misunderstandings that often lead to disputes."[34]

The abuse of partnering has bred in some organizations an institutional reluctance to collaborate and, somewhat inadvertently, reinforced a by-the-book mentality.

When Partnering Doesn't Work

There are three main situations where partnering doesn't work.

1. It's done just to "check the box."

Yes, time is everyone's most valuable possession, but at what point does cutting corners on the process compromise its effectiveness? Lee Evey explains: "There's partnering and then there's partnering. Games and nice-sounding phrases don't make much of a difference. And some people don't put their heart in it and put on a role. You need goals and action plans backed up by personal commitments." Paradoxically, as more public agencies mandate partnering on projects, the more likely the process can digress to just another administrative requirement to be crossed off the list. Ideally, partnering is initiated by all major project stakeholders voluntarily committing to engage in the process. In my personal experience, when the key stakeholders are willing to initiate a formal interviewing process for the selection of their facilitator, much as the owner would for a CM or designer, that says a lot about their collective commitment to the process.

2. The process is abandoned, is cut too short, or is not a priority.

Developing a team in any endeavor takes a certain amount of time and commitment. Some project stakeholders have asked me if we can do the partnering session in one hour because "that's all the time we can afford." My response: "Well, if that's your commitment to partnering, then even that one hour is probably going to be a waste of time."

Project stakeholders need to see the teaming process as being one of the top two or three priorities of senior management. If review workshops are constantly rescheduled or dropped, there's a good chance of the team defaulting to Business as Usual.

3. Principals do not participate and genuinely engage in the process.

Principals of all the major stakeholders must attend the full workshop. If they won't, what does that say about the organization's commitment? Ash Wason of Carollo Engineers says, "My presence in the team-building or partnering process is important to the team. If I'm there and make the time for this, I believe this communicates that this teaming process is of a very high level of importance to our firm. Also, in situations where I can be helpful, I am not reluctant to participate."

Suboptimizing Partnering

One of the most common shortfalls is failure to sustain or follow through on the partnering process. Teams can often fall into two traps after an initial workshop:

1. Things are going so well that they don't see the value in continuing. This action, in turn, fails to take into account two realities:

a. I have never seen all the individuals at a review session unanimously agree on what is working and what could be improved.

b. It violates the notion of continuous improvement, and partnering becomes a reactive process. If the goal is to achieve and sustain World Class teamwork, partnering needs to be a proactive tool. In other words, use it to anticipate how a team will deal with future challenges and opportunities.

2. Rarely, as I've noted, does a team achieve World Class status after the first session. If they do, they did not set their stretch goals high enough.

Mike Aparicio of Skanska notes: "A partnering process provides a disciplined framework to make sure the team culture is staying in place. It's also about holding yourselves accountable, as a team, once a quarter. This ensures alignment, renewed energy, and continued focus."

The Value of a World Class Partnering Process on the Jet Propulsion Laboratory's Flight Projects Center Project

The partners expressed these values at the close-out partnering session:

- It enabled direct communication among the team.

- I was able to meet and talk with people I might not otherwise have met.

- We set measurable deliverables for the team.

- Ideas/issues were brought up with everyone present to buy into the solution.

- It enabled the group to get it off their chest.

- The frequency of review sessions (every 3–4 months) was about right.

- It allowed me to put a face on the organizations involved in the project.

- The sessions were project-specific: no games, no concepts, no Kumbaya.

- We were all driving toward common goals.

- We got a perspective from all, especially the subs.

- It enabled commitment to the project and follow-up on Issues.

- We left meetings with a list of items to work and improve on.

- You get exposed to people across contractual lines, which allows you to hear from other people's point of view.

Conclusion

I would like to close on a note of both caution and optimism. As a caution, I would like to dispel the notion that World Class teamwork is a surefire formula for unqualified project success and personal well-being. As we have seen, striving toward World Class teamwork is challenging work and requires extraordinary commitment, as does achieving excellence in any endeavor. There will be moments of personal doubt, stress, uncertainty, and even project results that may fall well short of expectations.

Even with the relatively consistent achievement of World Class teamwork which a few organizations have come close to sustaining, "the bar," as one of them put it, "keeps getting higher." Owner needs and expectations and the competition never rest. Nor is World Class teamwork a one-time event. It is a process that can be and needs to be reinvented each time you begin a new job. The result? Your organization develops a culture of excellence and continuous improvement. World Class teamwork offers the opportunity for personal creativity, self- expression, and growth. Or as one veteran superintendent told me, "I get to do another project with friends."

I hope and expect that the ten behaviors described in this book might look entirely different both to me and to others in five years or so. Defining World Class teamwork should be an ongoing conversation among all project stakeholders both at the industry and project level.

PART FOUR

———

Appendixes

APPENDIX A
World Class Teamwork Case Study:
St. Joseph Hospital Patient Care Center Project

How Builders Brought Off and Benefited from a World Class Team
at St. Joseph Hospital Patient Care Center

**by C. Patrick Peterson, Project Director, McCarthy Building Companies,
and John Pangrazzio, FAIA, FACHA**

This case study was published in the March 2008 edition of *HealthCare Design*.

St. Joseph Hospital Patient Care Center

A healthcare icon in Orange County, California, St. Joseph Hospital celebrated its seventy-fifth anniversary in March 2004 during the groundbreaking of the hospital's new Patient Care Center. This momentous occasion kicked off the master facility plan for the medical center and marked a major milestone in the organization's history.

The new Patient Care Center project entailed construction of a four-level, 248,000-square-foot hospital tower featuring an expansive main entrance and lobby, 150 critical care and medical surgical inpatient beds, 14 operating room suites, a central sterile and supply department, and a freestanding central plant. The project team was charged with building this state-of-the-art facility, as well as setting a positive example for future projects in the campus and St. Joseph Health System facility master plans.

Furthermore, the Patient Care Center project was expected to uphold St. Joseph Hospital's seven-decade-long reputation for patient care and community service. Meeting the challenges of minimizing impact to the nearby facilities while maintaining all existing services was no small feat because of the nature of the project, as well as its tight site surrounded by the existing St. Joseph Hospital facilities, Children's Hospital of Orange County (CHOC), businesses, and residences.

The St. Joseph Hospital Patient Care Center offered numerous challenges, all met through a fully integrated partnering approach. Through this strong commitment to partnering, the new Center was built on time, within the original project budget, and without any claims. The team's success is further highlighted by a recordable safety incident rate of *zero*.

Project Background

The project team for the Patient Care Center had to coordinate with two hospitals that surrounded the site and connect them to the new facility. To complicate preconstruction further, just four months before construction was to begin, the general contractor stepped down and McCarthy Building Companies was hired.

To start building trust and collaboration among the group, the hospital voluntarily initiated a professionally facilitated partnering program. The project team agreed that the time investment in a partnering program, along with incremental cost of one that was professionally facilitated, were time and money well spent considering the potential benefits. To kick off the program, the team held three week-long partnering sessions that brought everyone up to speed quickly and seamlessly. These sessions successfully turned the somewhat disparate groups into a unified team firmly on track for achieving success.

During the first partnering workshops, the team discussed what was working and what was not. The team then came up with nine major areas of focus, which were deemed the project's "Big Hairy Audacious Goals" (BHAGs)—a term coined by authors Jerry Porras and Jim Collins in their book *Built to Last: Successful Habits of Visionary Companies.*

The project's nine BHAGs were formalized on a partnership charter and included:

- Substantial completion including all changes to date no later than the approved Prime Contract Change Order date.
- Project completion at contract value plus a maximum of 16%.
- Project wins an ASHE Award for teamwork (still in process).
- Recordable incident rate less than one and zero lost-time accidents.
- All issues/disputes resolved at the project level.
- Punch list complete no later than 30 days after substantial completion and close-out.
- Office of Statewide Health Planning and Development (OSHPD) issues resolved within two weeks. OSHPD design write-ups resolved within 30 days.
- Patients, staff, and neighbors involved, informed, and minimally impacted by noise and parking. Zero early incidents because of mistakes.
- Transition plan executed on time and with zero last-minute user changes.

During partnering meetings, the team initially identified the project Strengths, Weaknesses, Opportunities, and Threats (SWOT). On a 1-to-10 scale (where 1 = Combative and 10 = World Class), the items were individually scored and then team-ranked/aggregated. If the identified item scored between 1 and 3, it was flagged as an issue that could derail the attempt to achieve the BHAG, and a subgroup was formed to resolve the issue. Subgroup meeting dates were immediately arranged so the issue could be resolved as soon as possible after the partnering session. The issue would then be revisited at the next partnering session, and the team would score it again, with subgroup meetings continuing until the issue was resolved to the team's satisfaction.

One of the project's partnering goals was to resolve all disputes at the team management level with a representative from St. Joseph Hospital Design and Construction, NBBJ Architects, and McCarthy. In the rare instances when an outstanding cost issue had the potential to go to claim, the management team held a special meeting, typically including the applicable subcontractor(s), and worked through the issue until a mutually satisfactory agreement was reached. This proved extremely successful, resulting in zero claims on the project.

Take, for example, mechanical/electrical/plumbing systems coordination, a complex work activity that doubled the time allotted and added additional materials to the project. The first analysis of additional manpower and materials added close to $3 million in extra value to the project. The team agreed to break each trade's systems down individually and analyze the additional cost with proper backup from the subcontractors, and determined that if each member provided all the proper information and analysis, the cost resolution would not be delayed. Through a series of meetings, fair and appropriate valuation was assessed, and all cost issues were resolved and paid in a timely manner, eliminating any risk of project claims at the project close-out.

Involving everyone in partnering—from the crafts workers to the project executives, end-users, and even the jobsite neighbors and local community—ensured that the goals were met and that all stakeholders would be pleased with the process and end result.

At project completion, Jim Eisenhart, the team building facilitator from Ventura Consulting Group (see "Healthcare Project Partnering: The Five Key Elements," *Healthcare Design*, February 2008, p. 22) stated, "What made this project team particularly unique was not only did their teamwork scores improve dramatically over the course of the project, but they achieved all of their initial partnership goals. I challenged them in the initial workshop to set measurable goals that called for nothing less than

World Class performance and World Class teamwork. Most of our partnerships usually hit 70 to 90 percent of their goals, but this team nailed every one."

Partnering Charter

The partnership team had multiple meetings in 2006: January 25, March 29, June 14, and December 4. A partnering charter was prepared, tracing and evaluating the project goals every couple of months through an electronic survey system created by Ventura Consulting.

One of the project goals developed during the initial partnering session was to achieve a recordable incident rate of less than one and a lost-time accident rate of zero. As it turned out, with more than 175 workers during the project's peak and a total of 700,408 man-hours, the project boasted a *zero* recordable safety incident rate and a *zero* lost-time rate.

The subcontractors were challenged by McCarthy to go above and beyond their existing safety policies, and many implemented additional safety regulations for their crafts workers. All major meetings and daily meetings started by addressing safety, so safe work practices and accident prevention were constantly on the minds of everyone on the project. Some of the specific techniques used to ensure a safe work environment on the Patient Care Center Project were: safety meetings, safety lunches, monthly merchandise awards to encourage employee participation in safe work methods, correct on-site conditions, and celebrating major achievements and milestones.

All new hires were identified by wearing red hard hats for the first three months so seasoned employees (in white hard hats) could mentor them while working on site. In addition to new hires, any employee identified to be in an area where there was danger of being struck by equipment or overhead loads was required to wear high-visibility clothing to aid in constant awareness. A comprehensive job-site safety inspection program was implemented, with scheduled and surprise inspections conducted regularly to identify potentially unsafe conditions and to provide immediate correction.

Partnering and Budget Control

The projected budget for the project was $203.7 million, and the budget forecast at completion is currently under $195 million. The partnering process helped maintain the project budget goals by identifying issues early in the partnering meetings and resolving all issues at the project level. Additionally, the team's decision to have an expert from every construction specialty on site at all times was possibly one of the most significant cost- and time-saving approaches of the entire project. The effects of this decision were countless and far-reaching and, in the end, were greatly responsible for bringing the project in under budget.

Also, through partnering, a solid foundation of trust among the project team, and a proactive approach by the facility, the team achieved an early buyout of core construction materials, such as steel and concrete. This was an important cost-saving mechanism, as it enabled the team to secure reasonable prices early on and avoid any escalating costs of building materials, which at the time were rising rapidly.

Partnering and Maintaining Schedule

The first partnering goal was to complete the project, including all changes, no later than the approved Prime Contract Change Order date. The project took 38 months to build and was substantially completed on June 26, 2007, meeting its goal for on-time completion after additional scope had been added. Meeting this goal was no small task, especially since the project was delayed 35 days because of saturated site conditions resulting from several days of rain. The rains occurred near the beginning of construction and created a massive pool of water in the newly excavated hole. If this difficulty hadn't been resolved, the rains would have cost the team a half million dollars and a 45-day scheduling setback.

However, the team mitigated the damage and immediately recovered 21 days by working through selective overtime and conducting a schedule impact analysis that identified the delayed construction activities that could push the total schedule past the contractual end date, thus allowing McCarthy to focus the team's efforts on those specific activities. The rest of the time and money were made up through teamwork and commitment to the partnering goals during the course of the project.

Another time-saving solution was localizing the Construction Administration team on-site. This laid the early groundwork for success and cut the review process for architectural and engineering field directives and RFI responses from the typical three weeks to a short five days. In addition, communication lines were always open, which kept the project running smoothly, even when changes arose. For example, when a foundation concern surfaced on the north side of the building, the geotechnical engineers and structural engineers were immediately called and were able to solve the problem within a couple of days. Without the engineers on site, that section of the project could have been delayed for weeks, depending on how long it took the engineers to travel to the site, assess the problem, and develop and communicate a solution. In addition, the on-site team was available to meet with the State of California OSHPD field staff on a regular basis to address field conditions quickly.

Additional Goals Achieved

Additional partnering goals contributed to completing the project on schedule. These included partnering commitments to resolve all issues at the project level, complete the punch list no later than 30 days after subcontractor completion and close-out, resolve OSHPD issues within two weeks and OSHPD design write-ups within 30 days, and execute the transition plan on time and with zero last-minute user changes.

Involve All Stakeholders

Craft workers were extremely important to the success of this project and the partnering program. The subcontractors' foremen participated in the partnering meetings, and then the foremen would meet with their craft workers to relay the partnering goals and strategies when necessary. Input from the craft workers was also obtained for discussion at each partnering session. For example, when McCarthy challenged the subcontractors to institute a safety program above and beyond their current program, the craft workers came up with ideas to create safer work environments and then carried the ideas into action and monitored one another to ensure compliance.

The field crews were also responsible for implementing efficient material procurement and installation means and methods to achieve cost and schedule goals established in the Partnering Charter. When a proposed change order was drafted by the owner or design team, the field management and craft workers would have a meeting, review the proposed change, and provide timely feedback defining the impacts on the job of implementing the proposed design revision. If they saw a negative effect from the proposed change, they would provide material and installation solutions to the owner and design team that would achieve their design intent but minimize the cost or time impact on the overall project.

The major subcontractors and specialty trade subcontractors were also an integral part of the project team responsible for meeting the partnering goals. They participated in all of the partnering sessions and helped to establish the goals in the Partnering Charter. The subcontractors also participated in the evaluation surveys and provided input related to their specialty, all of which helped to achieve the project goals.

Partnering Leads to Innovation

Every innovative idea on this project was supported by the goals and spirit established through the partnering process. Some of the innovative ideas developed through the course of the St. Joseph Patient Care Center project included helping to fund Zone Four seismic compliance under the California Senate Bill 1953. An unfunded mandate, the Bill became effective in March 1998 and requires all hospitals to withstand the maximum potential earthquake and continue to be operational immediately afterward. To help offset the cost of building a seismic-compliant facility to house inpatient beds, the team conducted service-line assessments for the hospital that evaluated and designed capacity in the new Patient Care Center for service (business) growth in surgical services. These studies led to the decision to add 150 patient beds and 14 operating suites to increase the hospital's capacity and service capabilities. The increased revenue from these services will pay the debt on the new building.

Challenging MEP Systems

The mechanical, electrical, and plumbing systems on this project were challenging and could have resulted in lost time and an increased budget if not coordinated and implemented correctly. The existing utilities were in the path of the new construction, and exact design and coordination were needed to successfully adjoin the utilities to the new hospital building without damaging or interrupting the existing infrastructure. As a result of partnering, constant communication and coordination among the design and construction teams, the MEP challenges were successfully overcome and resulted in no additional funding needed.

Project Commissioning and Start-Up

There was no formal commissioning plan for the project, so the team implemented its own process. From generating a start-up schedule months in advance to developing a detailed testing verification book prior to start-up, the team was able to successfully commission the project and obtain a final OSHPD sign-off with no delays.

Outside Communications

Because of the proximity of the Patient Care Center to two high-volume hospitals, a parking structure, an office building, an elementary school, and residential buildings, it was important to keep a positive relationship among all parties. Therefore, one of the partnering goals was that "patients, staff, and neighbors should be informed and minimally impacted by noise and parking." The team created a comprehensive communication plan, which continually relayed pertinent and timely information to all parties and provided everyone with a personal contact who was available at all times to meet in person, listen to feedback, and discuss any concerns. Before construction, the project team held week-long Visioning Sessions with the neighboring children's hospital to develop the most effective plan for working together throughout construction. Similar meetings were held with the Sisters of St. Joseph Hospital, the nearby residents, and businesses and school administrators. Quarterly Community Forums also were held to discuss construction progress and upcoming work, and members of the team went through the neighborhood several times, answering questions one-on-one with community residents. In the end, the construction phase of the project had *zero* delays because of community complaints or interferences, and the neighboring hospitals remained 100 percent functional during construction.

Another important aspect of the project was to mitigate construction noise, vibrations, and/or effects on traffic and throughways. The team held weekly meetings with the hospital facilities team to communicate upcoming construction activities and to alleviate any concerns. In addition, extensive planning and make-ready work were completed ahead of major construction activities to ensure access for staff and patients to all parts of the existing hospital. A detailed site-logistics plan was also developed to mitigate traffic; it included road rerouting, providing off-site staging areas for construction materials, resourceful scheduling of construction deliveries, and providing convenient pick-up and drop-off areas for patients.

Partnering and Quality Construction

McCarthy established a multiple-staged Quality Control and Inspection Process:

Step #1: Subcontractors send McCarthy a Quality Control report stating that they have completed their work.

Step #2: McCarthy completes a secondary Quality Control list in the rooms that the subcontractors have reported complete.

Step #3: After the subcontractors have completed work per the Quality Control list, McCarthy submits a final in-wall inspection to the Inspector of Record (IOR) for final corrections and sign-off, and then closes up walls. This process was conducted for both in-wall and overhead close-up and was completed per the schedule completion dates.

The project team also implemented a Quality Control program including:

1. Trade-specific pre-installation meetings.

The general contractor, designer, trade-specific contractor, and inspectors meet to review the contract documents (plans and specs) to make sure that everyone understood each other's expectations from a design intent and means and methods of installation perspective. This would also provide a forum for Q&A by the field management team as it related to all 16 divisions of specifications before building materials were bought and installed.

2. First-installed field visits and analysis.

The project management team would conduct an early punch list on each building system the first time it was installed in the field to make sure that baseline quality was established at each step of construction. After the first-installed meeting, the results would be communicated to the balance of the trades so that they all understood intent of the final product.

3. Field mock-ups.

Each major room, redundant building system, and exterior enclosure system was completed in a expedited manner so that all trades could establish a sequence of installation and standard of quality and the designer and owner could see the final product of the repetitive building systems rooms' high-end finishes. This allowed early adjustments to be made by the craft workers along with the designer and owner so that the final product met everyone's expectations, and corrections did not delay the overall project.

4. Fabrication plant visits.

The general contractor, inspectors, owner, and design team traveled to all major equipment and material fabrication plants to ensure that the products being produced from raw material were meeting the standards and quality that was intended in the plans and specifications, both aesthetically and functionally.

The *true* test of quality, though, is the approval of the people who are using the facility after it is built. Patsy Brandenburger, a long-time Critical Care Services RN at St. Joseph Hospital, shared her excitement about the new hospital: "The new Patient Care Center is phenomenal.

The amount of space and the [space plan] flow in the patient care units has created an excellent environment for critical or intensive patient care. The integration of the latest technology along with the thoughtful healing design of the building has given us [the caregiver] and the patient the best tools for healing."

Chuck Coryell, St. Joseph Hospital Director, Design and Construction, summed up the importance of partnering to the quality of the project: "The project team was highly collaborative at every stage of the construction process. They started strong and finished strong with consistent performance throughout the 38-month project. The team provided resources with the right skill set at each level of the field operations for both the new Patient Care Center [hospital tower] and the supporting central utility plant [Facilities Services Building]. From the project executives to the job-site foremen, each staff member displayed a genuine interest in their role at meeting our goals of high-quality facilities delivered on time."

Partnering Develops Ongoing Relationships

The project team has created strong relationships with one another through developing skills they learned during team-building and partnering sessions that will carry with them long into their next endeavors. At the start of the St. Joseph Hospital Patient Care Center project, relationships had to become synchronized very quickly because a new general contractor was brought on board late in the preconstruction process after another general contractor left the team. However, after the partnering sessions began, a process was created to form trust and respect among team members that helped streamline procedures, expedite the schedule and achieve project goals.

Team Building and Motivational Activities

Team building and motivational activities were an important part of forming a cohesive project team capable of bringing this challenging project to a successful completion. Some of these activities included:

• An initial partnering session.

• The design team studied and read *The Compassionate Presence*, a book documenting and illustrating the Sisters of St. Joseph's 78-year history. This book became an important tool throughout the design process, and through partnering meetings, the information from the book was instilled into the mindset of the project team.

• Weekly meetings between the client and project team to keep the communication lines open.

• A barbecue with the project team and the hospital staff and caregivers with 250 people attending.

• Project team baseball games and lunches. These offered the team a relaxed environment in which to share diverse viewpoints, build common ground, and ensure that everyone's voice was heard.

• The trades nominated individuals from other trades for a crafts worker of the week award, and a T-shirt was given to the worker that best exemplified good craftsmanship and/or safety.

• McCarthy gave monthly safety awards to its employees whenever there were no job-site accidents during the month. Stemming from the project's safety challenge, several of the subcontractors stepped up and added new safety requirements and gave incentives to their employees similar to McCarthy's incentive program.

McCarthy had golf and other team-building outings with the owner, architect, and mechanical engineer. At each partnering workshop, the partnership voted and acknowledged the "best partner" or the individual who in the preceding three months had been the best team player.

The project team developed and implemented a Patient Activity Program for the Children at the neighboring children's hospital that overlooked the construction site. The program included several architecture- and construction-themed activities and donated construction-related toys to the hospital playrooms. The project owner, architects, engineers, and subcontractors all volunteered and assisted with this program, which was implemented quarterly for two years.

The project team provided volunteer services and donations to the neighboring Ronald McDonald House and supported St. Joseph Hospital in its efforts for the American Heart Association by participating in "Go

Red for Women Day" and raising more than $150,000 during two Orange County Heart Walk events.

In support of the construction industry, the project team shared its project expertise with the industry by providing numerous job-site tours for OSHPD office and field personnel, students participating in the ACE mentoring program, architects, and engineers.

The team engaged an outside team building facilitator in January 2006, who worked closely with the team during the entire final year of construction.

Innovative Construction Techniques

Innovative construction techniques were developed through partnering with subcontractors, who initiated their ideas on this project. They included:

• Changing the Cast In Place (CIP) basement walls to Shot Crete, which shaved 30 days off the entire project schedule and saved money. This benefit was realized because the means and methods of installing a Shot Crete basement wall system are much more efficient and take less manpower than a formed CIP wall system.

• Using deck inserts to support MEP systems.

• Changing to a PVC roof system, which was superior in quality to the initial roof specified and also easier to work around. To do this, McCarthy proposed taking money budgeted for a temporary roof and investing it in a more durable PVC roof system. The substrate of this roof system can act as a temporary roof system, and the finish product is a higher-grade product, both in material, maintenance, warranty, and long-term durability. The owner, designers, and contractor maximized the design intent, construction logistics, and product for the end user without increasing the overall project budget.

• Using blue-board (mold resistant) for drywall areas allowed for early installation of interior walls to start before the entire building was protected from weather or moisture (i.e., dried-in). With this early build-out, the project either accelerates or builds float into the schedule, thus benefiting the overall project schedule.

Recruitment Draw for SJHS

The new state-of-the-art Patient Care Center has already become a great recruiting tool for St. Joseph Hospital. The building design is an integral part of their marketing tool kit, and the special attention to staff amenities and patient-centered care have received high remarks from new recruits and current staff. When St. Joseph Hospital held their "sneak peek" recruiting fairs, which gave attendees an opportunity to experience the quality of the new facility first-hand, they were astounded by the response. Hundreds of recruits turned out for the two events, and 91 new employees were hired, making these the hospital's most successful recruiting fairs to date.

One Final Note

In February of 2009, the St. Joseph Patient Care Center was selected by the Associated General Contractors of America as one of six awardees of the prestigious Marvin Black Award given out nationwide for excellence in partnering.

APPENDIX B
Contributors

NOTE: Approximately 95 percent of these individuals I have had the privilege of working with on World Class construction project teams over the past five years. Roughly the same percentage of their comments have come from in-person or telephone interviews. The balance have come from their written comments.

Michael Abeln, Director of Construction, U.S. Army Corps of Engineers, Mobile, Alabama

Jake Adams, Program Manager, Los Angeles World Airports

David Allen, Architect and PM, U.S. District Court, San Diego

Mike Aparicio, Vice President for Transit Operations, Skanska

Glenn Ballard, Cofounder, Research Director, LEAN Construction Institute

Wylie Bearup, City Engineer, City of Phoenix

Scott Ashton, Industrial Division Manager, Berg Electric

Alan Bliesmer, Operations Manager, Hensel Phelps Construction

Steven Boehm, South Region Director of New Construction, Los Angeles Unified School District

Jim Bostic, Vice President for Facilities, St. Joseph Health System

Sylvia Botero, Senior Vice President, RBB Architects

Joe Brown, former Deputy Director of Construction, Caltrans District #4, San Francisco

Brian Cahill, Director of Operations, Barnhart Balfour Beatty

Ron Calkins, Project Manager, Briggs Electric

Arturo Castro, President and COO, Tucker Sadler Architects

Dave Cavecche, Executive Vice President and General Manager, Suffolk Construction Company

Don Chee, former Senior Project Manager, City and County of San Francisco

Larry Cochran, Vice President, Kiewit Companies

Jim Cowell, Associate Vice President for Facilities, Caltech, and U.S. Navy CEC Captain, retired

Virgil Curtis, Project Sponsor, Balfour Beatty

Vijay Daniel, Senior Project Manager, Whiting Turner

Bill Davis, Inspector of Record, Los Angeles Unified's Central Region Elementary School #14

Pete Davos, Vice President, DeSilva Gates Construction

Perry Dealy, CEO, Dealy Development

George Delano, Senior Project Manager, Granite Construction

Brian DerMatoian, Vice President, SJ Amoroso Construction Company

Robert Develle, Manager of the Facilities Division, NASA Jet Propulsion Laboratory

Betsey Dougherty, FAIA, LEED, AP, Principal of Dougherty + Dougherty Architects, and former AIA National Board Member

Doug Duplisea, Senior Vice President and Southwest Regional Manager, Kiewit Companies, Phoenix, AZ

Sue Dyer, President, Orgmetrics, and CEO, International Partnering Institute

Maurice El Hage, Area Construction Manager, Caltrans

Don Eng, Director, Construction Management Division, City and County of San Francisco

Lee Evey, former Program Director, Pentagon Renovation (PENREN), and former President, Design Build Institute of America

Tony Ferruccio, Executive Vice President, Mactec, Atlanta

Mark Filanc, CEO, Filanc Construction

Bob Finney, District #4 Deputy Director for Construction, Caltrans, San Francisco Bay area

Thomas Fodor, Project Manager, Granite Construction,

Mike Forner, head of the Caltrans Toll Bridge Program

Bob Fouty, Senior Project Manager, Archer Western Construction

George Furnanz, Senior Vice President, Stacy and Witbeck

Mike Ghilotti, CEO, Ghilotti Brothers Construction

Dan Gilbert, Project Director, Ontario Medical Center, Kaiser Permanente

Carlos Gonzales, Senior Project Manager, Clark Construction Group

Kim Grant, Vice President and Operations Manager, Swinerton Builders

Tom Gusich, Vice President of Water Resources and Industrial Projects, University Mechanical & Engineering subcontractors, Phoenix

Ron Hall, Regional Manager, McCarthy Building Companies

Nabil Hissen, Principal Engineer, Zoon Engineering, Inc., and consultant to San Francisco Presidio Trust

Kirk Hazen, Vice President and Southeast District Manager, Hensel Phelps Construction, Orlando

Boone Hellmann, Campus Architect, University of California, San Diego

Mehdi Hehdari, Vice President and Regional Director, Vanir Construction Management

Jim Houchins, Vice President, JE Dunn Construction

Greg Howell, Managing Director, LEAN Construction Institute

Ray Hughes, Regional Manager, Flatiron Corporation

Steve Iselin, Executive Director of NAVFAC (Naval Facilities & Engineering Command) in Washington, DC

Tim Jacoby, Vice President of Facilities, Rady Children's Hospital

Gary Janco, Executive Vice President, CC Myers, Inc.

John Jansen, Senior Vice President, Kiewit Companies

Brian Jordan, Senior Vice President and Regional Manager, AECOM

Mike Kerchner, Project Executive, Tutor Perini Corporation

Issam Khalaf, Principal, Jacobs Construction Management

Steve Kimball, Project Director, Hensel Phelps Construction

Larry Kolves, Superintendent, Pinner Construction

Jeff Lage, Vice President, Skanska

Paul Ligocki, Operations Manager, Hensel Phelps Construction

Boon Lim, Construction Manager for Wastewater, San Francisco Public Utilities Commission

Wayne Lindholm, Executive Vice President, Hensel Phelps Construction

Jim Link, Vice President, Skanska

Jim Linthicum, Director of Engineering and Construction, San Diego Association of Governments (SANDAG)

Bart Littell, Vice President, Parsons Brinckerhoff

Mike Llamas, Vice President of Operations, Ghilotti Brothers

Sara Loughead, Project Manager, Rady Children's Hospital
David Mallik, Senior Project Manager, Whiting Turner Construction
Kathy Mayo, Vice President, AECOM
Joanne McAllister, Senior Project Manager, Anshen + Allen architects
Mike McKinney, Operations Manager, PCL Construction, Inc.
Cynthia Meinhardt, Project Officer, City of San Diego New Central Library
Frank Miller, Vice President, DynaElectric
Kevin Mitchell, Senior Project Manager, Kiewit Pacific
Peter Mondery, Project Manager, Southern Contracting
Lonnie Morelock, Project Director, Kiewit Companies
Andy Morgan, Vice President, Vanir Construction Management
Dennis Mori, Executive Officer and Project Director, Los Angeles County
    Metropolitan Transit Authority
Roland Muller, Project Superintendent, Swinerton Builders
Steve Murray, President, Murray Company
Beverly Nelson, Contracting Officer, U.S. Bureau of Reclamation, Lower
    Colorado Region
Dave Niese, Area Manager, Flatiron Construction
Mark Norris, Assistant Public Works Director, City of Oxnard
Alix O'Brien, Construction Manager, URS Construction Management
Chad Olson, Senior Project Manager, Suffolk Construction
Les Osterberger, Vice President, A. O. Reed
Lou Palandrani, Senior Vice President, Clark Construction Group
Patrick Peterson, Vice President, McCarthy Building Companies
Perry Petersen, Principal, Petersen Construction Services
Johnny Pinner, President, Pinner Construction
Fred Powell, Senior Associate, NBBJ Architects
Josh Randall, Vice President, Tutor Perini Corporation
Rob Robinson, Vice President, URS Construction Management
Commander Whit Robinson, Resident Officer in Charge of Construction,
    U.S. Naval Hospital Camp Pendleton
Ed Ruckle, U.S. Navy Civil Service (retired); Principal, Ruckle
    Construction Management

Ron Rudolph, Regional Vice President, Turner Construction

Vitas Rugienius, Operations Manager, Hensel Phelps Construction

Ken Schacherbauer, Vice President of Field Operations, Perini Building Company

Mike Scott, Assistant Vice President, Parsons Brinckerhoff

John Sealey, former head of the Federal Bureau of Prisons Construction branch, Washington, DC

Pat Shafter, Senior Project Manager, Swinerton Builders

Stephen Sharr, GKK Works, formerly Director of New Construction for the Central Region of the Los Angeles Unified School District

Jack Shewmaker, Construction Manager, Granite Construction

Craig Shulman, Senior Project Manager, LPA Architects

Greg Simons, Executive Vice President, Bernards Construction

Sue Stewart, former Senior Vice President, McCarthy Building Companies, St. Louis

Doug Strout, Principal and Director of Healthcare, KMD Architects

Dave Takamoto, Principal, Takamoto Ventures, Inc.

Dave Tatevossian, South Region Deputy Director for New Construction, Los Angeles Unified School District

Barry Thalden, Partner, Thalden•Boyd•Emery Architects, St. Louis and Las Vegas

Rick Thorpe, Chief Executive Officer, EXPO Authority, LA METRO

Larry Timmer, former Vice President, Harris & Associates, construction managers

Dennis Turchon, Principal Construction Manager, Caltrans

Mike Tylwalk, Division Manager, Summit Builders

Steve Van Dyke, Project Director, McCarthy Building Companies

Robert Van Kirk, Construction Administrator, Mazzetti and Associates

Len Vetrone, Senior Vice President, Webcor Builders

Ash Wason, Chief Operating Officer, Carollo Engineers

Bill Welch, Project Manager, Hensel Phelps Construction

Richard Welsh, Regional Construction Engineer, U.S. Bureau of Reclamation

Jerry West, former NBA All-Star, former manager and GM of the Los Angeles Lakers, and current owner/GM of the Memphis Grizzlies

Chet Widom, FAIA, President of the American Institute of Architects, current Vice Chancellor of the College of Fellows with AIA, and Consultant to Los Angeles Community College system

Captain Mike Williamson, CEC, U.S. Navy

Don Wright, Program Manager, Bechtel

Jim Wyatt, Director of Field Engineering, Eastern Municipal Water District

Notes

1. Jon R. Katzenbach, *Teams at the Top* (Boston, Mass.: Harvard Business School Press, 1998), 130.

2. Carol Eaton, "Bimla Rhinehart Balances Multiple Interests at CTC," *California Constructor* (February 2010): 5.

3. Barbara Jackson, *Design-Build Essentials* (Florence, Ky.: Cengage Learning, 2010).

4. "Construction and the Internet: New Wiring," *The Economist* (Jan. 13, 2000), http://www.economist.com/node/273886?story_id=E1_NSPRRG

5. Richard McGill Murphy, "Why Doing Good Is Good For Business," *Fortune* (February 8, 2010): 92-93.

6. Richard Korman with Jim Parsons, "The Post Traumatic Construction Disorder," *The Engineering News Record* (March 15, 2010): 24.

7. Vineet Nayar, "Trust through Transparency," *Harvard Business Review* (January 2, 2009), http://blogs.hbr.org/hbr/nayar/2009/01/trust-through-transparency.html

8. Peter Drucker, *Managing the Non-Profit Organization* (New York: Harper Collins, 1990), 18–19.

9. Philip Howard, *The Death of Common Sense: How Law Is Suffocating America* (New York: Random House, 1995).

10. Dennis Prager, *Happiness Is a Serious Problem: A Human Nature Repair Manual* (New York: Regan Books, 1998), 39.

11. Daniel Pink, *Drive: The Surprising Truth about What Motivates Us,* (New York: Riverhead Books, 2009), 117.

12. Pink, *Drive*, 36.

13. Pink, *Drive*, 37.

14. Economic Intelligence Unit of PricewaterhouseCoopers, "Managing the Risks and Rewards of Collaboration," June 2008.

15. Jon R. Katzenbach and Douglas K. Smith, *The Wisdom of Teams* (Boston, Mass.: Harvard Business School Press, 1993), 3.

16. Howard, *The Death of Common Sense*, 179.

17. Patrick Lencioni, *The Five Dysfunctions of a Team* (San Francisco: Jossey-Bass, 2002), 213.

18. Howard, *The Death of Common Sense*, 30.

19. Prager, *Happiness Is a Serious Problem,* 61.

20. Katzenbach, *Teams at the Top*, 95.

21. Pink, *Drive*, 106.

22. Stanley A. McChrystal, "It Takes a Network," *Foreign Policy* (March/April 2011): 46.

23. Thomas Davenport and Jeanne G. Harris, *Competing on Analytics: The New Science of Winning* (Boston: Harvard Business School Press, 2007).

24. Joanna Masterson, "All for One, One for All," *Executive Construction* (Jan. 2010)

25. Jim Collins, *How the Mighty Fall* (New York, Harper Collins, 2009), 77.

26. Jeffrey L. Rodengen, *Kiewit: An Uncommon Company* (Fort Lauderdale, Fla.: Write Stuff Enterprises, Inc., 2009).

27. Sue Dyer, "Collaborative Construction," International Partnering Institute Special Report (2008): 11.

28. Judy Schriener, "Millenniums Bring New Attitudes," *Engineering News Record,* February 28, 2011, 22.

29. Schriener, "Millenniums Bring New Attitudes," 25.

30. Stephen M. R. Covey, *The Speed of Trust* (New York: Free Press, 2006), 313.

31. Lt. General J. Hatch, Commander, U.S. Army COE, Policy Memo, August 1990.

32. International Partnering Institute, *Collaborative Construction: Lessons Learned for Creating a Culture of Partnership* (June 2008).

33. *Collaborative Construction,* 1.

34. U.S. Army COE Alternative Dispute Resolution Pamphlet #4, Revised, May 2010.